STRESEMANN
AND THE REVISION
OF VERSAILLES

"Instinct and experience alike teach us that human nature is not logical, that it is unwise to treat political institutions as instruments of logic, and that it is in wisely refraining from pressing conclusions to their logical end that the path of peaceful development and true reform is really found."

SIR AUSTEN CHAMBERLAIN
before the House of Commons,
March 24, 1925

"Wenn man sich die Möglichkeit deutscher Aussenpolitik vor Augen führt, wird man klar entscheiden müssen, wohin der Weg gehen soll . . . . Selbst wenn Deutschland ein militärischer Machtfaktor wäre, müsste man sich . . . . darüber klar sein, dass man (mit einer Politik der Revanche) . . . . einen ganzen Weltbund gegen Deutschland erneut auf die Beine bringt. Denn das ist ja gerade die diabolische Art des Versailler Diktats gewesen dass sie an allen Ecken und Enden Unfrieden zwischen Deutschland und allen seinen Nachbarn geschaffen hat."

GUSTAV STRESEMANN
September 14, 1925

STRESEMANN
AND THE REVISION
OF VERSAILLES

A Fight for Reason

HENRY L. BRETTON

STANFORD UNIVERSITY PRESS
STANFORD, CALIFORNIA

TO THOSE WHO MIGHT
HAVE LIVED

PREFACE

This study is concerned with the peaceful revision of a major treaty, the Treaty of Versailles. In general, it addresses itself to the political and diplomatic phases of the process of revisionism through which that treaty passed in the first decade following World War I. In particular, the study is concerned with one policy maker, and is limited to the examination of the role which he personally played in the making and conduct of a revisionist foreign policy.

While there are undoubtedly other aspects of German revisionism, this study is restricted to those features which are directly and indisputably traceable to Gustav Stresemann, German foreign minister from 1923 to 1929. As Stresemann showed an inclination to concentrate on political issues, and to leave such highly technical matters as the financial aspects of the reparation settlement to other ministers, the latter and similar technical matters have not been covered in this work in any detail. They are considered, however, if their political significance came to Stresemann's attention, and if they constituted a significant part of his revisionist policy. In such cases, the study analyzes only their political contents.

The study aims at the discovery of a pattern in international relations. From the beginning of the research the effort was made to ascertain whether Stresemann, in charge of German foreign policy for six consecutive years, had applied a set pattern in his revisionism and, if so, what that pattern was. Furthermore, there was reason to believe that, once a pattern had been discovered, certain basic diplomatic and political analogies could be drawn with respect to present-day Germany and her international position. Specifically, this study seeks to discover the sequence in which the several attacks against the peace treaty—and against the political order resulting from it—were launched. An attempt is made to examine the national and international background of the strategy applied and the particular objectives which Stresemann had in mind. In addition, an attempt is made to analyze the methods employed by Stresemann in his struggle to modify the political and legal order imposed upon Germany by the Treaty of Versailles.

With respect to organization and treatment, it was believed that a chronological presentation of the materials would not have permitted sufficient emphasis of the several elements, methods, and objectives of Stresemann's policy of revisionism. In order to emphasize such matters as Stresemann's own political background, the roots of his concepts of Germany's international position, and in order to permit a separate examination of the several political and diplomatic facets of his policy, a topical approach was preferred. At the same time, to avoid breaking up connected historical sequences, where such a process would prove harmful to the over-all pattern of the study, topical subdivisions were arranged in such a manner as to preserve the historical context.

The study is prefaced by a biographical introduction. Chapter I covers the period from his birth to the date when Stresemann, relieved of the additional responsibilities inherent in the chancellorship, was finally placed in a position of direct control in the realm of foreign policy. Chapter II carries the biographical survey from 1923 to his death in 1929. The following two chapters are devoted to a close examination of the bases of his foreign policy and of the methods applied by him. The fifth chapter considers the war guilt question separately because of the fundamental bearing which this dispute had upon the entire problem of revisionism. From then on, the study proceeds to examine Stresemann's foreign policy point by point. Chapters VI to IX are devoted to the consideration of matters of greater immediate importance, while the remaining chapters deal with matters of relatively lesser significance.

Because of the essentially biographical nature of this study, research was confined to an examination of source materials directly and conclusively traceable to Stresemann, with other documentary and secondary materials utilized to provide the necessary background.

The study is based, along with other source materials, on the published collection of Stresemann papers entitled *Das Vermächtnis* as well as on the unpublished—now microfilmed—papers, the *Nachlass*, which were found in the Stresemann file in the captured archives of the German foreign office. Mr. E. Taylor Parks of the Department of State was most helpful in arranging access to these materials. Additional Stresemann materials were consulted at the Hoover Institute and Library on War, Revolution, and Peace at Stanford University, Stanford, California. The writer wishes to express his gratitude to the officers and members of the staff at the Hoover Library who so generously contributed of their time and effort to facilitate the necessary research at that institution. The writer's special gratitude goes to Dr. Charles Easton Rothwell and Dr. Fritz Epstein, both of the Hoover Library. At the latter institution and at the General and Law

Libraries of the University of Michigan, an extensive and exhaustive study of the parliamentary records of the German Reichstag and National Assembly was undertaken. This study covered the Debates and Supplements of the several German parliaments from 1917 to 1929. At the Newspaper Annex of the New York Public Library leading German dailies were consulted for the years 1918 to 1929. These newspapers included, among others, *Die Frankfurter Zeitung*, *Das Berliner Tageblatt*, and *Die Vossische Zeitung*. The published records of the German Commission to Investigate the Causes of World War I were consulted at the General Library of the University of Michigan. All translations of source materials published in the German language were made by the present writer.

Aside from its contribution to the field of international relations, the study seeks to fill an existing gap in the documentary coverage of Stresemann's foreign policy. None of the existing biographies of Gustav Stresemann extends beyond the general, popular level of writing, and none can be considered useful for the requirements of scholarly research except as background material. For that reason, it was deemed necessary to provide an academically acceptable and useful foundation for further scholarly research on the statesman who occupied a key position in Germany between the wars. Also, by providing an exhaustive analysis of available documentary sources on Stresemann, the writer hopes to clarify the many emotional and speculative judgments of the man and his policy.

Furthermore, all the existing biographies on Stresemann fail to separate the various phases of his foreign policy, and in particular no publication works out his relationship, and that of his policy, to the peace settlement of Versailles. This study seeks to contribute to the field of international relations by presenting a concentrated research effort in that direction. Although a careful reading of *Das Vermächtnis* may facilitate a general appreciation of the basic aspects of Stresemann's foreign policy with respect to the Treaty of Versailles, it does not represent more than an incomplete, chronological arrangement of Stresemann's writings, speeches, and other materials. It was considered desirable to prepare a specialized study on Stresemann with reference to other documents and source materials so that no statement on the man or his policy, no judgment, and no evaluation remain undocumented. This endeavor was of course limited to Stresemann's revisionism. Moreover, *Das Vermächtnis* does not cover the period prior to 1923, except in a summary fashion. By undertaking a careful study of the earlier years of Stresemann's public career, with the ultimate purpose of the study in mind, it was believed that significant relationships, not otherwise established, could be discovered.

Thus this study aims at making an original contribution in the following respects: (1) it is the first exhaustive, documentary analysis of a given aspect of Stresemann's foreign policy; (2) it seeks to work out a pattern of pacific revisionism of a major peace treaty by a key figure in European international politics.

The present writer is greatly indebted to Professor Arnolf Wolfers of Yale, who was influential in the choice of the topic; to Professor Howard M. Ehrmann of the Department of History at the University of Michigan, who assisted with valuable suggestions and encouragement; and to Professors James K. Pollock, Lawrence Preuss, Marshall M. Knappen, and Russell H. Fifield of the Department of Political Science at the University of Michigan, who passed judgment upon the manuscript at various stages. Special thanks go to Consul Henry Bernhard of Stuttgart, Germany, formerly Stresemann's private secretary, and to Dr. Edgar Stern-Rubarth, now of London, who was also closely associated with the German foreign minister. Both gentlemen, in correspondence with the present writer, and in the case of Consul Bernhard by a review of the manuscript, made valuable suggestions based on their intimate knowledge of the period and the person to which this study addresses itself. Dr. Eugene Fischer-Baling of Berlin, Germany, also proved to be most co-operative when approached by the present writer.

The maps of Western Germany and of Danzig and the Polish Corridor, on pages 62 and 63, have been reproduced from a publication of the United States Department of State, *The Treaty of Versailles and After, Annotations of the Text of the Treaty* (Washington, 1947).

Henry L. Bretton

University of Michigan
Ann Arbor, Michigan
March 1953

CONTENTS

xi

MAPS

STRESEMANN
AND THE REVISION
OF VERSAILLES

CHAPTER I

THE PREPARATORY YEARS

In many ways, Gustav Stresemann was an outstanding figure among German political leaders and statesmen. Whatever ulterior motives one might attribute to him, the total record of his public career and private life bespeaks a spirit of conciliation, international co-operation, and humanism. His record in those respects stands unsurpassed in the annals of German history. He combined an unusual political acumen with an astonishing mental agility to swing himself to the top of German political life and to maintain himself there for a remarkably long period. Engaging at times in what might be called a kind of acrobatics, he accomplished seemingly impossible feats that found him representing the extreme Right at one time and the Left at another. All of this had apparently no detrimental effect upon his career. He changed from an attitude approaching chauvinism to one of enthusiastic, intense internationalism; revengeful at first and demanding retribution from Germany's enemies, he subsequently became a devotee of pacifism and rapprochement. According to the hour and the opportunity, Stresemann's political insight permitted him to perceive Germany's changing position on the international scene, and his flexibility enabled him to adjust himself rapidly to the different tasks arising from new conditions.[1]

Gustav Stresemann was born on May 10, 1878, seven years after the founding of the German Empire and in the year of the Berlin Congress. Coming from the middle class—his father was a retailer of bottled beer—the young Stresemann found himself at a disadvantage in an essentially aristocratic society. Moreover, the trials and tribulations of the small businessman, in an age of industrial and commercial combinations and monopolization, imbued young Gustav with a passion for the economic and social underdog, the "little man." It can be said that Stresemann was literally born a Liberal.

In 1897, Stresemann went to the University of Berlin where he studied economics, public finance, political science (*Staatsrecht*), international law, history, and literature. Although the latter two were his favorite subjects, his practical sense, emphasized as it were by a romantic frustration, led him to write his doctoral dissertation on the development of the bottled-beer industry. His first job, at twenty-three, brought him in close contact with organized small business. As assistant manager of the Association of German Chocolate Manu-facturers, he sparked the fight against heavy industry, a fight which was to assume nation-wide proportions. His subsequent positions and industrial connections all stood under the sign of economic liberal-ism, of protection for small entrepreneurs against the inroads made upon their trade by heavy industry. The finishing industries, which he represented, were languishing under a national trade policy main-tained under pressure from powerful political and economic interests. While the small industries depended upon a constant flow of cheap raw materials from abroad, heavy industry and agriculture insisted on a policy of high tariffs. The experience accumulated in the course of that struggle tended to shape the future foreign minister's views on international trade and may well have been responsible for his abiding faith in economic interdependence as a healing factor in international relations. Although he was subsequently obliged to recognize the pri-macy of politics in the realm of foreign policy, he never lost sight of this early training.

In 1906 he married Käthe Kleefeld. This marriage became a source of strength for Stresemann, contributing to his success in later years to an extent that cannot be overestimated. His wife, together with their two sons and the faithful and efficient private secretary, Henry Bernhard, made up a team of friends, advisors, and confidants that evoked the envy of many among Stresemann's contemporaries.

Stresemann's parliamentary career began in 1907 when he was first elected a deputy to the Imperial Reichstag. He represented the National-Liberal Party, whose leader was Ernst Bassermann. Failing to be re-elected in 1912 against Social-Democratic opposition, he trav-eled to North America, returning prior to the outbreak of the war. In December 1914, he was again elected to parliament. From that time on, until his death, he retained a seat in the Reichstag.

Germany's position during the early phases of World War I war-ranted extreme optimism and resulted in the advancement of far-reaching annexationist designs by leaders of the government, the several political parties, and economic and other voluntary organiza-tions.[2] The military high command was, of course, no exception. The most active propaganda agency among the annexationists was the Pan-German League. The political party showing closest affinity to it was the National-Liberal Party.[3] That party had been in the forefront of the domestic struggle for political reforms and in that sense had become an outspoken opposition party. However, in the field of foreign policy and with regard to war aims, it stood firmly on the grounds of a "Greater Germany" and substantial annexations. It was in this latter field that Gustav Stresemann at first established his qualifications for political leadership.

Following his apprenticeship as assistant secretary of the Association of German Chocolate Manufacturers, Stresemann had advanced to the leadership of the Union of Industrialists, an organization of the manufacturing branches of German industry. After the outbreak of the war, the Union became affiliated with the Central Union of German Industrialists, which in turn became one of the most powerful forces in the Pan-German League. In addition, Stresemann joined, in January 1917, what became known as the "Commission for a German Peace." Taking its cue from the Pan-German League, the Commission pressed for a negotiated peace, which was to give Germany the desired extensions of the eastern and western boundaries, control over Belgium and Poland, the coast of Flanders, and expanded colonial possessions. It demanded that the costs of the war be borne by the "vanquished." By affiliation a Pan-Germanist, and by political choice a National-Liberal, the Stresemann of the early war years can thus be considered an annexationist.

Aside from his parliamentary and party activities, Stresemann was also a member of an interparty club, the "Wednesday Society."[4] This club, founded by Ernst Bassermann and Ludwig Stein early in the war, sought to promote a universal will to resist, and to preserve national enthusiasm and unity in Germany on a nonpartisan basis. Frequent meetings with club members and an occasional assignment as secretary of the club permitted Stresemann to become acquainted with a great variety of German leaders in all walks of life. Among the members of the Wednesday Society were Friedrich Naumann, Walther Rathenau, Ludwig Stein, Count Ulrich von Brockdorff-Rantzau, Albert Ballin, Albert Südekum, Otto Hoetzsch, and Georg Bernhard. Stresemann's subsequent rise to prominence must be attributed to this phase of his life as well as to his astonishing command of parliamentary procedure and oratory, to his close association with several important commercial and industrial enterprises and organizations, and to his prominent role in the German-Canadian and German-American economic associations.

Stresemann's wartime role is best summarized by four events: his disapproval of the peace offer of December 12, 1916; his opposition to the Erzberger Peace Resolution of July 9, 1917; the assumption of the leadership of the National-Liberal Party following Bassermann's death on July 27, 1917; and his participation in the overthrow of Bethmann-Hollweg, then German chancellor, during the government crisis of July 1917.

Stresemann objected to the several peace proposals because of the prevailing uncertainty regarding the ultimate achievement of annexationist war aims in the event of a negotiated peace, and because of his faith in the invincibility of German arms.[5] Bassermann's death, while giving Stresemann the title of the departed leader, did not necessarily assure him the undivided support of the party's rank and file. From July 1917 on, it became imperative for Stresemann to prepare himself for continued leadership by full consideration of all major trends within the party, precariously trying to maintain a balance between the forces of radicalism of the Right and Left. He proved himself eminently qualified for such a task.

The government crisis of July 1917 concerned Stresemann in his capacity as leader of one of the strongest parties. His active participation in the retirement of Bethmann-Hollweg, however, especially in the light of the existing military situation, was indicative of a willingness to end the war short of a German victory.[6] Stresemann attacked Bethmann-Hollweg on July 9, 1917, on the floor of the Reichstag. Testifying in 1927 before the Commission to Investigate the Causes of the German Collapse, he asserted that his opposition to the imperial chancellor had been based upon the latter's promotion of an independent kingdom of Poland, a policy which tended to prevent a separate peace with Russia at the time.[7] The move against the chancellor was Stresemann's first attempt to inject himself directly into the sphere of higher, domestic politics. Bethmann's subsequent resignation tended to improve Stresemann's chances for high office, since his move was seconded by Field Marshal von Hindenburg and General Ludendorff.[8]

Immediately preceding the military collapse and the Armistice, Stresemann learned that his annexationist background would prevent his holding a government position in any coalition designed to assure Germany favorable peace conditions.[9] Subsequently, instead of entering the government, he became a leader of the opposition, leading the imperial forces in a parliament dominated by the Social-Democrats. In that position, Stresemann experienced the collapse of the Empire and the emergence of the Weimar Republic.

On November 20, 1918, nine days after the Armistice, the National-Liberal Party reconstituted itself under a new name, the German People's Party.[10] Attempts to merge the National-Liberals with the Progressive People's Party failed, primarily because of dis-

agreements over domestic matters.[11] In the shadow of the peace conference convened at Paris on January 12, 1919, Stresemann's political
fortunes took another turn when a merger of the German People's
Party and the Democratic Party became a possibility. The new party,
so it appeared, would be composed of a majority of Democrats, with
Stresemann excluded from the General Executive Committee. The
fact that the merger did not materialize was in no small measure due
to Stresemann's refusal to assume an active role in the proposed
party.[12] Two months after the proceedings at Versailles had begun,
Stresemann was elected first chairman of the People's Party at the
first party conference. The threat of a new party, without him or with
him only in a minor role, was safely warded off.

On February 6, 1919, the Constituent National Assembly convened at Weimar with nineteen People's Party deputies out of a total
of four hundred twenty-one. Stresemann represented his party, small
as it was, on two major committees related to foreign affairs, the Committee on Peace Negotiations and the so-called Supervisory Committee. Membership in these committees permitted him to increase his
knowledge of the elements of foreign policy under republican conditions during the initial phases of the Weimar Republic. Here it must
be noted that although the primary objective of the National Assembly
had been the drafting of a constitution for the Republic, the negotiations over the peace terms and the signing of the Treaty of Versailles
expanded the scope of its activities. Thus, Stresemann was intimately
concerned with German foreign policy from the very beginning of the
new German republic.

During the period of the National Assembly, Stresemann kept his
party out of the so-called Weimar Coalition, made up of Social-
Democrats, Democrats, and the Center Party. Following the success
of the People's Party in the elections to the first Reichstag, on June 6,
1920, the party entered the government, and Stresemann moved temporarily from the opposition to a position of qualified support of the
Republic. Having been elected to the Reichstag at the head of his
party's ticket, Stresemann was soon after elected to the chairmanship
of the powerful Committee on Foreign Affairs.[13] While the People's
Party withdrew from the government in May 1921, over an issue of
foreign policy, he continued as chairman of that committee until August 1923, when he assumed the chancellorship.

Stresemann's chancellorship and his subsequent establishment of a
virtual monopoly over the conduct, if not control, of Germany's foreign policy represent the next major steps of his career. When President Friedrich Ebert, on August 12, 1923, asked Gustav Stresemann

to attempt the formation of a cabinet, the leader of the German People's Party had indeed come a long way since the days of Pan-Germanism. He had become the acknowledged leader of a parliamentary group, the Great Coalition, which constituted the only workable majority in the Reichstag. The preceding cabinet, led by Dr. Wilhelm Cuno, had resigned under the impact of the Ruhr occupation by French, Belgian, and Italian troops, with the intent of widening the parliamentary basis of German foreign policy. The vote of confidence for the first Stresemann cabinet, on August 14, 1923, brought him a majority of 52 percent of the total membership of the Reichstag.[14] The fact that the former nationalist-annexationist now had the confidence of the Social-Democrats was indicative of his accomplished political metamorphosis. Yet the new Stresemann was not inconsistent with the old. There was a distinct demand for militant liberalism in the Republic. The expected social revolution had not materialized and the superficial political changes merely tended to extend the old struggle between the classes. The Republic was far from being secure, and in order to avoid a total collapse, a middle course had to be chosen. A man like Gustav Stresemann, identified neither with the forces of social revolution nor with those of political reaction, was clearly the answer.

Stresemann had succeeded Chancellor Cuno not only because he commanded the confidence of a sufficient parliamentary majority, but also because he had risen to a position of pre-eminence in the field of foreign affairs and had the confidence of the industrial leaders of the Ruhr and the Rhineland, the most critical areas in the summer of 1923.[15] Last but not least, the fact that Stresemann also enjoyed the confidence of the British Ambassador at Berlin, Lord D'Abernon, had some bearing on his appointment.[16] Germany was in need of an ally against France, and Britain had on several occasions shown a tendency to support the German point of view. A German chancellor acceptable to Great Britain was a most valuable asset to German foreign relations at such critical times.

As chancellor—and foreign minister, since Stresemann had reserved the latter portfolio to himself—he struck out boldly for an economic understanding with France over the Ruhr and reparation questions. However, before seven weeks had passed, difficulties of a domestic nature threatened the newly installed cabinet. The right wing of the People's Party, primarily the representatives of heavy industry, revolted against Stresemann's policy of appeasing the Socialists. Thus, comparatively early in his career as architect of German foreign policy, Stresemann found it necessary to extract concessions from the Social-Democrats in order to keep his own party together and, on the other hand, to fight the right wing in the People's Party to the point where they would be prepared to work with the Socialists in the interest of a strong and uniform foreign policy. In this particular instance, compromises on the labor-management front, concerning the length of working hours, had to be reached in order to assure an early evacuation of Allied troops from the Ruhr. Extension of the working day, as the Ruhr and Rhine industrialists demanded, threatened to force the Socialists out of the Great Coalition, and tended to weaken the foreign policy pursued by Stresemann. Reduction of the working day, as the Socialists demanded, would have led to a widening of the split within Stresemann's own party.

The Stresemann cabinet lasted one hundred days. It fell primarily because the chancellor was convinced that intra- and interparty conflicts over domestic issues had weakened the Great Coalition to the point where the foreign minister could no longer count on a firm parliamentary backing for his policy.[17] Stresemann the chancellor was sacrificed to Stresemann the foreign minister.

CHAPTER II

THE FRUITFUL YEARS

The change-over from purely nominal to actual control of the foreign office found Stresemann face to face with a group of men who were to a certain extent quite strange and unfamiliar. As a descendant of a middle-class family, he harbored certain suspicions concerning the nobility and the diplomats. In spite of the constitutional changes, the German foreign office had remained essentially an assemblage of aristocrats. The son of a beer distributor could not avoid a feeling of uneasiness among the scions of an aristocratic society. Yet it did not take him long to bridge that gap. As soon as he had become convinced that men like Von Bülow, Count Zech, Von Richthofen, Von Schubert, Von Dirksen, Von Maltzan, to mention only a few, were honest, hard working, and loyal officials, he permitted a friendship to develop that lasted throughout the years of his incumbency. Such a cordial relationship was of mutual benefit to the minister and to his staff. As leader of a political party, as member of parliament, and as a cabinet member, Stresemann had to rely heavily upon his staff. On the other hand, the foreign office stood to gain by the minister's political power and influence. Under the circumstances, even his frequent absences for reasons of health were not held against him. One of his staff described the relationship in these words: "His most outstanding characteristic was his ability to grasp political ideas and to apply them to prevailing domestic and foreign policy requirements. . . . His talent to fashion thoughts that were presented to him into surprising, convincing, and acceptable concepts, was virtually amazing. During the sessions of the League of Nations Council, he surprised his colleagues —who had prepared careful notes for him, covering all points on the agenda—by his rich imagination. Ignoring the prepared notes, he would present a given case in a manner that was totally different from that expected and planned by his technical advisers." The applause which greeted his remarks at international conferences convinced doubters that his was a useful approach.[1]

Stresemann was not incapable of developing ideas all his own. The basic concepts of German foreign policy were of course determined by forces beyond the control of a minister. However, the manner in which given demands or proposals were presented to the world, the element of timing, the degree of emphasis placed on a demand, and all other manifestations and prerogatives of a decision-maker bore the unmistakable imprint of Stresemann's imaginative, even idealistic, character traits. There is evidence that he originated many of the foreign policy moves himself, or, conversely, that many of the key moves would not have been made had it not been for the fact that it was Gustav Stresemann who occupied the position of foreign minister. Determined to follow a theme through to its conclusion, and with an element of personal courage, he frequently assumed personal responsibility for foreign policy stratagems which were highly unpopular, even dangerous. His untimely death was no doubt hastened by his inclination to favor a speedy but more dangerous solution over a slow, but personally less strenuous and safer approach.

Following his "retirement" to the foreign office, Stresemann found himself confronted by this situation: the country had just emerged from the nightmare of inflation and it had become a matter of greatest urgency to arrive at a lasting and financially bearable reparation settlement with the Allied Powers. The foremost task in this respect was the creation of a sound basis for reconciliation between Germany and France. In general, Germany had to be led back into the community of nations, the most powerful members of which insisted on treating the vanquished nation as an outcast and untrustworthy international brigand. Here Stresemann encountered what he deemed to be a dangerous attitude prevailing among members of his foreign office staff. Hoping for further beneficial developments along the lines of the Rapallo Treaty of 1922, men like Count Brockdorff-Rantzau, ambassador at Moscow, and Baron von Maltzan, career officer in the foreign office, leaned toward an Eastern orientation. As Stresemann saw it there was no immediate danger in a policy based on correct and friendly relations with the Soviet Union. There could only be advantages in such an approach. However, opposed to military solutions of Germany's foreign policy problems, he viewed the military aspects of a close alliance with the Soviet Union—as was envisaged by the leadership of the *Reichswehr*—with grave concern. Throughout his tenure at the foreign office, he shrank away from what he considered to be a potentially fatal embrace of the Russian bear. The strengthening of age-old bonds which tied Germany to the West became therefore the basis for Stresemann's foreign policy.

The attempts at settling the reparation question provided the foreign minister with his first opportunity to meet face to face with his counterparts in Britain and in France. The first London conference of the reparation experts lasted from July 16 to August 1, 1924. Here the victors met with the vanquished under the sign of Anglo-French unity and understanding. Stresemann, unfamiliar at first with the procedure and the diplomatic figures, found it difficult to utilize his talents. However, before the first series of meetings was over, he had scored his first diplomatic triumph.[2] A question was placed on the agenda which the British and French delegates had agreed beforehand not to discuss. Contrary to Allied intentions, the question of an early evacuation of Allied troops from the Ruhr area was permitted to crop up on several occasions.

It was as a result of his conferences with the French premier, Herriot, and with other foreign diplomats, that Stresemann developed a predilection for informal, direct, and personal contact as an effective medium of diplomacy. He was not at all averse to frank and open exchange of information with the press. But Herriot's predicament, as a representative of a most sensitive parliamentary system of government, impressed the German with the need for cautious, exploratory conversations.[3] He never failed to consider that aspect of diplomacy.

On the whole, the London meetings left Stresemann with the impression that the road back to respectability was wide open for Germany, provided that he was able to keep his foreign policy on a steady, consistent course. Back in Berlin, he threw himself into the parliamentary and political battle for ratification of the agreements signed in London on August 30. It was to be a hard and bitter fight, but when it was all over and the Dawes Plan had been ratified, Stresemann had "arrived" on the international scene. He had proven to the world that he was capable of translating his given word into action.

As the year 1924 drew to a close, and following one of those strenuous election campaigns to which he and the nation were to be so frequently subjected, Stresemann initiated what was to become one of the greatest achievements of his career: a real treaty of peace among the Western powers. When the initial move was made, on February 9, 1925, Germany was without a government and Stresemann was out of office. This did not deter him, however. The country was seething under a renewed postponement of scheduled troop evacuations by the Allies. But the foreign policy had to be pushed forward; delay could prove fatal. That the audacious undertaking, designed to cement relations with the West, was crowned with success, amounted, under the circumstances, to a virtual coup on Stresemann's part.

The Locarno treaties constituted not only a proof of the foreign minister's political courage and daring but also a manifestation of his revisionist intents. He was opposed to the Treaty of Versailles with all of its unpleasant ramifications. As a pacific revisionist, however, dedicated to peaceful change rather than change by force, he preferred to alter the status imposed by Versailles by the substitution of other, more equitable and more dignified instruments of peace. The Locarno agreements represented such instruments.

The conference at Locarno provided Stresemann with an opportunity to meet with the other two statesmen who were to become his close collaborators in the fight for a normalization of Europe: Aristide Briand of France and Sir Austen Chamberlain of Great Britain.[4] He went to Locarno as a German, offering a German solution to the problem of peace. He returned as a European. Encouraged by the understanding attitude and willingness to accept compromises as evidenced by his conference partners—and perhaps also as a result of the truly European atmosphere which was so evident at Locarno—he raised his sights from relatively narrow revisionism to the greater, more lasting objective of a European union. Of course, as foreign minister of a democracy he could not afford to return without some concrete advantages. His efforts to obtain some concessions which could be used in the domestic campaign for ratification met with failure. As in the case of the previous London agreements, he had to use all of his political skill in order to weather a new internal crisis. Once again, he emerged victoriously. The Reichstag accepted the treaties and Stresemann could depart for London to set his name to the documents.

The year following Locarno saw Germany's entry into the League of Nations. Stresemann's first brush with an assembly of this sort strengthened his belief that little could be accomplished at large, unwieldy meetings. He was certain that the temporary rejection of Germany's application in March 1926 could have been avoided if the decision to admit her would have been left to a meeting of the "big three," namely, Briand, Chamberlain, and Stresemann.[5] But the ultimate triumph was much more satisfactory. When the German delegation, led by the foreign minister, made its entry into the hall of the League Assembly on September 10, 1926, a bitter and thorny road lay behind them. Germany had once again returned to the community of nations. Stresemann was ready to forget the past and to concentrate on the restoration of a world still bleeding from the wounds of a universal conflict. His partner, Aristide Briand, greeted Germany's admission with an enthusiastic appeal to the nations represented at the

League of Nations: "Away with rifles and cannon; make place for arbitration and for peace." The echo of that appeal was to resound long after the memorable occasion. But it was to be a hollow sound, only a memory of a glorious but lost opportunity.

What was true of the spectacular entry into the League of Nations was also true of the equally spectacular tête-à-tête with Briand at a small inn outside Geneva. The far-reaching understandings, plans, and promises that passed between the two statesmen at Thoiry remained hollow and unfulfilled. France and Germany had never seemed closer than at that time. But Briand was not France and Stresemann was not Germany. The tragic misunderstanding which kept the two nations apart took no account of the harmony and friendship reigning on this occasion. A short time later Stresemann was to ask: "*Gallia, quo vadis?* Is the deadly spirit of war to prevail, or the spirit that will open a new chapter in history of which the first words shall be: The peace and freedom of all peoples? We are justified in putting this question; not only we, but all peoples that want peace are waiting for an answer."[6] There was only silence from across the Rhine.

How did the diplomatic failure affect the man? Stresemann still enjoyed life. A typical product of the metropolis, he had acquired a taste for that unabashed, uninhibited conviviality that has always been associated with Berliners. A glass of beer or wine, a good dinner and a cigar, and the company of friends, were enough to make him forget the disappointments of his career. Whether it was in the small cafe in Locarno, at the frequent teas given for the press, or in the close family circle, Gustav Stresemann radiated an enthusiastic appreciation of the lighter side of life. In private conversation or at public appearances, he liked to surprise his listeners with his accomplished observation on German history or literature. Whether the topic was Goethe's writings or the historical significance of a given incident from the past, Stresemann was equally prepared to expound a sound thesis and to defend it against all comers. Instead of quoting homespun proverbs in support of his points, he spiced his political discourses with pertinent quotations from his favorite literary sources. In that respect, he had no peer among German leaders of his day. In general, whatever the fortunes of diplomatic warfare, whatever the disappointments of his profession, Stresemann remained an optimist until the last possible moment.

When the "Locarno spirit" seemed to have evaporated, Stresemann could have retired from the political scene. His health was poor. His family and his doctors counseled him to shorten his working days and to take a much needed holiday in Egypt to cure the kidney ailment from which he had suffered for so long. He could have written his memoirs and recouped the financial losses which he had incurred while in office. But he persisted. It is here that the charge that he was a nationalist at heart can be repudiated. If he had been determined to prevent a conciliation between France and Germany, to sabotage efforts to lay to rest the ghost of 1914, and to undermine the then existing international order, his retirement could have accomplished all that. His abdication would have been the signal to nationalists and chauvinists in all European countries to rise and to give the *coup de grâce* to the delicate structure erected at London, Locarno, and at Geneva. He could have sat back and watched the flames of hatred and revenge consume the remnants of a weakened Europe. The fact that he literally risked his life in the attempt to save the peace is a stronger testimony to his pacific intentions than all the documentary evidence taken together. There is no greater sacrifice possible than the sacrifice of one's life.

It was indeed a tragic event when the deathly sick man appeared before the Nobel Prize Committee on June 29, 1927, to receive and to acknowledge that great distinction conferred upon him for his efforts on behalf of peace. His life's work was crumbling as he reflected: "The years that have . . . passed have brought mountainous seas and deep abysses; they brought the beginning of confidence on which soon fell the snow of mistrust and war-psychosis, and at present seem to indicate a crisis of confidence in the whole attempt to establish peace."[7] His appearance in Paris, in August 1928, for the purpose of putting his signature on the Kellogg-Briand Peace Pact, was equally tragic. The treaty to outlaw war as an instrument of policy was meaningless by and of itself. The stricken man could have spared himself the torture of an uncomfortable train trip and the hustle and bustle which always accompany official appearances. Yet he left his sickbed, a dying man, to keep his word.

In August 1929, he undertook another journey, to The Hague, to participate in the negotiations on the Young Plan. Only his tremendous will power kept him alive. The agreements arrived at contained a modest measure of success. But it was too late. His final appearance before the League of Nations shocked all observers, and the world was witness to his death agonies. When a stroke ended his life on October 3, the light of peace went out all over Europe. A phrase that he addressed to his faithful friend Lord D'Abernon should be his fitting epitaph: "See, the great moment found a small-souled race."

CHAPTER III

THE FORMATIVE STAGE: POLICY

I. *The End of the War.* The foreign policy of Gustav Stresemann was formed during the closing stages of the World War, which
saw Germany defeated by the armed forces of the Allied and Associated Powers. The knowledge and experience gained by him as member of parliament and as party leader proved to be of the greatest
value once he was charged with the conduct of German foreign policy
in the year 1923 and after. Many thoughts, ideas, and concepts, which
matured under the impact of an unexpected military defeat, became
part of the future minister of foreign affairs, and of his foreign policy. It is for that reason that this part commences with the closing
phases of the World War, the ensuing Armistice, and the peace negotiations.

The year 1917 saw Gustav Stresemann in the role of a most
vociferous annexationist and militarist. He based his demands for
continued military efforts, in spite of evident reverses suffered by
German arms on land and on the seas, on certain economic considerations. Not even the threat of American intervention in the war could
deter him. To his mind, Germany had to win a military victory in
order to strengthen herself economically against a world which would
still be united against her after the war.[1] He regarded the war as a
struggle for the domination of the overseas trade routes, as a struggle
for the markets of the world. To him, the war was primarily a conflict
between Germany and Great Britain, the trading nations of the world.
Lecturing to the propaganda division of the war office in 1917, he
stated his views quite plainly: "This war is an economic struggle, and
the next one most likely, too."[2]

As leader of the conservative National-Liberal Party, he was
obliged to defend the vested interests of the light industries and to
seek consideration of their collective interests in the war and peace
councils of the nation. The war aims which he sought to secure were
primarily related to industrial and commercial interests and to questions of postwar international trade. On April 20, 1917, he reminded
the military leaders: "Longwy, Briey, and Courland are economic

problems, first; military, second; and sentimental, last."[3] His critique of the propaganda efforts of the military authorities centered on their failure to stress the economic aspects of the war.

Convinced that Great Britain was the principal adversary, he did not shrink from advocating unrestricted submarine warfare when the over-all military situation seemed to warrant desperate measures.[4] The price to be paid for this move, namely, the entry of the United States into the war, seemed to be negligible to Stresemann, especially because he held the American war potential, and in particular her shipbuilding capacity, in exceedingly low esteem.[5] Reliance on Germany's military and naval strength caused him to state that a sustained submarine offensive against Great Britain would force that nation to surrender within six months.[6]

The combination of the economist-industrialist and parliamentary deputy made up the Stresemann of 1917 and 1918. This, together with close ties to the military and naval authorities, created the basis for his strategic concept of Germany's military and economic position. Preoccupied with Napoleon's struggle against British sea power, but with the limited military knowledge of a politician and without insight into the realities of naval warfare, he could not raise himself above the situation of 1815. He tenaciously held to the theory of an exclusive conflict between Germany and Britain and utterly failed to take into account the rise of the United States.[7]

His annexationist program was sweeping indeed. In the West he proposed the annexation of the French industrial areas of Longwy and Briey, economic domination of Antwerp, and demanded that arrangements be made to perpetuate the long-standing conflict among the Flemish and the Walloons in order to assure the future neutrality of Belgium.[8] In the East he proposed annexation of Courland, utilizing the Bolshevik Revolution as an excuse to allow German troops to march into the provinces of Livonia and Estonia.[9] In the course of the negotiations leading to the Treaty of Brest-Litovsk, he went so far as to recommend that "close attention be paid to the Dvina-Dnieper Canal."[10] He recommended annexations at all costs, even against the wishes of the population. When certain political leaders became inclined to forgo war gains as a result of popular pressure, Stresemann remained adamant.[11] He showed no scruples about annexing foreign territories simply because such undertakings would tend to obstruct international reconciliation after the war. Having no faith in anything but power—economic, military, and naval—he considered any thought of international understanding on premises other than those of *Machtpolitik* idle and detrimental to the best interests of the nation.[12] He was not prepared to return to the *status quo ante bellum* because Germany had been exhausted economically and was now in bitter need of rehabilitation and replenishing of her resources. Whatever the outcome of the war, Germany had to face the postwar world on at least an equal footing.

For Stresemann the revolution in Russia was a most opportune event. In his opinion, it improved Germany's military position and bargaining powers vis-à-vis the Western Allies and Associated Powers. Already in April of 1917, he had advised the war office not to interfere with the revolution, but to consider it the equivalent of a German military victory on the Eastern Front.[13] By July 1918, he demanded that the German government come to a friendly understanding with the Soviets as soon as possible. The real enemy was in the West, as far as Stresemann was concerned. He saw no irreconcilable conflict between the German and Russian people, but a need for an understanding to save the peace in a continental sense. In order to avoid long, drawn-out discussions over the terms of the Treaty of Brest-Litovsk, he was even prepared to make considerable concessions to the Soviets in the form of substantial pledges regarding the eventual return of "purely Russian territories."[14] An understanding with the Soviets meant to him a strengthening of the continental economies for the economic struggle in the postwar world. In particular, he maintained that such an understanding would render an economic boycott of Germany by the United States and Great Britain exceedingly difficult, if not altogether impossible.[15] On the other hand, the proposed understanding could not and should not develop into a formal alliance, and neither should it preclude some annexations of Russian territories. Stresemann believed that annexations did not necessarily preclude friendly relations with the state from which territories had been detached. To prove his point, he called attention to the fact that Russia had fought alongside Japan in spite of the loss of Port Arthur and in spite of the Treaty of Portsmouth of 1905, and that Italy was fighting alongside of France and Great Britain in spite of her failure to regain Savoy and Nice. To him, compensations for the sake of alliances or understandings were meaningless and without effect. Instead, so he stated, the hour called for strength and self-assurance, both of which counted for more in the realm of international relations than weakness expressed by concessions. Soviet-German relations would have to be based on the recognition that power relationships follow power consciousness.[16]

II. *The Armistice.* Stresemann's position with regard to the conduct of the war was based on the assumption of the invincibility of

German arms. When it became evident to him that he had been deceived by the military, not only did he have to discard his wartime program of annexations, but his prestige and reputation as a reliable parliamentarian also suffered heavily. The policy which he developed in consequence of his political misfortune marks the real beginning of the Stresemann with whom this study is concerned.

The first doubts whether victory could be achieved came to him on August 21, 1918, when the secretary of state, Von Hintze, informed him of the true military situation.[17] Soon afterwards, the change in Germany's fortune was brought home to him by another event. The question of the eligibility of the National-Liberal Party to participate in a projected coalition government "to save the peace," caused one leader to suggest to parliament that no government should be burdened with the annexationist Stresemann.[18] There is evidence, however, that high government circles and some military leaders considered Stresemann for the foreign ministry until October 2.[19] On that day, Prince Max von Baden, the new chancellor, informed a "disappointed" Stresemann that the latter could best serve the nation as leader of the opposition.[20]

In the newly assigned role, and partly as a result of his deep disappointment over the failure of the army command to advise him correctly on the military situation, he now embarked upon a campaign of criticism against the military leaders. One of the first demands advanced by him concerned future military appraisals by the high command of Germany's and the enemy's capabilities. He insisted that generals and their staffs be required to submit their views in writing, and that they deliver their communications in person.[21] Furthermore, he accused the army high command of having lost its sense of balance in the decisive moments, and pressed for additional assurances regarding the military situation. As a leader of the opposition, he concerned himself with clarifying the question of responsibility for the military disaster that had befallen Germany. Taking the side of the military and of parliament on political grounds, he ventured to observe on November 12, 1918: "In our case, the front has held in a manner which no saga of heroic acts could describe. But the home front collapsed in the interior, blow by blow."[22] This participation by Stresemann in the fabrication of the *Dolchstosslegende* was soon to be followed by other acts designed to salvage the prestige of the Empire and its armed forces. To be sure, during the period of transformation, Stresemann was guilty of some remarks and moves which lacked clarity of purpose. Only the coming months and years could establish clearly in which direction he was heading.

The second major objective to which Stresemann addressed himself was the proposed armistice itself. As opposition leader, he considered it his duty to warn the country of the consequences should the armistice be signed on the basis of Wilson's Fourteen Points. Aside from purely tactical considerations, he warned that the projected loss of Alsace-Lorraine would tend to cut the main arteries of German industry. The eventual loss of Upper Silesia, Posen, and parts of West Prussia were also singled out as reasons for a German refusal to accept Wilson's Fourteen Points unconditionally.[23] On the other hand, the signing of the Armistice found Stresemann devoid of all annexationist designs so far as the West was concerned. He did not wish to give the Allies cause to press their own demands.[24]

In addition to shifting responsibility for the military defeat to the home front and obscuring former annexationist designs, he added a third plank in the platform upon which a postwar foreign policy could be erected. He sought to cast doubt and suspicion upon Allied war aims in the eyes of the German public and the world at large. Stresemann's line of departure for this attack was the basic contention that Germany deserved a place of prominence in the world and that her military endeavors to secure that place had been thoroughly in keeping with moral standards governing international conduct. Accusing Wilson and the Allies of lack of good faith by claiming that the idealism expressed in the Wilsonian proposals had been dropped as soon as the balance of power had shifted in favor of Germany's enemies, Stresemann assumed the role of the injured and warned Germany never again to place her trust in speculative assumptions about world psychology.[25] In the same vein, he also noted that Germany's adversaries had failed to take cognizance of changed political and constitutional conditions, thus giving the lie to their contention that they had merely opposed the imperialist designs of the Hohenzollern dynasty. Finally, he expressed regret over the demobilization of Germany's armies in the light of the alleged lack of good faith on the part of the Allied and Associated Powers, a move the full significance of which was only to become apparent after the Treaty of Versailles had been signed.[26]

III. *Versailles*. The first news which Stresemann received from Versailles was that the German delegation had offered one hundred milliard gold marks as the upper limits for reparations. In an editorial, he pointed out that it was poor strategy for Germany to fix a sum on her own account; it was expressive of some guilt, or acknowledgment of a guilt which he, Stresemann, did not recognize and which no right-minded German should recognize. Furthermore, he maintained that an offer of a fixed sum would weaken the German argument that Germany could only be held accountable for civilian damages. Since the full extent of these damages could not readily be ascertained in terms of fixed sums, Germany should withhold any estimate of damages until the other side had come forth with a proposal.[27] His point was clear. He feared that German concessions tended to legalize Allied demands and that they would deprive of needed ammunition the opponents of a punitive treaty. In keeping with his wartime position on German naval strength, he also expressed opposition to the proposed surrender of the German fleet.

There is no doubt that Stresemann disapproved of the peace terms as they were handed to the Germans on May 7, 1919. In fact, he advised the government to reject the terms. Referring to the pre-Armistice negotiations, he charged that the treaty ignored the "specified conditions" on the basis of which Germany had laid down her arms. "Seen in the light of these conditions," he declared, "the treaty is the greatest swindle in history."[28] He singled out the clauses forbidding the *Anschluss* with Austria, and the provisions dealing with Danzig, Memel, overseas cables, and colonies, and warned: "Economically speaking, this treaty means the 'Egyptization' of Germany." In an editorial in his own periodical, *Deutsche Stimmen*, he went so far as to hint that the several Allied commissions "might very well be prepared to assume the responsibility of government in Germany, for no German government would be able to govern under the conditions imposed upon the country."[29]

Lest the debate should be turned to his own war record, Stresemann spent considerable effort on the task of castigating the Allied terms as "fraudulent," "economically and financially impossible," "illegal," and "immoral." Replying to attacks by leaders of the Democratic Party, who denied him the right to criticize Versailles in view of his past annexationist background, he pointed out that political views had no bearing on the subject. The treaty violated international law and deserved to be attacked on those grounds.[30]

On June 22, 1919, the Constituent Assembly, by a vote of 237 to 138, agreed to the signing of the treaty and voted 235 to 89 to declare its confidence in the conduct of the negotiations by the government. Both votes found Stresemann in the opposition.[31]

The essence of Stresemann's legal argument against the treaty was contained in his address before the party conference of the German People's Party in 1921:

The peace of Versailles is based on a violation of law. It is not true that Germany laid down her arms unconditionally. Even the laying down of

German arms occurred only after an indisputable exchange of notes valid under international law had taken place between the German Government of the day and Secretary of State Lansing, acting on behalf of the Allied and Associated Powers, and which had stipulated conditions upon which the peace was to be concluded.[32]

Elaborating upon this point, he stated subsequently that it had only been the laying down of German arms which had enabled the Entente to set the peace terms. Since the military surrender had been decided on the basis of pre-Armistice conditions, mutually agreed upon before the peace conference had convened, any peace terms not in keeping with those prearranged conditions lacked moral and legal force.[33]

In addition to attacking the treaty on legal grounds, Stresemann sought to fight it on economic and cultural grounds. He held that the economic and financial clauses rendered the world economy chaotic and that consequently a fight against the treaty would be a fight for normal conditions in international trade and for the safeguarding of the world's cultural treasures.[34]

Dr. Edgar Stern-Rubarth, for a time one of Stresemann's closest assistants in the field of press relations, summarized the future foreign minister's revisionist objectives with regard to the Treaty of Versailles in this manner:

Stresemann's ultimate hope, as he once confessed to me, was: To free the Rhineland, to recover Eupen-Malmédy, and the Saar, to perfect Austria's *Anschluss*, and to have, under mandate or otherwise, an African colony where essential tropical raw materials could be secured and an outlet created for the surplus energy of the younger generation.[35]

As early as October 8, 1919, Stresemann applied the theory of the concept of change in the international community to those peace terms seeking to secure a status quo. At that time, he warned the "five gentlemen who sat down at Paris to carve up the world," that they would see the day when the world's development would change the course of events as they had pictured it.[36] One of the primary factors, in Stresemann's opinion, which would tend to accelerate a change of terms set forth in the peace treaty, was the anticipated ending of Allied unity once the common rival had been eliminated. As a result of Allied rivalry and competition, Germany's postwar position would be enhanced and a new period of economic development would ensue in which Germany would no longer be confronted by a united body of nations determined to stifle and to destroy her. Stresemann prophesied a three-cornered conflict between the United

States, Great Britain, and Japan, between the great colonial powers and Italy, and predicted that American financial power would threaten Great Britain's economic expansion to a far greater extent than Germany ever could have accomplished.[37]

Once more, he returned to the pre-Armistice agreement and demanded that the peace arrangements should conform to the contents and the spirit of the note addressed to the German government by Secretary of State Lansing. Further reason for an early revision of the treaty, so he claimed, was the fact that it had been imposed upon Germany as punishment, and that Germany's signature had not been voluntary.[38] Finally, he appealed to the Allies to give the new, democratic government of Germany a peace which would serve to strengthen it in the eyes of the German public.[39] The basis for his future policy of revisionism was thus established by 1921.

IV. *The League of Nations.* The realism evident in Stresemann's early pronouncements applied also to his views on the projected League of Nations. Replying to the speech delivered by President Wilson on January 22, 1917, he had nothing but irony for Wilson's reference to the League of Nations. Citing his favorite poet, Goethe, Stresemann quoted from *Faust*:

> Dream ye of peaceful days?
> Let him dream then who can.
> War's the word that solves the crux;
> Victory,—that's the slogan.

He concluded that power had always been the determining factor in international relations and that this would always remain so. The fate of states could not be made dependent upon the terms of a League of Nations charter, for those terms would be torn up as soon as the vital interests of a strong power were at stake.[40]

In formulating his attitude toward a League of Nations, Stresemann noted that the spiritual ties among the nations of the world had been shattered beyond repair by war propaganda and its effect upon the minds of the populations. He could not see how a bridge could be erected after the war if the German people were likened to Huns and barbarians. Moreover, he firmly believed that Germany could stand cultural and political isolation if necessary. Already in 1916, he had told the Germans that they should not expend their energies after the war in an attempt to gain the recognition of their former adversaries. The latter would soon realize how much they stood to lose if they should insist upon the isolation of Germany.[41] Psychological injury and lack of faith in anything else but power, as far as international relations were concerned, made him observe, "I cannot imagine the future of Germany based exclusively on international covenants." He was not prepared to submit the consideration of Germany's vital interests to an international organization. Guaranties for Germany's security could only be obtained through reliance upon the innate strength of the nation, and not through leagues or similar international bodies.[42]

In the course of the great debate on Article Four of the proposed German constitution, Stresemann had further occasion to develop his thoughts on the League of Nations and on international law in general.[43] Stating that the proposed article was dangerous, he pointed out that the principles of the League were not yet fully known to the Constituent Assembly and that this combination of ignorance as to the full meaning of "the generally recognized rules of international law" and the proposed article, could well turn into a noose around Germany's neck. Sanctions provided under the League Covenant against acts of aggression were utilized by Stresemann to demonstrate the dangers inherent in the proposed acceptance of the concept of "generally recognized rules of international law." Characterizing the League as being "of Anglo-American origin," he warned that Germany would be forced into a most embarrassing situation should the Anglo-Saxon powers decide to apply a boycott against the Soviet Union, a power with whom Germany maintained friendly relations. "It would be foolish," so he stated, "to permit others to drive Germany into aggression against other systems of government in the name of a vague concept of international action." Concluding his remarks on Article Four, he warned further that, "unless generally recognized rules of international law" were only such as had been expressly agreed upon by Germany, the article would be likely to drag Germany into unforeseen dangers.[44]

In spite of his misgivings, however, Stresemann did not object, in principle, to an eventual accession by Germany to the League of Nations. As long as it was understood that there was nothing binding about the Covenant or the decisions arrived at by the League, he saw some use for it. In particular, he visualized a general improvement of Germany's international position once she was an equal member of the League. For that reason, he stated that Germany's entry into the League was only possible if accession did not imply recognition, by Germany, of specific treaty provisions or of the Treaty of Versailles itself.[45] Accession under stipulated nonrecognition of the peace treaty, with the understanding that Germany be an equal partner, promised to facilitate revision if not of particular clauses, then certainly of the spirit of the Treaty of Versailles. Since it was Stresemann's conviction that Germany could well afford to stay aloof from the League unless accession brought certain advantages, he fought hard to have his conditions for entry accepted in spite of the opposition of pro-League elements in the country. Replying to the contention that it would be an honor to become a member of the League, he pointed out that full equality would only be attained if Germany was granted a permanent seat in the League Council. Membership in the Council would then facilitate equality in the general community of nations. The Social-Democrats, intent on having Germany join the League at the earliest possible time, objected to Stresemann's policy of requiring the fulfillment of certain conditions prior to accession.[46] As foreign minister, unable to make his observations as candid as before, he sought to justify his refusal to beg for admittance by referring to the failure of the League powers to approach Germany through proper diplomatic channels.[47]

Speaking in retrospect, in 1925, Stresemann gave his reasons for his League policy in 1923 and 1924. He pointed out that a situation acceptable to Germany in 1925 could have turned out to be disastrous in 1923. If Germany was to function properly in the League, it was necessary for her not to enter in a humble, subdued fashion, but to achieve equality prior to the entry; to enter through the front portals, not through the back door. Concerning the principles involved in this controversy, he remarked, in 1925, that he was never concerned with the ideals inherent in an international organization, but that the sole criterion for him was the utility of a membership in the League. "I ask myself only whether it is of use to Germany if we are in the League or whether it is better if we remain outside, and I decide the question from that point of view."[48]

The bases of Stresemann's revisionism were apparent before 1923 when he became responsible for the conduct of foreign affairs. They emerged in outline during the closing phases of the World War, became more recognizable in the course of the pre-Armistice and Armistice negotiations, and were fully matured, as springboards for subsequent moves, by the time the treaty had been signed.

Regardless of the outcome of the war, Stresemann was at first a convinced adherent of the doctrine that *Machtpolitik* was the sole determining factor in international relations and that only a nation's power potential could determine its standing in the world. Relying upon Germany's importance in Europe, and thinking in terms of international trade, he believed that the victorious powers could not easily afford to ignore or even destroy her. To assure a rapid return of defeated Germany to a position of first rank, he was prepared to utilize the resources of the young Soviet Republic and advised that friendly relations be maintained with the Bolsheviks.

Having been relegated to an opposition role in the new Weimar Republic, he felt free to advance revisionist arguments and to pursue from the very beginning a policy designed to change the peace settlement. His early revisionist policy was composed of two major elements: (1) the promotion of the legend that it had only been because of the collapse of the home front that Germany's armed forces had been compelled to surrender; (2) the charge that Allied motives underlying the peace settlement were base and immoral.

As soon as the treaty terms became known to him, he attacked them on a variety of grounds. (1) They were illegal and immoral because they violated the pre-Armistice agreement and because they gave the lie to Allied contentions that the war had been a struggle against the Hohenzollern dynasty. (2) They were detrimental to sound economic and financial considerations, and threatened to disrupt international trade beyond repair. (3) They ignored the fact that political and economic conditions can never be tied to a legal status quo. Change was certain to come because of the anticipated disunity in the camp of the Allied and Associated Powers and because of the native strength of Germany.

Stresemann applied his realism also to the League of Nations and to international law in general. Unconditional adherence to the generally recognized rules of international law and to the League of Nations Covenant was detrimental to the best interests of Germany. The rules of international law were to be valid only if expressly recognized by Germany. The only utility which Stresemann could see in the League, prior to 1924, was that of a medium through which the war guilt hypothesis, the basic assumption underlying the peace arrangements, could be repudiated.

CHAPTER IV

THE FORMATIVE STAGE: METHODS

I. *Parliament and Party.* Stresemann's views on the function of parliament in the state, especially as related to the conduct and control of foreign policy, were to a considerable extent developed during the closing stages of the World War. These views are of greatest importance in the analysis of Stresemann's foreign policy with regard to the Treaty of Versailles, as will be shown subsequently. Stresemann's firm grasp of the rules of party politics and parliamentary procedure and tactics enabled him to weather many future political storms over matters of foreign policy. His concept of diplomacy is also significant inasmuch as it brought a number of innovations to the international scene. A study of the parliamentary methods and political tactics he employed in his struggle to revise certain parts of the Treaty of Versailles promises to be particularly useful because, as foreign minister, Stresemann had to rely exclusively on political and diplomatic techniques for want of a strong armed force to back him up.

Stresemann's first opportunity to develop constructive thoughts on the role parliament was to play in a modern state came with the progressive deterioration of the political structure of the Empire. Blunders committed by the imperial government in the realm of foreign policy seemed to call for substantial and thoroughgoing reforms in the direction of increased parliamentary controls. The National-Liberals, committed to safeguard the interests of the *bourgeoisie*, sensed the coming storm which threatened to tear down the very bases upon which the Empire had risen. They sensed that events threatened to undo the careful balance established by Bismarck's constitution of 1871. They learned to value the balance provided by that document, which carefully checked the several reigning dynasties by a Reichstag, a *Bundesrat* based on Prussian hegemony, and by an army and an officialdom reared in Prussian traditions. On the other hand, they saw that the ruling clique, without the benefit of parliamentary advice and counsel, was driving Germany ever closer to an abyss.[1]

Stresemann followed the party line closely. In addition to party-political considerations, and largely because of his own middle-class background, he harbored a certain suspicion of career diplomats and war leaders of noble ancestry who dabbled in foreign policy. He regretted in particular the methods of selection of diplomats and foreign service officers, methods which seemed to work to the disadvantage of the middle class, and castigated the lack of appreciation shown by those in charge of foreign policy for the world-wide connections of German merchants. As early as 1916, when it had become apparent that the prewar foreign policy had not been very successful, parliament attempted to secure an increase of control over foreign policy. In this attempt the young National-Liberal deputy, Gustav Stresemann, assumed a leading role. Speaking on a proposed measure which would have permitted discussion of foreign policy by a parliamentary committee, while parliament was in recess, he pointed out that the record of the imperial regime showed that Germany had lost such long-term allies as Italy and Russia. Therefore parliament should be permitted to exercise greater control over the conduct of foreign affairs.[2]

Following the Russian Revolution, the question of political reform became ever more urgent. On March 14, 1917, the Social-Democratic opposition was joined by the National-Liberals in a vote favoring substantial changes in the franchise and in popular representation. Gustav Stresemann was again in the forefront of the movement. Cautiously avoiding a direct attack on the imperial prerogatives, he nevertheless came out strongly in favor of parliamentary rights and privileges.[3] Parliament, so he held, had been circumvented for too long. Lack of liaison between those in charge of foreign policy and parliament had undermined the people's faith in the government and had dangerously weakened public morale.[4]

Corresponding to the progressive deterioration of the military phases of the struggle, there developed in Stresemann an ever greater desire for methods and techniques to strengthen the home front. Again, he scrutinized the conduct of foreign policy and discovered that it lacked popular support because of the limited franchise which tended to relegate large segments of the population to a position of political impotence and disinterest. Universal franchise, he maintained, had a direct bearing on the success or failure of foreign policy. A successful conclusion of the war, he warned, depended upon the fullest utilization of all domestic forces. The effort was doomed to failure unless more expression was given to the people's representatives, more universally chosen.[5] The trinity of democracy, public morale, and foreign policy—the hypothetical basis for military victory

—became almost a fetish with Stresemann as the end came in sight. By October 1918, he went so far as to state that "the system which has brought us this state of affairs has forfeited its right to further existence."[6] He was particularly irked by the failure of the "system" to educate the country properly in the fullest utilization of available resources, thus permitting "the amateurs of military science in Great Britain and the United States" to beat Germany at her own game. This sentiment was in keeping with thoughts expressed by him as early as March 1917, when he had publicly demanded a reorientation toward increased co-operation among government, parliament, and people.[7] The industrialist in Stresemann, impressed by the power of advertising, had recognized the potentialities of the parliamentary system in modern warfare, diplomatic and otherwise.

In the course of the political debate following the proclamation of the Weimar Republic, Stresemann had occasion to state his political and constitutional credo quite clearly. Following a skirmish with members of the left wing of the National-Liberal Party over the recognition of the new political system, he succeeded in softening that recognition by making the pertinent party proclamation read: "We stand on the grounds of the democratic form of state created by the fact of the revolution. . . ."[8] Aside from that qualification, Stresemann saw no reason to criticize the new constitution in detail, at least not at the time. His real attack on the Weimar constitution awaited the convening of the Constituent Assembly on February 6, 1919.

The first constitutional issue attracting Stresemann's attention concerned the creation of a permanent parliamentary committee on foreign affairs under Article 35, Paragraph 1 of the proposed constitution. Even though he felt strongly about that subject, Stresemann himself did not take a stand. Instead he left it to the chairman of the parliamentary group of the People's Party, Dr. Heinze, to propose that the article be stricken. In spite of the fact that he was the chairman of the party and had been his party's representative on the committee debating the issue, before it came to the floor, and thus had been responsible for the party's decision to oppose the institution of the foreign affairs committee, he was not prepared to identify himself with the rejection. However, Dr. Heinze's justification for the rejection sounded very much as though a future foreign minister had prepared it. The justification addressed itself to "a dangerous control" which such a committee would exercise over the foreign policy "of an able and farsighted foreign minister," while inefficiency of a minister would not be remedied by such a "control committee."[9] This pronouncement stood in direct contradiction to the position held by Stresemann while the issue had concerned an increase of parliamentary powers under a monarchy. Now that the wheel had turned a full cycle, Stresemann was opposed to parliamentary controls over the conduct of foreign policy on a mandatory basis. In the same vein, he also voted against a motion to give parliament the power to subpoena documents pertaining to the conduct of foreign affairs.[10]

The independence of the office of foreign minister under the republican form of government was the subject of one of the first pronouncements made by the leader of the People's Party in the newly convened Reichstag in June 1920. Expressing regret over the failure of the new constitution to "de-politicize" the office of the foreign minister and foreign policy in general, he went so far as to state that it would be downright foolish to inquire about the political connections of the head of the foreign office. In this case, he observed, *la recherche du parti est interdite.*[11] There is sufficient evidence to warrant the assumption that Stresemann had in mind an extrapolitical foreign minister of the type prevailing under the Empire.

The official debut of Gustav Stresemann, following the period of apprenticeship in the National Assembly, took place on the day he was elected chairman of the standing committee on foreign affairs of the Reichstag, the very committee against the creation of which he had raised his early objections.[12] This was a most significant step, the culmination of years of oratory and literary effort in the field of foreign policy. Thanks to the majority vote in the National Assembly, when Article 35 had been voted upon, Stresemann now found himself in the position of a key figure on the parliamentary scene, with considerable power and influence in the making and control of foreign policy.

The newly elected chairman injected himself now into the center of foreign affairs by virtue of his controlling position and his longstanding experience. After the London Ultimatum of March 3, 1921, which demanded acceptance of Allied reparation claims by Germany, he insisted that the debate on the London negotiations be postponed until the committee on foreign affairs had had a chance to discuss the matter *in camera.*[13] Defending the government's right to conduct negotiations abroad without direct and immediate reference to parliament, he departed even further from his previous position by stating flatly that parliament as such was incapable of governing. "If the government has the confidence of the House," he explained, "then it must have the right to carry on with the affairs of the state until that confidence is withdrawn."[14] This was a declaration worthy of the best tradition of British parliamentary practice. On the other hand, to forestall any charges of unconstitutionality, he attempted, on two occasions, to come to the assistance of the government. He scheduled meetings of the committee at which government representatives were to be given an opportunity to explain the situation to avoid unnecessary disclosure of plans before a plenary session of parliament.[15] On another occasion, he proposed that a vote of confidence in the foreign policy of the government be passed upon in committee to prevent an anticipated adverse vote on the floor.[16] Thus, even his greatest political enemies had to admit that he was not prepared to follow unconstitutional lines in the conduct of his office. As foreign minister, he followed the same procedure unless premature disclosure of foreign policy plans was detrimental to the best interests of the nation.[17] Even then, however, he did not violate the letter of the law, but consulted with appropriate parliamentary bodies and party committees to obtain sanction for his actions.

Viscount Edgar Vincent D'Abernon, British Ambassador at Berlin, 1920-26, indicates in his memoirs that the party did not necessarily influence Stresemann's foreign policy. As British Ambassador, it was his duty to support a man whose views were acceptable to His Majesty's Government. In spite of the fact that the People's Party followed almost extremist lines, standing on the ground of monarchy and conservatism, Lord D'Abernon supported the candidature of Stresemann when the latter vied for the foreign ministry in 1921.[18] It stands to reason that D'Abernon knew a different Stresemann from the one who delivered fiery orations at party rallies. The British Ambassador traced this evident independence of the leader of the right-wing People's Party to what he called "his background of pugnacious nationalism." He reasoned that it was that background which strengthened Stresemann in the eyes of the nationalists, within the party and outside. Stresemann could do no wrong so far as the Right was concerned. If he followed a nationalist policy, he could count on the support of the rightist elements in the party; if he followed a conciliatory line in his foreign policy, then they would assume that he must have adopted these principles for imperative reasons of political expediency.[19]

Stresemann himself made no secret of his determination to attain his objectives by compromises with conflicting elements within the party. He was not prepared to waste his energies and his principles by fruitless battles against forces opposed to his policy. Even in a compromise, so he reasoned, there was still opportunity to attain one's objectives.[20] On one occasion, replying to charges that his own party was a party of compromises, he pointed out that no other policy was possible in a nation as badly split as the German. Moreover, only a firm, determined foreign policy could be successful. To assure that firmness and determination, it was necessary to arrive at compromises in order to guarantee continuity and stability of the domestic situation, the very backbone of a foreign policy. Once the domestic situation had been brought under control by compromises, the country could be represented abroad in a dignified, unified manner.[21] Domestic wrangling had to cease, once an issue crossed the national boundaries. With Stresemann, domestic policy was purely of secondary importance; it merely served as a backdrop to more significant, more vital national objectives.[22]

II. *Press and Propaganda.* The merger of domestic and foreign policy in the name of the newly established democratic society was not the only one of Stresemann's contributions. His middle-class social philosophy, coupled with a recognition of the diplomatic values inherent in modern industry, caused him to emerge with another corollary of German liberalism, namely, an increased reliance upon mass media such as the press and radio.

After 1923, as foreign minister, he was to become famous for his press conferences, his friendly relations with the press in general, and his expert use of propaganda devices both at home and abroad. Since the success or failure of his foreign policy depended heavily upon the degree to which he could mobilize public opinion abroad, and to a considerable extent, at home, mass media became tools of the first order in Stresemann's diplomatic kit. Peaceful revision of a major treaty in the face of almost insurmountable obstacles erected by the status quo powers, became largely a matter of mass appeal and propaganda.

In 1916, Stresemann delivered a speech in parliament on the subject of public opinion and diplomacy. Calling the attention of his audience to British propaganda practices, he noted with regret that "England knew how to appreciate the value of public opinion even in times of peace." Now that the two nations, Britain and Germany, were engaged in a life-and-death struggle, Germany was losing the battle for world opinion by applying antiquated methods to the propaganda defense of her cause. He noted that Great Britain was utilizing cables, telegraph, motion pictures, and "all other means given to the human race," in order to suggest certain ideas to her own citizens as well as to the peoples of the world. The most significant remark coming from that speech, however, was his reference to the British technique of "hammering propaganda into the brain."[23] In another Reichstag speech, made in 1920, he expressed a certain fascination for techniques applied by American advertisers and their relation to modern propaganda.[24] Here again it was the element of repetitious application of a given idea which attracted his attention. In later years, as will be shown subsequently, the dissemination of certain themes by repetition and magnification became standard procedure with Stresemann. To encourage new propaganda methods in the service of the war machine, he suggested, in 1916, that press attachés be assigned to each embassy and legation.[25] The future foreign minister and his propaganda technique are most clearly outlined, however, in the closing remarks of an address on "The World War and Public Opinion": "Oh, if the soul of the German people would only be a harp in the hands of the Foreign Office, an instrument which the Foreign Office knew how to play."[26]

The basic suspicion of the liberal for anything coming from the privileged classes, emerged again when Stresemann turned public attention to the evident inability of German leadership to study, influence, and utilize foreign public opinion. "Press and parliaments abroad are against us because we are lacking the intimate touch with their representatives, an advantage which foreign leaders have with regard to our press and our parliament." He traced this apparent inability to what he called "the social prejudice" of the carriers of German diplomacy, and warned that a reform "of head and limbs" of the foreign service would be inevitable after the war.[27]

The extent to which Stresemann valued the explanation over the act becomes apparent if one considers his emphasis on propaganda in connection with military action. It appears that he considered Chancellor Bethmann-Hollweg's unfortunate remark about the "scrap of paper"—which that German statesman had applied to the treaty guaranteeing the neutrality of Belgium, just before Great Britain declared war on Germany—the source of all evil in the war of propaganda between the Allies and Germany. He concluded from that incident, and from its consequences, that Germany had lost the war on the diplomatic front before the military phase had begun.[28] In addition to that initial blunder, he noted other failures on the part of responsible authorities to utilize public opinion and propaganda and to correlate them with military actions, in the interests of a more effective realization of the over-all objectives of German foreign policy. He warned the army press office, in 1917, that its failure to provide the public with visible and concrete evidence of the deadly struggle in which German armies were engaged, would inevitably lead to an underestimation of the true state of national security on the part of the home front. Pointing to Great Britain, he observed that lights were dimmed in that country, while theaters, motion-picture houses, and gala receptions continued in Germany as though the country were at peace.[29]

Concerning the German distribution of speeches made by British leaders, he demanded that the official German replies be less tardy and that they follow the distribution within twenty-four hours. German replies to foreign attacks, he observed, resembled, in their effectiveness, the legendary horn which emitted in the spring the tunes that had been blown into it in the winter.[30] In principle, he was not opposed to the distribution of foreign speeches in Germany; he merely wanted more effective counterpropaganda. He suggested that speeches and proclamations by German leaders should take into account possible adverse effects upon morale at home, something which British statesmen had realized all along. Above all, he sought to convince those in positions of responsibility that a democratic century had arrived, and that public opinion had become a major factor which could no longer be ignored.

At the third party conference in 1920, he demanded on behalf of the People's Party that the revision of the Treaty of Versailles be made the center of a propaganda campaign conducted by the government, "which should hammer into the conscience of our people and of the entire world, the fact that an injustice has been done to Germany." He further proposed the utilization of a central office for home service which would accomplish two major objectives; it would fight communism at home and the Treaty of Versailles abroad.[31] To commence with the propaganda campaign at once, he demanded that Germany publish a list of payments already made to the Allies in pursuance of reparation agreements. At the same time, he also demanded that a list of Allied war criminals be handed to those demanding prosecution of members of Germany's armed forces for alleged war crimes.[32]

Stresemann expected a great deal from those propaganda moves for he was convinced that the cause of German revisionism was best understood by the masses in the former enemy countries. All that was needed to undermine the Allied position was to present the German side of the argument to the masses in France, Great Britain, Japan, Italy, Belgium, and elsewhere, and to do that by a well-oiled, well-co-ordinated propaganda machine. For that reason, he advised the German government in 1922 to be less boastful about Germany's ability to pay reparations. "I believe," he stated before the Reichstag, "that a policy of total frankness concerning our financial weakness would . . . have a better effect on future decisions and on the estimates of Germany's ability to pay than the gesture by which we said that the first gold milliard has been raised by the stated date and has also been paid."[33] In further support of his point of view, he urged that the German government distribute passages of Bonar Law's speeches delivered at the Paris conference on reparations, and of resolutions adopted at the meeting of the International Chamber of Commerce at Rome, and of the British Bluebook on Reparations, all of which tended to support the German position on the reparation question.[34]

Stresemann's personal relations with the press were also indicative of his deep appreciation of that modern medium of information. His diaries show innumerable entries of names of outstanding domestic and foreign correspondents with whom he discussed problems of the day—at luncheons, over the breakfast table, and at the regularly scheduled press teas given at the foreign ministry.[35]

As chairman of the Reichstag's Foreign Affairs Committee, and later on as foreign minister, Stresemann contributed frequently, whenever his delicate health would permit, to a number of papers and periodicals. *Deutsche Stimmen* was the periodical most frequently used by him; papers and periodicals carrying articles signed or merely inspired by him were: *Das Hamburger Fremdenblatt*, the *National-liberale Korrespondenz*, *Nationalliberale Blätter*, *Hannoverscher Kurier*, *Magdeburgische Zeitung*, *Deutsche Allgemeine Zeitung*, *Kölnische Zeitung*, *Tägliche Rundschau*, and *Die Zeit*. Whenever he was unable, or unwilling, to place an article over his signature, he contributed anonymously or asked one of his closer associates to sign it for him. Henry Bernhard, his private secretary, Dr. Edgar Stern-Rubarth, press liaison official, or Baron Rochus von Rheinbaben, member of the People's Party and Reichstag deputy and associate in the foreign office, frequently planted the "master's voice" either in written form or as a hint or rumor among the foreign colony in Berlin.[36]

It is clear, however, that Stresemann's attitudes toward parliament and press were very similar: he preferred to utilize both as sounding boards, and no more. The bitter attacks launched against him and his policy in later years led him dangerously close to a demand for press censorship. Addressing a group of students in 1926, he formulated his thoughts in this manner:

When you read that Stein—fortunate statesman—was in a position to subject the press to pre-censorship on all foreign matters and to prohibit the writing of anything detrimental to France, then you can see how Prussia made foreign policy in those days. . . . If one has lost a war and is struggling for one's existence, then it is impossible for everyone to say what he thinks; then it is patriotic to keep one's mouth shut. . . .[37]

The question of an official organ at the disposal of the foreign minister plagued Stresemann throughout his public career. By 1925 he expressed regret that the Reich's chancellor appointed the chief of the joint press division, while the division itself was under the foreign minister.[38] He held, as he had maintained before, that the foreign ministry was essentially a nonpolitical office, and that this situation necessitated the removal of the press division from a source of political controversy into the hands of the "neutral" foreign minister.[39] Unsuccessful in this attempt, he searched for a suitable newspaper of his own. In reply to a parliamentary inquiry in 1926, he admitted, before the Foreign Affairs Committee of the Reichstag, that the government had in fact purchased the *Deutsche Allgemeine Zeitung* in April of that year and that this had been done with secret funds at his disposal.[40] In a letter to an industrialist, two years later, he again voiced a desire to have for his own use a newspaper which could afford to carry "news items designed to further international understanding, [items] which would normally not be considered as newsworthy by the highly competitive daily press."[41]

Judging by the sums allotted to the foreign ministry in the annual budget, sums which were not subject to examination by the *Rechnungshof*, and the disposal of which was entirely within the discretion of the foreign minister, Stresemann did not lack funds to propagate his ideas at home or abroad.[42] Between 1926 and 1929, the money available to the foreign minister and earmarked for propaganda, press relations, or secret purposes, ranged from eighteen to twenty-six million reichsmark per annum, and covered such diverse spheres of propaganda as German schools in foreign countries, support of destitute Germans abroad, cultural and humanitarian relations with foreign countries, commercial news services, and domestic and foreign regular news services, as well as many undisclosed agencies, agents, and channels. In the light of Stresemann's known convictions concerning the use of mass media in modern diplomacy it stands to reason that a considerable part of the public and secret funds was applied to the propagation of his ideas, i.e., toward the preparation of public opinion at home and abroad for an eventual revision of the peace arrangements. Also, it appears that he was instrumental in the creation of the several funds, since he held the office of foreign minister from 1923 to 1929, the years during which the foreign ministry was developed.

Replying to a charge made by Raymond Poincaré in 1929 that government funds were being used to extend "Germanism" abroad, he gave an accounting of the use to which the "informational" funds of the whole German government had been put. He stated that the entire appropriation for propaganda purposes amounted to only 21,638,000 reichsmark, and that only a small part of this sum was earmarked for use outside the Reich. The Ministry for the Occupied Territories, for example, had four million marks, of which three million had been set aside for "cultural" purposes. The German Minister of the Interior had at his disposal another two million marks for the same purpose. The foreign ministry had been allotted a secret fund of six million marks for "the advancement of humanitarian and cultural relations with foreign countries," 4,500,000 of which were set aside for use in schools, and 416,000 marks for dissemination of information within Germany. In addition, the foreign ministry had a sum of 2,400,000 marks for the dissemination of information about Germany in foreign countries.[43] This statement, of course, did not represent a full accounting of the use to which the secret funds had been put. Stresemann's own words on the importance of propaganda, and on the subject of public opinion and diplomacy, would indicate that the funds at the disposal of the foreign minister of a country striving to revise a complex international situation, were not exclusively used for "cultural and humanitarian purposes." There is evidence that foreign office funds were used to subsidize foreign editions of German newspapers like the *Alemania Illustrada Gaceta de Munich* in Spain. In 1927, the German Ambassador at Bern informed Stresemann that a certain anti-Poincaré press apparatus was experiencing financial difficulties and stood to lose its influential role in French politics unless aid was forthcoming from Berlin. Stresemann at once authorized the payment of 100,000 RM as a first installment of a one million RM assistance project.[44]

III. *Diplomacy.* The length of Stresemann's tenure in the foreign ministry gave him the right to consider himself the first German foreign minister who fully applied the new democratic form of government to a German foreign policy. While he was not the only democratic German foreign minister, nor the first one, his long stay in the ministry served to produce a new type of foreign policy and diplomacy based on the new political structure. The new policy, however, not only took into account the newly established republic and its domestic requirements, but also the particular international situation in which Germany found herself after the war. The diplomacy evolved by Stresemann was that peculiar to a country which had lost a war and which was striving to regain a lost power-position without the benefit of an armed force to back up its demands.

In an anonymous article, written in 1925, Stresemann outlined his diplomatic strategy as follows: "Germany's basic military weakness spells out the limits, the nature, and the methods of Germany's foreign policy."[45] Based on that hard-rock foundation, a German foreign policy was then to achieve five major objectives. First of all, it was necessary to fight French aggressiveness and to protect Germany's territorial integrity by the use of allies yet to be found. Second, Germany was to become the center of German minorities in Europe, the core of the German cultural community, the protector of German minorities against those powers which had received these minorities as a result of postwar treaty arrangements. Third, it was necessary to revise the eastern boundaries. Fourth, Germany was to prosecute her claims to colonial activity and to regain some of her lost possessions. Fifth, Germany was to become a pioneer in the fight for full recognition of the rights of European peoples to self-determination, especially as applied to German-Austrian relations and the desired *Anschluss.* If Germany followed these general lines, and did not permit herself to be distracted, she would not be alone in her struggle. If, on the other hand, Germany attempted a frontal attack upon the established order in Europe and sought to regain such regions as Alsace-Lorraine or Eupen-Malmédy from France and Belgium, she would only find herself opposed to the entire group of Versailles powers, powers whose vested interests spelled maintenance of the status quo. As Stresemann saw it, observance of these principles would not arouse the opposition of the powers, while, on the other hand, it would allow Germany slowly to regain a position of equality and influence in the concert of nations.

The foregoing chapter would indicate that Stresemann himself was convinced of the need for a revision of the Treaty of Versailles, but this revision would have to be a peaceful one, and would have to be based on a policy of reconciliation with at least some of the former enemy states. Painfully aware of the lack of a strong military and economic backing for such a policy, Stresemann developed the concept of fulfillment of Allied demands in return for piecemeal concessions. However, in his endeavor to follow his over-all strategy of an inoffensive foreign policy designed to realize greater objectives, he encountered strongest opposition from nationalist circles in Germany. This development led to a most important corollary to the policy of pacific revisionism, namely, fulfillment of basic demands advanced by the nationalist opposition at home.

However, nationalist demands would not be met to the point where Germany's vital interests would be endangered. As Stresemann saw it, there would always be a contradiction between the national conscience of a people as sensitive as the Germans and the impotence and dishonor arising from a lost war and the acceptance of a damaging peace treaty: "No one knows," he wrote in 1924, "how narrow the path of active German foreign policy is bound to be, how necessary it will be to maneuver the ship of state (*lavieren*) whenever the grand gesture would only be ridiculous because it would lack the grand deed."[46] There was no other policy but that of renouncing the use of "grand gestures," and of "sabre-rattling."[47] Pomp and glory were not to be the elements of a foreign policy designed to lead a beaten people back to self-respect; instead, the new foreign policy would have to be based upon the swift utilization of given opportunities, upon foresight and expediency. Addressing himself to the political Right, at an election rally, he pointed out that under the circumstances confronting postwar Germany, not even Bismarck would have followed his policy of "blood and iron," but instead would have stood for "*Realpolitik*." In this instance, Bismarck would have based his policy on the use of ideas instead of arms.[48]

The policy of fulfillment of Allied demands with full regard for the aspirations of the nationalists was bound to lead to the accusation of opportunism and wavering on Stresemann's part. He sought to ward that off by referring once more to his great predecessor, Bismarck, quoting him as having said: "Who, after all, is an opportunist? He is a man who awaits a favorable opportunity to carry out what he considers useful and purposeful, which, after all, is the task of all diplomacy." Concerning the closely related charge that he lacked principles, Stresemann referred to another of Bismarck's remarks: "If I should go through life with principles, I should imagine myself walking through a dense forest with a long pole between my teeth."[49]

The concept of realism and opportunism in Stresemann's diplomacy was based on a number of observations and convictions, the roots of which lay in the final phases of the World War and in the period of peace negotiations. Based on the already stated concept of anticipated disunity in the camp of the Allied Powers, he forecast a speedy end of vindictiveness on the part of Germany's former enemies.[50] The Allies and their associates, so he believed, could not be certain of developments in Central Europe. This was especially so in the light of the Bolshevik Revolution, political fermentations in the Balkans, and the emergence of new political factors in Asia and in the United States. Therefore the Allies would have to secure close ties with defeated Germany, which, after all, was more of a Western than an Eastern country.[51] Furthermore, he was convinced that the threat of a French hegemony on the European Continent was anathema to Great Britain, and that it was mandatory for any German statesman to utilize this fact to the utmost.[52] Then there was the new political factor of the Soviet Union's known opposition to the European status quo, a factor which also was to be utilized in the scheme of German foreign policy.

A corollary to the policy of utilizing the existence of another revisionist power in the interest of German revisionism was the reliance on French and British fears of communist revolutions outside of Russia. Following the riots of the 1920's, in which Communists and other radical elements sought to seize power in Germany and to establish a German Soviet Republic, Stresemann observed: "What a splendid opportunity to make German foreign policy."[53] He advised the Social-Democratic government that the Entente had always claimed that the alleged danger of a bolshevization of Germany was in reality nothing but a figment of German imagination. Now it should be stated, Stresemann demanded, that there was a real danger to German and European culture, that this danger was the result of Allied postwar policy toward Germany, the product of the "crime of Versailles," and that the survival of Europe depended upon the strength of Germany's economy to resist revolution and anarchy. Because it was one of the greatest fears of the Western Allies that the German Republic would succumb to a revolution, he demanded that German leaders inform the rest of Europe that Germany was capable of erecting an effective wall against further bolshevization, provided that she was left strong and viable enough to do so. An economically weak and disarmed Germany, so Stresemann maintained, could not prevent the inundation of Europe by the Soviet flood.[54] Stresemann's entire political and social philosophy would bear out the conclusion that his appraisal of the utility of the Soviet Union in relation to German foreign policy was far more sincere than the threats uttered earlier to the effect that Germany might ally herself with the Soviets against the West.[55]

The above-mentioned concept of fulfillment of the reparation clauses of the peace treaty became an integral part of German foreign policy and became known as *"Erfüllungspolitik."* The need for fulfillment of contracted obligations had been recognized by all responsible German leaders once the terms had been accepted and the Treaty of Versailles had been signed. It had been recognized that nonfulfillment would inevitably lead to the application of sanctions and penalties by the Allied and Associated Powers. Stresemann took no exception to that rule. He voiced his agreement, in principle, once the treaty had been signed, but made certain reservations. As early as October 1919, he expressed himself publicly to the effect that it would be foolhardy to resist fulfillment. At the same time, however, he made it clear that no one had ever thought in terms of fulfillment without reservations and eventual revisions.[56] In other words, Stresemann established, comparatively early, the concept of "reasonable fulfillment" or fulfillment in part only. Of course, this policy was subject to change since Stresemann, as foreign minister, was confronted with certain domestic and foreign events and developments, and had to adjust his policy to these changing circumstances; nevertheless, partial fulfillment remained the basis for most of his subsequent official acts. In 1921, in view of Germany's severe financial crisis, he added to this policy the concept of conciliation with France as an expedient to effect a temporary relief.

Economic concepts and considerations played a great role in Stresemann's diplomatic strategy. His own background and understanding of economic and industrial relationships contributed to an ever growing realization that the economic interdependence of nations could well be utilized toward an improvement of international relations. It was only a small step from that realization to a renunciation of war as a means to advance national policy objectives. It might well be said that Stresemann's understanding of the role of political economics in international affairs strengthened his belief in pacific revisionism as opposed to change by force.

By 1910 he expressed the belief that Great Britain would only lower her own standard of living if she would attempt to reduce Germany's economic strength.[57] In 1915 he warned that the United States was threatening to confront the Old World with a comparatively undisturbed, even immensely strengthened economy, a development that would necessitate closer economic ties among the European powers.[58] More specifically, he proposed, in order to resist economic pressure by the Entente after the war, a customs union or understanding among the Central Powers which would ultimately lead to a political "*Mittel-Europa*," a new central-European constellation to be composed of Germany, Austria-Hungary, Bulgaria, and Turkey.[59] Reliance on the strength of economic and industrial bonds among the nations caused him to take a relatively optimistic view of the postwar world, provided of course that Germany was left in a position to compete effectively with other trading nations.[60]

All of the foregoing sentiments and observations had a direct bearing upon Stresemann's subsequent moves. Immediately after the war he sought to have the concepts of economic interdependence applied to Allied-German relations. On the one hand, the Allied and Associated Powers stood to gain by a peace settlement that did not cut the economic ties which had existed before the war. A Germany bled white by reparation payments would soon constitute a dangerous sore on the European body. On the other hand, Germany's political recovery, her return to a position of equality would of course be considerably enhanced by a planned and purposeful utilization of her economic strength. That strength, he maintained, was bound to lead to political concessions on the part of the nations depending upon German trade and industry. All that was required for a speedy political recovery was a rapid solution of the basic question of procurement of raw materials, procurement of credit for purposes of reconstruction and for the purchase of raw materials, a supply of coal, and an enthusiasm for work.[61]

The idea that economic interdependence among nations tended to obscure other considerations of national policy, found its most prominent expression in Stresemann's thoughts on Franco-German relations. By 1919 he was firmly convinced that Britain had embarked upon a course that was to lead to the utter destruction of Germany's economic potential, that her policy was based on the concept, *Germaniam esse delendam*. France, on the other hand, had little to gain from a Carthaginian peace. If the German government withheld concessions and forced France to take stock of her economic interests, the latter would inevitably tend to abandon all thoughts of revenge and exaction of retributions.[62]

In his analysis of French thought, he differentiated between political leaders intent upon revenge and fulfillment of military objectives, and the economists and industrialists who were aware of the vital connections of long standing which had served to weld France's industry and her financial structure to that of Germany.[63] He assumed that a diplomacy based upon these calculations would be successful because economic thought would outweigh military thought in France; this was an attitude characteristic of the young Liberal in the imperial Reichstag who strongly believed that merchants and industrialists were far more qualified to conduct international relations than career diplomats and politicians per se.[64]

The United States of America occupied an important place in Stresemann's postwar plans. He assumed that this country, as powerful as it was, had the greatest interest in an increase of the purchasing power of those nations which had been its customers before the war.[65]

There was reason to hope for American intervention on Germany's behalf.

In the wake of the spreading economic crisis following the end of the war, Stresemann's confidence in the prospect of a universal understanding on economic questions grew rapidly. Under the impact of the Ruhr invasion by Allied troops, he redoubled his efforts to have German foreign policy conform with his concept of the role of economics in international relations. Taking into account the benevolent attitude of the United States and the assumed hostility of Great Britain, he developed his theory of a *rapprochement* with France, based on the significant fact of a close affinity of iron, coal, and indigenous populations in the Rhine, Ruhr, Alsace-Lorraine triangle.[66] Speaking in retrospect, in 1927, Stresemann noted with satisfaction that the war had encouraged the emergence of trusts, which had in turn served to advance the cause of European unity beyond all expectations. Furthermore, he noted that the nations of Europe were drawing closer together in an effort to protect themselves against the more powerful nations in control of the raw materials: "Although this fact might be of doubtful utility as far as economics have a bearing on politics, it does nevertheless constitute a step forward in the direction of peace and international understanding."[67] As late as September 1929, one month prior to his death, he was still referring to the need for economic unity in Europe, a unity based on the economic integration of Europe, and designed to counteract "the Balkanization of Europe brought about by the Treaty of Versailles."[68]

In a general summary of Stresemann's foreign policy, Dr. Edgar Stern-Rubarth analyzes its economic aspects in this manner: "Stresemann realized the danger of a Balkanization of Europe with two unaffected power centers remaining outside: the United States of America and the growing Union of Soviet Socialist Republics. It was his objective to create a protective society of European nations to stem the influence of the two superpowers."[69] A different view, expressed by Dr. Walther Schotte, held that Stresemann sought to attain some degree of European unity in order to guarantee a dominant position for Germany. Germany's organizational talents and her economic strength would move her naturally into a predominant position among European nations. If the rest of the world insisted upon making Germany the universal workshop, the rest of the world would soon become dependent upon German production.[70] Whatever the correct interpretation of Stresemann's objectives may be, it was clear that, from the point of view of a politician, it was his prime objective to develop a diplomacy which took economic realities into account and which would base political understanding as well as maneuvers in the field of foreign policy, on the known affinity of international industries regardless of national boundaries. All of which, of course, was to create a favorable basis for bargains toward a revision of the Treaty of Versailles.

The methods used by Stresemann as foreign minister are clearly discernible in the earlier stages of his career. Among these methods, the parliamentary approach to the conduct of a foreign policy was most significant in the light of previous German experiences. Although his concept of the role of parliament in the conduct and control of foreign policy was based on the liberal German tradition prevalent in the ranks of the opposition under the Empire, he permitted himself a number of variations and digressions which lent his foreign policy a peculiar character almost singular in the history of Germany. Between 1917 and 1919 he moved from a position of supporting a predominant role of parliament in foreign affairs to one of limiting it to a sounding board and mere agency for the expression of public opinion. At the outset of his public career, he favored the removal of foreign affairs from all political and parliamentary controls. The consideration, conduct, and control of foreign policy were to be matters beyond domestic strife and party-political ambitions.

The German People's Party was primarily a means by which Stresemann could secure his position of influence in the field of foreign policy, before and after his assumption of office. As its leader, he set the party position on matters of foreign policy; he did this, in spite of the strongest opposition within the party, by deft compromises and timely concessions. In order to assure the success of his foreign policy, he was always willing to make concessions and to arrive at compromises with parties of either the Left or the Right. All that mattered to him was that the foreign policy should be continuous. Political parties were but means to organize the country behind a given foreign policy.

Because the country lacked the unity necessary for a stable and continuous foreign policy, and because of unexpectedly violent opposition to his policy from the ranks of the nationalists, Stresemann departed slightly from his earlier position with regard to the role of parliament in foreign affairs and strove, successfully, to extend his influence over the several parties. By deft political maneuvers, he succeeded in gaining the support of the majority in the several parliaments without, however, taking the latter into his confidence.

To further the objectives of his foreign policy, Stresemann came to rely to an ever increasing extent upon press and propaganda. Thinking of ways to improve the effectiveness of German diplomacy, he drew heavily upon American advertising techniques and British propaganda practices. Taking another hint from the United States, he endeavored to maintain the most excellent relations with the press, utilizing domestic and foreign correspondents for purposes of advancing his diplomatic objectives. He was also known to contribute frequently to a number of newspapers and periodicals at home and abroad.

One problem which he was never able to solve to his complete satisfaction was the ownership of a newspaper as the official organ of the foreign ministry. On the other hand, while he was in office, he had at his disposal considerable sums of money, voted to the foreign ministry by parliament, the disposal of which was completely at the discretion of the foreign minister, and not even subject to the ordinary auditing processes. The money was used for propaganda and informational purposes as far as can be ascertained.

With regard to Stresemann's diplomatic methods, in the strictest sense, three major approaches can be singled out: (1) exploitation of Allied disunity and rivalry in the interest of a quick return of Germany to a position of power; (2) maximum utilization of the Russian Revolution and of its consequences in a campaign to frighten Western European countries into a more considerate policy toward Germany; (3) utilization of Germany's strong economic position and potentialities, and of her economic ties and affinities with other European nations, in order to nullify certain peace arrangements and treaty provisions.

CHAPTER V

THE WAR GUILT QUESTION

The question of guilt, responsibility, and causality for the World War, 1914–18, has become the subject of a considerable literary and political debate. This study concerns itself with one aspect of the question only, namely, the bearing which the war guilt accusation against Germany had on the fate of the peace settlement. In particular, this study is concerned with Article 231 of the Treaty of Versailles and its interpretation. The issue, as seen by the Germans, and especially by Stresemann, was as follows: if Germany could repudiate the charge of guilt, then the entire moral and legal armament of the Treaty of Versailles would collapse. Then it would be relatively easy to attack the separate provisions of the treaty itself.[1]

To be sure, Stresemann was not the only opponent of an assumption of war guilt by Germany. The opposition ranged from the extreme Left to the far Right. However, from the point of view of a consistent foreign policy, his was the most significant and constructive attitude. Aware of the fact that Article 231 had been designed as an introduction to, as well as a justification for damage claims by the Allies against Germany, he believed that the entire complex of reparation and damage claims would be deprived of a moral and legal basis by a refutation and repudiation of the accusation. Moreover, there was evidence that the Allied and Associated Powers traced other aspects of the peace settlement to a basic assumption of war guilt on the part of Germany. Stresemann reasoned therefore that a repudiation of the war guilt accusation would *ipso facto* serve to abolish additional claims and, at the same time, would lead to a revision of other inconvenient treaty provisions.[2]

With regard to the historical bases for the war guilt accusation, Stresemann rejected any attempts to blame a particular country or personality for the outbreak of the war. He believed that aside from the German failure to be levelheaded during the crucial weeks of 1914, there were many more forces at work to bring about an armed conflict. He cited the personality of Edward VII, the Great Coalition

46

against Germany, the French loan to Russia, the large-scale armaments in the countries arraigned against Germany as causes which had been just as effective as any moves or failures committed by German leaders.[3]

In his early attempts to refute the war guilt accusation, Stresemann sought to differentiate between what he called "remote causes" and "immediate origins." By the use of these terms, he sought to distinguish between long-range historical causes and immediate origins of the outbreak of the war. In this connection, he did acknowledge a certain responsibility on the part of Count Berchtold, Austrian foreign minister.[4]

During a debate on the floor of the Reichstag, Stresemann launched what can be considered his first, full-fledged attack on the war guilt accusation. He denied flatly that the Treaty of Versailles had any moral basis, and stated just as candidly that the war guilt accusation was a historical absurdity. Citing President Wilson's address before the Women's City Club of Cincinnati, in 1916, Stresemann noted that the American Chief Executive had then admitted that "no one could know how the war had begun and what had caused the conflict."[5] The move was designed to influence the negotiations on Allied reparation claims which had been advanced at London. On April 28, 1921, a few weeks after the Allies resorted to military sanctions in reprisal for alleged German default in reparation payments Stresemann demanded again that the foreign minister proceed actively to repudiate the war guilt accusation. Referring to the attempt by the foreign ministry to achieve reconsideration of the accusation by the publication of certain pertinent documents, he stated, "Even if the foreign ministry makes documents available, a word on the repudiation of the war guilt thesis would have been effective at London."[6] Little did he know then that some time in the future he would be confronted with similar demands for active diplomatic representation on the war guilt question and that he would then be most embarrassed by those moves.

Following his accession to the chancellorship and the foreign ministry in 1923, Stresemann struck out on the road to total abrogation of the war guilt clause. At first, he approached the subject obliquely. Instead of an outright denunciation of the clause, he declared that Germany was prepared to submit the question of war guilt to an impartial tribunal for objective examination and for a final judgment.[7] On September 2 of the same year, he advanced the proposition that all nations open their archives, as Germany had done already, to permit an impartial investigation of the causes leading to the war.[8] These attacks were intensified under the impact of French insistence on full payment of reparation by Germany. It was under the pressure of imminent danger from that source that Chancellor Stresemann ventured to repudiate the war guilt accusation forthrightly in a public address: "I reject the war guilt lie with all determination at my command." He was well aware of the French reasoning behind their adamant insistence that the war guilt accusation should stand as it had been developed at the end of the war. He knew that their policy of vigorous enforcement of the treaty terms stood or fell with the legitimacy of the war guilt doctrine. To carry the argument to the *reductio ad absurdum* he even advanced counterclaims on the grounds that the Allies also had inflicted injustice upon Germany, and were therefore liable to make restitution.[9]

Soon after he had entered the foreign ministry, he was made painfully aware of the fact that for a foreign minister the war guilt question assumed different proportions than had been the case before. Now it was he who was prodded by the opposition to raise the war guilt question in spite of high diplomatic considerations which counseled him not to do so.[10] In his reply to demands from the floor of the Reichstag that he inject the question into the then pending negotiations on a new reparation schedule, he avoided a firm stand. While he was fully aware of the advantage which the nationalists stood to gain from his failure to bring the war guilt question up at diplomatic conferences, he also realized that a premature raising of the controversial point was likely to endanger the precarious *modus vivendi* which the new reparation schedule sought to establish. The result of these considerations was a very weak statement by the foreign minister to the effect that he "was satisfied with the progress made by the problem in the direction of an ultimate solution."[11] However, the new reparation schedule, or as it became popularly known, the Dawes Plan, had yet to be ratified by the Reichstag and there was a growing sentiment to bargain German willingness to continue reparation payments in return for Allied repudiation of the war guilt accusation. To avoid serious consequences at home, Stresemann decided to appease the opposition by saying, "We draw the consequence from the lost war and are paying reparations but we reject the idea that we have to render war damages on the grounds of moral responsibility."[12] Such statements, however, did not succeed in stifling the opposition. The pressure for a stronger move did not abate. On the day of the final vote on the Dawes Plan, August 29, 1924, the Reichstag adopted a resolution instructing the government to work toward a solution of the question on every possible occasion. The resolution, including a statement demanding the "liberation from the burden of false accusation," was to have been delivered to all governments concerned. For one reason or another, however, it was merely published in the German press. Whatever the reasons for the failure to deliver the message, Stresemann had promised the Nationalists a *demarché* on the war guilt question in return for their affirmative vote on the Dawes Plan, and had failed to do what he had promised.[13]

Lord D'Abernon notes in his diary that Stresemann and Chancellor Marx had obtained Nationalist support for their initial journey to London by promising to raise the war guilt question in an official, unmistakable manner. Upon their return, they tried to evade this. Following the vote on the Dawes Plan, a note raising the controversial point was prepared but its dispatch delayed by Ago von Maltzan, then in sole charge of the foreign office. Maltzan asked D'Abernon to prevail upon Stresemann to delay the sending of the note so as to avoid international complications. D'Abernon goes on to say, "The truth of the matter is that Stresemann has always been himself a partisan of 'denial' (of the war guilt accusation). Apart from his personal opinion he has recently patched up his differences with the Nationalists and is anxious not to kill his new-born friendship."[14] The British Ambassador's observations tend to support the thesis that Stresemann, although he personally wanted to protest the war guilt accusation at that time, did not do so for reasons of diplomatic strategy.

The second opportunity to raise the war guilt question officially came with the projected entry of Germany into the League of Nations. On September 17, 1924, Stresemann told Lord D'Abernon that, in his opinion, Germany's entry into the League was directly connected with Article 231 of the Treaty of Versailles. He argued further that since the League Covenant was an integral part of the peace treaty, recognition of the Covenant by Germany would necessarily imply acceptance of the treaty and all it stood for. On these grounds, recognition of the Covenant would spell acceptance of the basic hypothesis underlying the peace arrangements, namely, the war guilt accusation.[15] Subsequently, on September 29, the German government addressed a note to the ten nations represented on the Council of the League of Nations. The note declared that Germany was willing to observe her international obligations on the condition that such a declaration "did not imply an admission by the German government of those assertions on which Germany's obligations are based and which place a moral responsibility upon the German people."[16]

A third opportunity to raise the war guilt question presented itself in 1925, when Great Britain and France showed a willingness to accept Stresemann's proposal to solve the security problem in the West by a multilateral pact. One of the conditions laid down by the Allies as a *conditio sine qua non* was Germany's accession to the League of Nations.[17] A further condition was the continued recognition by Germany of the Treaty of Versailles and related arrangements. At the very last moment, as the foreign ministers of the nations concerned prepared to meet, Stresemann caused an oral declaration to be submitted to London, Paris, Rome, and Brussels, wherein he repeated the statement on the war guilt question contained in the note of September 1924 and almost brought the coming conference to a premature failure.[18] Once more Stresemann informed the Allies that Germany's entry into the League should not be understood to imply German recognition of the assertions underlying the obligations assumed by her as a result of the lost war. The declaration, somewhat belatedly, sought to make amends for the wrong committed earlier when Stresemann had failed to satisfy nationalist demands by not presenting the Reichstag resolution to the several governments. Sir Austen Chamberlain, British secretary for foreign affairs, opposed the raising of the war guilt question at that time, and in the face of that resistance Stresemann abandoned the demand temporarily.[19]

There is no doubt that he postponed the move gladly, having done his duty toward the opposition at home. He was certainly not willing to endanger *"das Kind,"* as he and Lord D'Abernon had chosen to name the proposed security pact.

At Locarno, the chancellor, who had accompanied the foreign minister upon Stresemann's insistence, sought to press Stresemann into another *demarché* on the war guilt question. Chancellor Luther was worried lest failure to raise the question would have profound repercussions at home and would lend strength to the Nationalists, who had joined the cabinet in January. Stresemann, intent upon reaching agreement with the four Western powers on greater issues, reminded Luther of the cabinet decision which had left it to the discretion of the delegation to determine the time and manner in which the war guilt question was to be raised. He also assured the worried chancellor that the Nationalist member of the cabinet, Dr. Schiele, had signed the cabinet protocol in question. Stresemann did decide to raise the issue on October 8, to avert a threatening revolt by the nationalists in the cabinet and in the Reichstag, but softened the effect by basing his remarks on the previously submitted memorandum of September 1925, rather than putting the question directly.

It had become quite evident that Stresemann was not willing to endanger the negotiations for a security pact by giving in to the demands
of the Nationalists. Following the withdrawal of the Nationalists
from the cabinet, on October 22, Stresemann, no longer under their
pressure, dropped all pretenses in an off-the-record talk to the press
and admitted frankly that there was no hope ever to have the Allies
repudiate Article 231. "There is no chance in history," he stated,
"that if a hard peace is based on declarations by twenty-seven nations,
that these assertions are ever withdrawn by the signatories."[20] Furthermore, he declared that additional formal declarations on the subject were useless and that "enlightenment" was the only way to
remove the stigma of guilt from the German people.

On September 10, 1926, Germany occupied her seat as a member of the League of Nations, having been accepted on September 8.
There, in a highly dramatic setting, Stresemann did not avail himself of the opportunity to raise the war guilt question. Instead, he
waited one week before he touched upon that delicate matter, and
then in an indirect way. Speaking to members of the German delegation and to German correspondents at Geneva, and one day before
a historic meeting with Aristide Briand at Thoiry, he noted:

We wish to realize one thing: There is no more impressive repudiation
of the moral accusation than the acceptance of Germany (in the League of
Nations) as it occurred amidst applause from the nations of the world. It
is decisive for our attitude that future historians will instead emphasize
the question, how it was ever possible that Germany had the strength to
withstand a world of enemies.[21]

Clearly, Stresemann was vacillating on that issue. He had declared
it to be useless to press for a formal repudiation of the war guilt
accusation by the Allies, yet was not averse to bringing the matter
up shortly afterwards. The reason was clear: he did not wish to
press two issues at one and the same time if that could be avoided.
Thus, confronted by the fact that the Allies were not prepared to
repudiate the accusation, but were ready to come to an agreement
with Germany on another matter, he decided that the war guilt question had to wait. Once the Locarno agreements had been signed, and
Germany had become a full-fledged member of the League of Nations,
the question of war guilt would be taken up again.

When on September 18, 1927, the venerable German president,
Von Hindenburg, repudiated the war guilt accusation in an unmistakable manner on the occasion of the inauguration of a patriotic
monument, Stresemann declared his unqualified support.[22]

In June 1929, only five months before his death, Stresemann stood once again before the Reichstag seeking to have that reluctant house accept another reparations agreement negotiated by him in the face of strongest opposition from the Right. As he took the stand in defense of his policy, he turned to the one question which had helped him to overcome nationalist opposition in 1924, the war guilt accusation. Freed of all restraints, i.e., there was nothing or little to be gained any more from restraining one's language, he struck hard at the foundation of the Versailles settlement. He declared that he had never harbored any doubts about the reasons for which the war guilt clause had been introduced into the peace settlement. The concentration of all blame for the war upon Germany had been nothing but a ready-made excuse for a vindictive peace. Never would anyone in Germany recognize an exclusive war guilt or responsibility for the war. Moreover, he warned, the Allies would find him fighting against the war guilt accusation to the bitter end.[23]

On June 28, 1929, in the midst of a controversy with the nationalists, the German government once again issued a proclamation on the subject of war guilt just as it had done on the day when the Dawes Plan had been voted upon. "We know that we are in agreement with all Germans when we deny the accusation that Germany alone was responsible for the war. . . ."[24] On the same day, Stresemann referred to his own position as of the year 1923, when he had maintained that Germany was prepared to submit the historic question to an impartial tribunal. He concluded that Germany could not accept a verdict where one party was judge in its own cause.[25]

Concerning the substance of the war guilt accusation, Stresemann rejected any attempt to localize the origins of the World War, or to affix the stigma of guilt to any particular nation. Soon after the signing of the Treaty of Versailles, he commenced to attack Article 231 on the grounds that the charge had never been proven, that it could not be supported by evidence, and could not be maintained before a panel of impartial judges. Therefore the treaty, built upon the war guilt hypothesis, lacked any legal or moral basis. Moreover, he maintained that the war guilt accusation had been fabricated in order to justify the vindictive reparation claims and their corollary, the application of military sanctions.

As a minister, intent upon securing a working majority in parliament, and as a result of coalitions with the Right, he frequently raised the war guilt question, in conferences and in public. Because the nationalist opposition pressed hard upon the government—and

when they were in the cabinet, they pressed even harder—Stresemann, often against his better judgment, went so far as to endanger
delicate international negotiations in order to appease those clamor-
ing for repudiation. He raised the war guilt question officially in
conjunction with the Dawes Plan, his League of Nations policy,
the Locarno Pact, and the Young Plan. Disappointment over Allied
failure to provide him with political ammunition against nationalist reaction at home, coupled with particularly vitriolic attacks
against his person on the part of the Right, led him, in 1929, to come
out strongly in favor of repudiation.

While he had virtually given up hope of ever seeing the Allies
repudiate the war guilt accusation, he nevertheless fought on. There
was hope that public opinion in the former enemy countries would be
converted to the German point of view, thus preparing the way for
revision of less basic but nevertheless important provisions of the
peace treaty.

CHAPTER VI

REVISION OF THE SANCTION CLAUSES:
MILITARY OCCUPATION

The Treaty of Versailles, in its reparation clauses, provided among other things that the Allies had the right to resort to economic and military sanctions in order to enforce payment of reparations by Germany.[1] The political struggle which developed over this matter postponed any more far-reaching revisionist ambitions of German leaders, and of Stresemann in particular, obliging them to concentrate on the removal of foreign occupation troops before attempting any further steps on the road to revision of the treaty. In the course of that political struggle, however, Stresemann had opportunity to attack the very bases of the peace settlement in very much the same fashion as in the case of the war guilt accusation. The point at issue, namely, that nonfulfillment of treaty obligations by Germany entitled the Allies to military occupation of German soil as a measure of reprisal, turned out to be the crux of the entire argument.

By his attack on the penal clauses of the treaty, Stresemann attempted to undermine the entire moral and legal structure upon which the peace settlement had been erected. Success in the political struggle against the Allied interpretation would leave Germany free to default at will. Because France turned out to be the chief motivating factor behind the Allied interpretation, holding that if it became necessary she alone could enforce the sanction clauses, it became a matter of strategy for German statesmanship to attempt to isolate France from Great Britain and her remaining allies.

The problem of sanctions first arose in 1920, when the German government, seeking to quell an uprising, sent 20,000 troops into the zone demilitarized under the peace treaty.[2] In retaliation, the French sent troops to occupy Frankfort on the Main, on April 6, even though that area was not included in the zones of occupation under the terms of the treaty, nor was it, by common understanding among the treaty powers, to be occupied at all.[3] In this case, the French troops were forced to withdraw upon vigorous protests by Great Britain.

54

Subsequently, following a series of threats by the Allied governments, sanctions were again applied on the grounds that Germany had deliberately defaulted on reparation payments, and on March 8, 1921, the towns of Duisburg, Ruhrort, and Düsseldorf were occupied by foreign troops. Additional punitive measures accompanied the move. Sanctions were once more applied on January 11, 1923, when the French, Belgian, and Italian troops occupied the Ruhr industrial area. It was the latter event, more than anything else, which stirred resistance to the treaty to an unusual pitch and set in motion the forces which brought Gustav Stresemann to the fore.[4]

I. *The London Ultimatum.* On March 3, 1921, at a conference of creditor states at London, the occupation of certain Ruhr towns was decided upon in retaliation for what was considered voluntary default by Germany. As chairman of the Reichstag committee on foreign affairs, Stresemann took an unqualified position against the Allied move. He declared on the floor of the Reichstag that neither international law nor the peace treaties as such entitled any nation to further occupation of German territory. Moreover, he warned that punitive measures would be detrimental to world economy, and that they were self-defeating in the light of the industrial and social chaos which they would bring about.[5] However, the limited occupation of some Ruhr ports was merely a prelude of things to come. On May 5, 1921, the Supreme Council of the Allies, sitting at London in continuous session ever since March 1, decided to press for a more expeditious fulfillment of the treaty terms by Germans, and to make the scheduled settlement as complete and as definitive as possible. For that purpose an ultimatum was handed to the German delegation on May 5. The ultimatum charged Germany with neglect in the fulfillment of her international obligations and enumerated certain alleged violations of articles of the Treaty of Versailles.[6] In its penal provisions, the ultimatum declared: "Failing fulfillment by the German Government of the above conditions by May 12 [the Allies had decided] to proceed to occupy the valley of the Ruhr and to take all other military and naval measures that may be required."[7]

Under the impact of the ultimatum, a political crisis developed in Germany. The government fell, and on May 9, three days prior to the expiration of the ultimatum, Stresemann, in his capacity as chairman of the People's Party and as chairman of the committee on foreign affairs, went to see the British Ambassador. He sought to clear up certain points before he could recommend acceptance of the ultimatum to his party, and also was evidently inquiring whether the Allies would grant certain concessions to enable him to assume the chancellorship.[8]

Stresemann's four-point inquiry was highly indicative of certain conceptions and interests on his part which were to become basic elements in his later foreign policy. His first point concerned the interpretation of Paragraph 19, Annex II of Part VIII of the Treaty of Versailles, and dealt with the extent to which the Allies believed they were entitled to compensation for damages incurred as a result of military action during the war.[9] He inquired whether the passage dealing with the delivery by Germany of "such materials and labour as any of the Allied Powers may . . . require towards the restoration or development of its industrial or economic life," applied only to the restoration of damages caused by the war. Or did it mean any Allied Power could at any time require Germany to deliver goods necessary for the development of Allied industry or commerce? Stresemann held that the latter interpretation would mean that any Allied Power, e.g., Italy or Yugoslavia, could, for many years to come, demand delivery by Germany of any materials or services deemed to be necessary for the reconstruction of its economic life. Such an interpretation, Stresemann warned, would lead to a paralysis of German industry, and therefore acceptance of the ultimatum would be impossible.[10] The third point of the inquiry addressed itself to the sanction provisions of the ultimatum and asked whether the sanctions imposed on March 8 would be canceled in the event Germany accepted the terms. Here he pointed out that acceptance of the ultimatum involved heavy responsibilities, and that it would meet with strong opposition. Unless a government, which assumed responsibility for acceptance of the ultimatum, was assisted by some concessions, it would be unable to obtain a majority in the Reichstag.[11] This argument was to become standard procedure with Stresemann in later years and was to be repeated again and again. The fourth point concerned Upper Silesia. In the event that the Allies, i.e., Great Britain and Italy, declared themselves ready to allot a substantial plebiscite area in that region to Germany, he and his party would be prepared to assume responsibility for the acceptance of the economic terms of the ultimatum. Again he warned that any government accepting the ultimatum, but faced with the loss of Upper Silesia, would not last a fortnight.[12]

This incident convinced Lord D'Abernon that Stresemann, in spite of the nationalistic inclinations displayed by the People's Party, was nevertheless prepared to follow and to support a policy of fulfillment, provided he could point to some concessions in support of his precarious position. It also indicated that Stresemann had more confidence in Great Britain than ever before.[13] Furthermore, the move indicated the high degree of political and personal daring of Stresemann, for the acceptance of that or any other ultimatum was likely to spell the death sentence, politically and physically, of anyone who publicly associated himself with such a policy.[14] Unfortunately, Lord D'Abernon did not receive a reply from the Foreign Office until May 10, too late for Stresemann's purposes, for the debate in the Reichstag had already begun, and it was necessary for him and his party to take a stand on the ultimatum as originally submitted.[15] Speaking in the name of the party, Stresemann voiced regret that no assurances of a more favorable meaning of the ultimatum had reached him at the time of the debate, and that therefore he and his followers within the party were unable to vote for acceptance.[16]

The course of Stresemann's actions between May 9 and 10, and the subsequent vote in parliament, indicate that initially he had been prepared to vote for acceptance and that he had been ready to assume personal responsibility for it. Because of a split within the ranks of the party, he had been obliged to bolster his position by the visit to the British embassy. When the necessary assurances were not forthcoming, he was forced to vote against acceptance in order to maintain party unity, and to secure his own position as party leader.[17]

After the ultimatum had been accepted by a majority and the storm had passed, Stresemann addressed the Reichstag once more. However, this time his speech was far more aggressive in terms of nationalistic content than had been the case before, when the speaker had been within reach of the highest position of responsibility. This time, unburdened by any diplomatic considerations, he lashed out at the Treaty of Versailles, demanding that Germany take advantage of every opportunity offered to her under the terms of the treaty, instead of attempting to fulfill impossible terms under conditions equally impossible. In keeping with previous observations on his part, he also noted, in passing, that there was a distinct difference of opinion between Britain and France concerning the effect which the ultimatum was to have upon the withdrawal of foreign troops from the Ruhr ports occupied on March 8, 1921.[18]

II. *The Ruhr Crisis.* On January 6, 1923, Stresemann held a press conference in his capacity as chairman of the Reichstag committee on foreign affairs. Reviewing the record of the past German governments and pointing out that they had reached the limit of what was possible in the way of fulfillment of Germany's international obligations, he noted specifically that the Cuno government, in 1922, had offered a "God's peace on the Rhine." In view of such a record of fulfillment and reconciliation, France was still intent upon applying forceful measures in pursuance of her security objectives. In conclusion, he warned that warlike measures would find the German people unwilling to support anything else but a government dedicated to a policy of determined resistance.[19] Four days later, French troops proceeded with the punitive occupation of the entire Ruhr area in pursuance of findings of "voluntary default" on Germany's part by the Allied Reparation Commission. They were soon joined by Belgian and Italian troops. While the British government refused to participate in the action, the United States withdrew its army of occupation from the Rhineland in protest.[20]

On January 13, Stresemann read a declaration on behalf of all *bürgerliche Parteien* and addressed to the Reichstag. The declaration attacked the violation of German sovereignty under false pretenses, went on to state that written treaties had been broken by the arbitrary action, and demanded that the German people and the world resist the act of aggression.[21] Betraying Stresemann's co-authorship, the declaration noted that France stood alone in the act without the approval of her allies, and that this fact of a disagreement among the former Entente powers was only natural since Germany had not laid down her arms unconditionally and was therefore entitled to the unqualified support of the other treaty powers. The latter point was subsequently elaborated upon by Stresemann in a speech at Dortmund on February 21: "We don't have to beg for their intervention [against French aggression], we demand it. . . ."[22] Subsequent development showed that "their" meant Great Britain and the United States. Again he referred to the famous Lansing dispatch on the basis of which Germany had accepted the Armistice, and to arouse British suspicions, he added soon afterwards that the French action in the Ruhr could very likely lead to the establishment of an operational basis for further aggression in Europe.[23] Finally, returning to a favorite device of his, he raised the possibility of a Russo-German alliance to ward off further French aggression.[24]

In spite of the determined attack against France, Stresemann did not fail to indicate a willingness to come to terms. Chances for an understanding between France and Germany had not been destroyed. He was well aware of the fact that France did not present a united front but was split along lines very similar to the political divisions in Germany. Both countries had a militant Right favoring a policy of revenge and aggression and of attaining security through the application of force, and a militant Left desirous of peace and the achievement of security by international co-operation and understanding. With his conciliatory gestures and remarks, he hoped to succeed in arousing the antimilitarists against Poincaré's policy of trying to enforce the treaty by military action. In support of his argument, he stressed industrial relations, financial considerations, warned of a collapse of French finance, and offered German assistance to help stabilize French currency through exchange agreements, aside and apart from the collection of reparations.[25]

The emphasis placed by Stresemann upon bilateral industrial agreements and co-operation was to a considerable extent the result of plans and projects developed by the strong industrial segment of the People's Party. Among the industrialists in the People's Party were Dr. Otto Hugo, Executive Committee of the *Reichsverband*, Export and Import; Dr. Otto Most, member of the Lower-Rhenian Chamber of Industry Association; Dr. Rudolf Schneider, Secretary General of the *Reichsverband*, German Industry; Dr. Kurt Sorge, Board of Directors of Friedrich Krupp, A.G., and Honorary President of the *Reichsverband*, German Industry; Hugo Stinnes, President of Stinnes Coal and Mining Combine; Dr. Otto Thiel, Chairman of the National Employees Association; Dr. Albert Vögler, Director General of United Steel, Dortmund. Among these prominent industrialists and leaders of trade associations, Hugo Stinnes was perhaps the most controversial person. In 1922 Stresemann publicly paid tribute to the advice and influence rendered by Stinnes in the course of the deliberations of the Reichstag committee on foreign affairs, of which Stinnes was merely an alternate member.[26] Furthermore, Stresemann's biographers and his own diary give evidence of close personal relations with French industrial leaders. Chief go-betweens, so it appears, were Louis Loucheur, industrialist and leader of the Left-Radicals, and Professors Hesnard and Haguenin. Dr. Edgar Stern-Rubarth states that Professor Haguenin was the "uncrowned king of Germany" before Stresemann became foreign minister, but retired before 1924.[27]

Specifically, Stresemann advised the German government to follow a more conciliatory policy so that the reparation question could be solved at the earliest possible time. Prospects for such a settlement would be enhanced if Germany's industrial capacity and credit potential would be exploited to the fullest as a bargaining point in the forthcoming negotiations. At the same time, no concessions were to be made concerning the unrestricted control by Germany over her own territories. In other words, Stresemann believed that Germany was now in a position to exact a price in return for the abandonment of militant resistance in the Ruhr. It would seem that his personal inspection tour through the Ruhr area, under the assumed name of Dr. Friedrich Erlenkamp, had served to strengthen his convictions in that respect.[28]

Concerning proposals to the effect that the Ruhr was to be administered by an agency under the League of Nations, Stresemann evidenced a distinct lack of faith in international organization. He considered occupation by enemy troops far less degrading than surveillance by an international police force.[29]

Taking note of a remark by Lord Curzon to the effect that the Ruhr occupation had proven to be wasteful, he quickly seized the opportunity to stress once more the existence of a split between the Western Allies.[30] At the same time, however, he expressed his regrets over Britain's inclination to confine her efforts to sympathetic speeches while her troops and her statesmen continued to assist France in the reduction of German sovereignty in the West. "This time," he warned, "negotiations will be conducted before the arms of passive resistance are laid down."[31] In other words, the lesson of the pre-Armistice negotiations of 1918 was to be observed, and there was to be no surrender of the only weapon left to Germany, namely, passive resistance, until the terms of the new peace had been settled.

Lord Curzon's biographer, Harold Nicolson, states that the British foreign secretary, knowing that he could not launch a frontal attack on Poincaré's policy, based his strategy instead upon "a wide encircling movement, keeping the French upon the unfavorable grounds of reparation, encouraging the Germans to offer reasonable conditions for an armistice, hoping to mobilize world opinion."[32] Stresemann's policy, while he was chairman of a powerful parliamentary committee, and leader of an opposition party, corresponded with Curzon's strategy. Holding on to the weapon of passive resistance, and supporting every government move in that direction, Stresemann nevertheless did not cease to stress the "open door" in a number of ways. In this endeavor he was backed by leading industrialists, among whom were several members of his party. On May 25 the National Association of Industrialists (*Reichsverband der Industriellen*) offered to assume a considerable part of the financial burden that would be incurred in the event of an adverse settlement of the Ruhr conflict. Stresemann declared that no economic sacrifice would be too high in order to secure the liberation of the Rhineland, the Ruhr, and the Saar.[33] This move represented an attempt to bolster Lord Curzon's position in Great Britain. As it became increasingly clear that Germany could not afford a continuation of passive resistance without dire economic consequences, he warned the British people that "German bolshevism means British bolshevism," and that the economic demise of Germany would soon be followed by a general European economic crisis. Furthermore, and also for the benefit of those in

Britain who feared a general European conflagration, he added that French policy had engendered a hatred in Germany to an extent unknown even during the war. The future Stresemann policy, however, was clearly outlined in the following remarks:

If there would be a statesman or a politician who could bring us *rapprochement* which would save the Rhineland and the Ruhr from further tortures, he would truly be guilty of criminal neglect if he failed to act in order to achieve such a *rapprochement*.[34]

This remark was of course also designed to declare Stresemann's candidacy for the chancellorship once again.

On the eve of Stresemann's ascendancy to the highest cabinet post, on August 11, he learned of a note sent by Lord Curzon to Raymond Poincaré. The note tended to bear out Stresemann's appraisal of the Anglo-French relationship, and was highly indicative of a veiled invitation to put pressure on France. The British foreign secretary developed a number of legal, political, and economic arguments against the Ruhr occupation, concluding that France had no right to apply sanctions under the Treaty of Versailles without the express consent of the other Allies. The part of the note bound to have the greatest effect upon the Ruhr conflict, however, stated that while Britain would never take sides against her own Allies, she was at the same time unable to advise Germany to terminate her passive resistance unconditionally.[35] This stand by the British leader, whether directly or indirectly, served to open the way for an armistice in the Ruhr. Moreover, it facilitated Stresemann's appearance on the diplomatic stage.[36]

III. *Toward Liquidation of the Ruhr Crisis.* Stresemann's one hundred days as chancellor of the Republic were almost completely devoted to the continuation of the Ruhr struggle. From August 13, 1923, the day of his accession to office, until November 23, both his domestic and his foreign policies were primarily dedicated to the attempt to force a withdrawal of the occupation troops, and to forestall future occupations and interventions by the Versailles powers. The early revision of the sanction clauses of the Treaty of Versailles remained his primary objective.

With his appointment to office, his strategy changed but slightly. He now advocated a dual solution of the conflict: submittal of the dispute to an international tribunal of arbitration,[37] and, at the same time, a sacrificial offer by German industry to satisfy French reparation demands.[38] This policy had two corollaries. On the one hand, Stresemann emphasized that a solution of the conflict concerned all the Versailles powers and not France alone, while on the other hand,

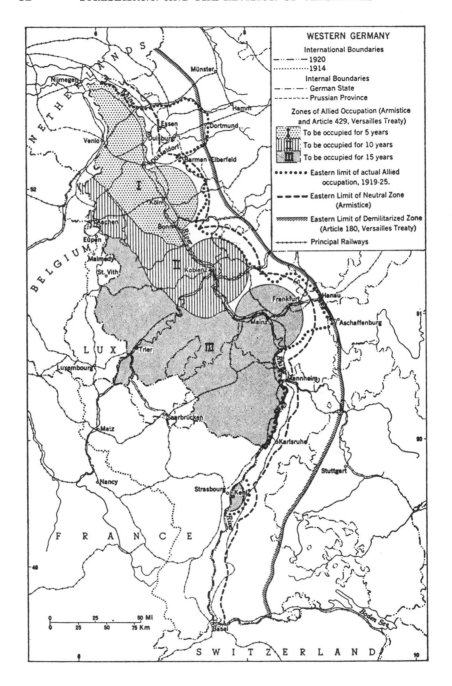

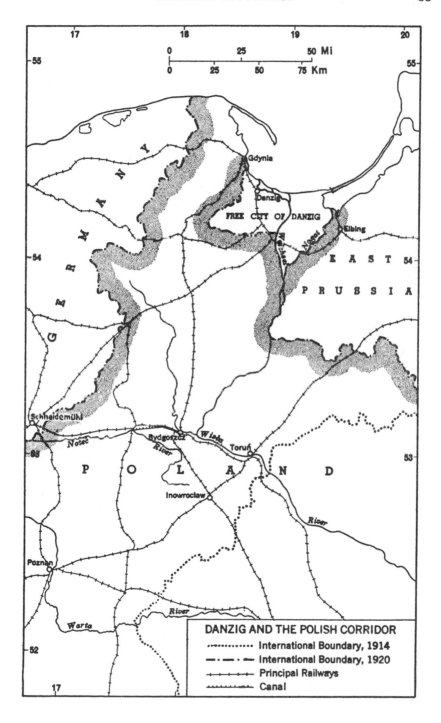

DANZIG AND THE POLISH CORRIDOR

·············· International Boundary, 1914

—·—·—·— International Boundary, 1920

+++++++ Principal Railways

·········· Canal

Great Britain was told that a strong and economically viable Germany was of vital importance to her. Once the tentative support of Great Britain had been obtained, Stresemann would not permit France to maneuver him into a quarrel with Britain through bilateral negotiations with France alone. Instead, he assured British statesmen of his good faith, and in order to allay any fears on their part that he would misuse British support, he informed the British Ambassador of his intention to be more discreet and more conciliatory in his diplomacy toward France than had been the case before he became chancellor.[39] To strengthen the German position against France even more, he not only suggested that the reparation question could only be solved if the Allies first negotiated the matter among themselves and then with Germany, but also that the United States of America should not be excluded from the negotiations.[40]

French security considerations were to be countered by a world-wide effort to confront military with economic and political argumentation. Since combined action on the part of the Allied Powers was a prerequisite for the successful curbing of French aspirations, Stresemann could well afford to deny any intentions to sow distrust among the Allies, for it was Germany's only hope, at the time, to see a settlement of the Ruhr conflict on a multilateral basis.

The proposal to submit the Ruhr conflict to arbitration was never seriously considered by France. However, the second offer, to settle reparation claims by mobilization of German industrial resources, came very close to realization.[41] It failed only because Stresemann, engaged in a struggle to deny France the right to occupy German soil in retaliation for nonpayment of reparation obligations, could not possibly accept the French demand for a lease on the Rhine and Ruhr industries as a guaranty for future payments. He insisted that no settlement of the conflict was acceptable to him, which tended to support the French view that the Ruhr and the Rhineland, under *de facto* occupation, were areas to be differentiated from the rest of Germany. Addressing himself to Raymond Poincaré, Stresemann stated, "For us in Germany there is no Rhine question which could be solved internationally."[42] The *sine qua non* for a settlement was still an admission by France that the Ruhr occupation had been illegal. In the absence of a French surrender on that point, passive resistance continued to harass French occupation authorities in the Ruhr, and found Stresemann's wholehearted support.[43]

Aside from passive resistance and some conciliatory proposals, Stresemann proceeded to follow a policy of active diplomatic opposition to the occupation. He informed the British Ambassador that, failing an early withdrawal of the occupation troops, Germany would be forced to consider herself no longer bound by the Treaty of Versailles.[44] He asserted that as long as Germany was not permitted to solve her own economic problems in her own way and under her own sovereignty, she certainly could not be expected to pay reparations. However, at a cabinet meeting, a week later, he strongly advised against rupture of diplomatic relations with the treaty powers and against rejection of the treaty itself.[45] The reasoning behind the apparent contradiction became clear when he addressed parliament a few days later. While he was prepared to pressure Great Britain into action on Germany's side by threatening repudiation of the treaty, he actually regarded the document as the best protection available to Germany at that time. "As long as the treaty is valid," he advised the Reichstag, "there exists a legal basis for intervention by foreign powers on behalf of Germany."[46] By "foreign powers" he meant, of course, Great Britain. In order to alleviate French fears, and at the same time to strengthen the British position, he offered a mutual security pact to France at a public meeting in Stuttgart.[47] The proposal was curtly rejected by Poincaré.[48]

The over-all diplomatic objective during the struggle against the French interpretation of the military sanction clauses was the attempt to convince the world, Great Britain in particular, that the French policy constituted a direct threat to European peace and world trade. Coupled with the propaganda move were constant representations to British diplomats to the effect that Germany would cease passive resistance, and would resume payments of reparations if she was given a guaranty against future French moves across her boundary.[49]

In his campaign to stir Great Britain into action against France, Stresemann resorted to a multiple propaganda barrage, ranging from purely economic considerations to legalistic arguments. In an interview with the correspondent of the *Daily Express*, he stated that since Germany was the United Kingdom's best customer, the latter could not well afford to permit Germany's economic collapse. He added, to smooth ruffled feelings, "While Germany is obliged to accept military occupation, she also has the right to demand that such occupation be inter-Allied and not by individual powers."[50] "Are not England's interests concerned?" he asked Lord D'Abernon on another occasion.[51] Finally, he sought to impress Great Britain with the idea that Germany was prepared to negotiate, provided that certain concessions were made by the other side. These concessions would have involved: liberation of all political prisoners in the Ruhr area, the return of expellees, resumption of official duties by German civil servants, a general amnesty for saboteurs, cessation of confiscations of German property by French troops, abstention from interferences in industry, and recognition of full German sovereignty over the Ruhr.[52] In the hope that British pressure upon France would lead to French concessions, he even advised continuation of passive resistance in spite of the fact that the end of Germany's financial endurance was in sight.[53]

When General Smuts of the Union of South Africa indicated displeasure over developments in Western Europe, Stresemann wrote to him at once, declaring his readiness to discuss the situation.[54] But all efforts were of no avail. Once passive resistance had come to an end, and when he was forced to admit failure, he wrote regretfully, "All attempts to interest England in the proposition that passive resistance could not be terminated except on certain conditions, failed because British foreign policy was not active enough at the time."[55]

Poincaré's triumph and Stresemann's defeat came suddenly. On September 27 Stresemann had to give the order for cessation of passive resistance, surrendering thereby the only reliable weapon available to him in the struggle.[56] On October 6 he admitted complete failure in the attempt to "utilize passive resistance toward a successful foreign policy."[57] The principle which he had fought to uphold, namely, that reparation payments, defaults, and Germany's territorial integrity were not intertwined but subject to separate considerations and quite independent of one another, had not been sustained. However, he was to have the last word. On the strength of Article 241 of the Treaty of Versailles, he informed the Allied Reparation Commission that as a result of the Ruhr invasion, Germany's financial affairs had been rendered too chaotic to permit continuation of reparation payments.[58] While this *non possumus* ultimately led to revision of the reparation schedule, the matter of military sanctions had not been settled.

The final diplomatic move by Stresemann as chancellor concerned French demands for coal shipments in payment for damage incurred as a result of the Ruhr occupation. Addressing the Reichstag, he asked, "If I accept the French view that these coal shipments are not to be taken out of the reparation account but are instead to be in payment of the Ruhr invasion, then I, as chief of the government, legalize that invasion . . . and that is out of the question."[59]

Aside from the fact that France seemed to be unalterably opposed to a modification of her policy in the Ruhr crisis, Stresemann faced the severest opposition at home. His policy designed to force revision of the sanction clauses by diplomatic methods was most vigorously attacked by a large segment of the political and industrial leadership at home. The opposition to his policy was so intense, and the situation so delicate that he was forced to conduct the initial exploratory talks with De Margerie, the French Ambassador, in secret. At the end of the first conversation he had to request absolute secrecy. "The situation here is so delicate," he explained, "that any government preparing to terminate passive resistance would come to fall at once."[60] A few days later, he addressed an appeal for objectivity to the press in the Ruhr area. He asked the journalists, gathered to honor him, to co-operate with him in his attempt to undo the harm done to European unity by the Ruhr occupation.[61] This was to be one of many such appeals for rationality which Stresemann was to address to the press in later years.

However, while some of the press co-operated, the rest of the country was by no means prepared to follow his appeal to reason. Leading the opposition was Alfred Hugenberg, publisher of right-wing dailies, whose newspaper chain was dedicated to ultranationalism and revenge.[62] The German National People's Party, through Hugenberg's press and in parliament, made it well-nigh impossible to give the outside world the impression that Germany had reformed and had peaceful intentions toward her neighbors. On the other hand, primarily to allay French fears, it was paramount for Stresemann to convey just such an impression.

To bring the nationalists into line, Stresemann resorted to a variety of parliamentary tactics. Blunting the edge of their anti-socialist campaign, he praised the Social-Democrats, whose votes he required to maintain his government, by pointing to their loyal conduct during the Ruhr struggle. Furthermore, in order to make it as difficult as possible for the nationalists to remain in the opposition, he called for national unity in the eventuality of a rejection of the Treaty of Versailles by Germany.[63] This was of course merely a tactical maneuver. As has been pointed out, Stresemann was not prepared to reject the treaty as a whole. The call for national unity, however, was based on dire circumstances. During Stresemann's chancellorship, and simultaneously with developments in the Ruhr, both the extreme Left and the Right sought to gain control of Germany by attempts at armed insurrection.[64] In addition, there were almost insurmountable obstacles in the sphere of domestic politics. The two cabinet crises experienced by Stresemann as chancellor, the second causing his downfall, had established one thing clearly. In order to carry out his foreign policy, Stresemann required the parliamentary support of the Social-Democrats. As a result, the severest opposition to his government developed among rightist circles, predominantly from representatives of heavy industry, including many members of his own party.[65] Giving in to the demands for an eight-hour day during the Ruhr crisis, for example, Stresemann lost the support of the Ruhr and Rhine magnates. On the other hand, if he had followed the advice of the latter group and had taken dictatorial measures to keep the Ruhr workers in line, he would not only have lost the confidence of the strong Socialist Party, but would also have played into the hands of French die-hards who charged that Germany was not to be trusted.

The Ruhr battle ended in defeat for Stresemann. Heavy industry, once the blow had been delivered and the Stresemann cabinet had resigned, turned around and granted France greater concessions than they had been willing to grant the coalition government at home. Yet Stresemann emerged far stronger from this crisis than he had ever been before. Through his political steadfastness, he had secured for himself the future support of the Social-Democrats and of the middle-of-the-road parties, the Democrats and the Center Party, as well as the majority in his own party, the German People's Party. It had become clear that Stresemann, as foreign minister, unburdened by direct responsibility for social and economic conflicts at home, was the best man for handling Germany's foreign problems.[66] One day before the second and final fall of his cabinet, Stresemann addressed a warning to Great Britain and France not to undermine the democratic elements in Germany by a policy of retribution. The rise of radicalism, he warned, could be avoided by a more conciliatory policy on the part of the Allies.[67]

The fall of the Stresemann cabinet was the result of his own doing. He explained to the press, "I had the feeling that my own majority would no longer have been sufficient for the important diplomatic negotiations and decisions called for in the immediate future."[68]

French and Belgian troops had entered the Ruhr on January 11, 1923. The coming negotiations, which Stresemann had spoken about on the eve of his departure from the chancellor's office, were expected to lead to the liquidation of the occupation. The following years were to see Gustav Stresemann freed from the responsibility of the highest government office, free to devote his time and energies to foreign affairs and to those aspects of domestic politics necessary to carry his foreign policy forward. Because he could devote all his available time to the foreign office, the next phase in the struggle against the Treaty of Versailles, limited as it was, was relatively speaking more successful.

As soon as the Treaty of Versailles had been accepted by Germany, it became clear what form Stresemann's attack on the peace settlement would take. Of all the undesirable aspects of the treaty, its penal provisions represented the most immediate problem and were therefore selected as the chief target. Consequently, Stresemann concentrated his early efforts on the task of restricting and limiting the application of military and economic sanctions by the Allies. For the time being, it seemed to be more important to blunt the edges of the treaty by reducing the direct consequences of nonfulfillment to manageable proportions, than it was to attempt a revision of the substance of the treaty.

In furtherance of this foreign policy, Stresemann developed four major strategic objectives before and after his appointment to the foreign ministry. (1) In order to cast doubt upon the utility of military sanctions, he attempted to prove that punitive measures designed to exact reparations were self-defeating because of the inevitably adverse effect such measures would have upon the economy of the state from which reparations were to be collected. On similar grounds, he called attention to the social, economic, and political reactions which a severe economic crisis in Germany would cause in the victor states. The chance of a bolshevization of Europe in the wake of a German economic collapse was an often repeated argument in that connection. (2) In keeping with the foregoing objective, Stresemann advocated, and supported, the resort to passive resistance during the greater part of the Ruhr occupation. This move was designed to render the application of military sanctions as costly and as difficult as possible and, at the same time, to gain the support of the nationalist elements in Germany. (3) Because it became apparent that the occupation of the Ruhr by France had failed to meet with British approval, Stresemann considered it opportune to attempt to drive a wedge between the two former Allies. The aloofness of the United States made it momentarily difficult to exploit the rift which had also developed between the Western powers and their North American associate. (4) In order to exploit any existing antimilitarist, conciliatory sentiments in France and in Great Britain, Stresemann's strategy called for restraint on the part of Germany and for repeated offers to effect a reconciliation with the former enemy states, primarily on the basis of industrial understandings and agreements.

To achieve the foregoing strategic objectives, Stresemann developed the following additional diplomatic tactics. (1) In order to restrict the application of sanctions in pursuance of treaty provisions, while at the same time preparing the ground for a general treaty revision, he commenced with an attack on the legality of military sanctions. This attack took two forms: (a) he attempted to establish the dictum that sanctions could not, and should not, extend to the point of violating Germany's territorial integrity; and (b) that no single Allied nation could unilaterally decide upon the application of sanctions. A successful attack on the legality of the penal provisions of the treaty would of course serve to undermine the entire peace structure, whereas the latter point would serve to prevent any resort to sanctions in general. It could confidently be expected that if *all* Allies had to agree to the application of sanctions, no sanctions would be applied. This would leave Germany reasonably free to interpret the remaining treaty provisions at will. (2) On the same grounds, and for similar reasons, Stresemann was not prepared to repudiate the treaty as such for the time being. Because Allied unity was no longer a factor to be reckoned with, he believed that the Treaty of Versailles constituted the only remaining legal protection for Germany, inasmuch as under the terms of that treaty, and only on those grounds, Great Britain was in a position to prevent France from engaging in additional military ventures against Germany. (3) Because it was necessary for a disarmed Germany to maintain a legal bulwark against French aggression, but not one which contained obnoxious sanction provisions and penal clauses, a new diplomatic concept emerged in outline. The oppressive treaty was eventually to be nullified, with full regard for its advantages, by the substitution of another legal structure. This was to be achieved by the conclusion of another treaty which was to have this dual effect: (a) on the one hand, it was to prevent another application of sanctions against Germany by a legal fortification of Germany's western boundaries; and (b) on the other hand, it was to be as effective as the Treaty of Versailles in discouraging unilateral acts by France, or if it could not prevent them, it could at least serve to render them morally and legally unfeasible. If it could be established that unilateral acts by France were "wrong" from the legal and moral point of view, it stood to reason that world opinion could easily be mobilized in favor of the German cause.

Stresemann's policy, either at the time he was in charge of foreign policy, or before, was of course partly conditioned by considerations of domestic politics. Because his own party was split over the basic question of fulfillment or nonfulfillment of the treaty terms, he had to exercise great restraint to avoid a widening of the rift. When it became evident to him that an impasse had been reached in the Ruhr struggle and that the policy of offering passive resistance had to be replaced by a more conciliatory attitude toward France, he strengthened his relations with the powerful Social-Democratic Party in order to assure himself of the necessary parliamentary support for his future foreign policy. He did this in spite of the nationalistic tendencies within his own party and in the face of a rapidly growing nationalist movement in the country as a whole.

Stresemann's exposed position and his struggle against his own nationalistic-militaristic past are occasionally reflected in the mass of private and official papers which make up the Stresemann file in the archives of the German foreign office, the *Nachlass*. The papers show evidence that the minister's loyalty to the Republic cannot be firmly established as of the time of the attempted rightist revolt in 1920, the Kapp *Putsch*. The recurrence in Stresemann's correspondence of the name of a participant in the affair, one Major Pabst, alias Peters, would indicate a more than casual interest on the minister's part in the fate of the exiled and hunted rebels. The relationship between Stresemann and Pabst appears to have been unusually close to permit the latter to exact a promise from the foreign minister to intervene in his behalf and to obtain an amnesty for Pabst and for his co-conspira- tors. There is also evidence of a certain nervousness on Stresemann's part regarding the trials of the so-called *Feme* murderers, especially the trial of Lieutenant Schulz. A statement made by the minister to the *New York Times* in 1924, to the effect that he was a monarchist at heart, coupled with the foregoing and additional evidence, would indicate that Stresemann found it difficult at times to extricate him- self from his past. As the anti-Weimar reaction began to form and to organize itself, there were in its ranks many individuals and groups who had at one time considered Stresemann as one of theirs. They continued to claim him and his sympathies. The fact that considera- tions of diplomacy and statecraft tended to alienate the man from his former associates—making them his bitterest enemies in the proc- ess—provides the principal element in the tragedy and the epic that was Stresemann.

CHAPTER VII

REVISION OF THE SANCTION CLAUSES:
EVACUATION OF ALLIED TROOPS

I. *Initial Strategy.* Following the Ruhr fiasco, a new cabinet came into existence. It was the first of six to which Stresemann was to belong as foreign minister only. It represented a coalition of the Center Party, the Democrats, and the German People's Party. Stresemann, still leader of his party, entered the new cabinet considerably stronger than before. As chancellor he had clearly demonstrated his resolute opposition to the radicalism of either Right or Left, and had also proven to be a staunch defender of the new republic. Old suspicions had gone by the wayside. He had won the confidence especially of the middle parties, but the Socialists also remembered his refusal to deliver Germany into the hands of French or German big industry. He was now prepared to continue the battle against sanctions, military occupation, and against the Treaty of Versailles in general.

In a much discussed letter to the ex-Crown Prince of Germany, written in September 1925, he stated:

The most important objective of German foreign policy is the liberation of German soil from foreign occupation. First of all we will have to get the yoke off our backs. For that reason it will be a requirement for German foreign policy . . . to maneuver (*finassieren*) and to avoid big decisions.[1]

For the next five years, following the Ruhr occupation, the liberation of German soil from foreign occupation was Stresemann's primary objective.

Aside from Paragraph 18, Part VIII of Annex II of the treaty, the sanction clause, which depended upon a declaration of default by the Allied Reparation Commission, was another obstacle, Article 428, which provided for the occupation of German territory west of the Rhine. This article read as follows: "As a guarantee for the execution of the present treaty by Germany, the German territory situated to the west of the Rhine, together with the bridgeheads, will be occupied by Allied and Associated troops for a period of fifteen years from the coming into force of the present treaty." If the provisions of the treaty were faithfully carried out by Germany, the northern section of the occupied area, which included Cologne, was to be evacuated at the end of five years, and the central section, which included Coblenz, at the end of ten years. Evacuated territory could be reoccupied either during or after the expiration of these fifteen years, in the event that Germany refused to observe her reparation obligations. On the other hand, should Germany before the end of fifteen years comply "with all the undertakings resulting from the present treaty," the occupying forces would be withdrawn immediately. These stipulations were given in Articles 429 to 432 of the Versailles Treaty. Stresemann's objective with regard to these provisions was to advance the scheduled dates of evacuation and if possible, on the basis of Article 431, to achieve a complete withdrawal of Allied troops before the expiration of the fifteen-year period.

Following the cessation of passive resistance in the Ruhr area and the coming into existence of the *Mission Inter-allié de Contrôl des Usines et des Mines*, the Rhineland and the Ruhr had for all practical purposes become "reparation provinces." In order to terminate this situation and to remove the customs barriers between occupied and unoccupied Germany, Stresemann now engaged in a campaign to restore the economic unity of all Germany. The first step in this direction was the request, addressed to the Reparation Commission, dated June 7, 1923, for a conference to determine Germany's capacity to pay.[2] This strategy was to tie the Ruhr conflict to the general reparations problem, and to force the evacuation of Allied troops by referring to the critical economic situation allegedly caused by the occupation.[3]

The international situation seemed to be favorable for the planned move. Great Britain, more than ever before, was keenly interested in a currency stabilization and a German economic recovery. A long moratorium appeared to be the best possible solution. On the other hand, France had reason to fear that at the end of the moratorium, she might find herself faced with a Germany more prosperous, more aggressive, and less inclined than ever to pay.[4]

Fully aware of the tensions in the Allied camp, Stresemann was determined to exploit the situation to the utmost. At one time, he even considered an alliance with the Soviet Union in order to forestall a Franco-Soviet alliance which seemed to be in the making. Such a "continental alliance," he believed, would find the support of Great Britain, "where the thought of war against France has not been ruled out."[5] He also carefully nurtured the impression in Lord D'Abernon's mind that he might enter into negotiations with Italy, which had approached him concerning the chances for an Italo-German alliance.[6]

On January 14, the Committee of Experts, convened by the Allied Reparation Commission, began its meetings under the chairmanship of Charles G. Dawes, a national of the United States. Its assigned task was to determine the resources and financial capacity of Germany in accordance with the provisions of Article 234 of the Treaty of Versailles.[7] While the committee was deliberating, Stresemann endeavored to prepare the international and the domestic scenes for the subsequent action. France was the first target for a subtle attack. In a talk to the foreign correspondents at Berlin, Stresemann connected the question of Germany's territorial integrity with France's economic system. The violation of the former, he maintained, would inescapably result in the destruction of the latter.[8] For home consumption, he stated that any economic sacrifices which might result from the experts' conferences would nevertheless assist in the attainment of foreign policy objectives, such as the regaining of German unity and sovereignty over the "lost territories."[9] Fully aware of French reluctance to agree to a modification of the reparation schedule, he embarked on a policy of giving maximum support and approval to the deliberations of the experts. The tone of his public addresses was optimistic, restrained, and conciliatory toward France. He appealed to France to realize that a Germany permitted to exist in peace would be a far better guaranty for French security than any alliance or treaties which she might want to conclude. Partly for home consumption, and partly directed to France, he explained that the findings of the experts' committee would show whether France wanted reparations or mere political power. Addressing himself to those at home who feared further losses of German sovereignty as a result of the reparations conference, he pointed out that Germany could well afford to let her fate rest in the hands of neutral experts. To head off any French objections to the anticipated judgment by the experts, he warned that failure to support democratic forces in Germany would inevitably result in a far greater threat to French security. This was his favorite point. In addition, he warned against attempts, proposed by France, to assure the survival of a democratic Germany by combined Anglo-French efforts. Such a move, he maintained, would be to the everlasting discredit of democratic ideals in Germany for an association of democracy with foreign powers would find the German masses opposed to democratic principles and methods.[10]

Thus, Stresemann's campaign, launched while the experts deliberated, sought to maneuver France into a position where she could no longer afford to insist on such forceful measures as the Ruhr occupation. Instead, she would be obliged to accept the judgment of the powers associated with her in the Reparation Commission. Stresemann's most telling victory during this period was his successful isolation of France and the fact that the United States had entered the negotiations.

II. *The Election Campaign and the Dawes Plan.* As a result of certain domestic difficulties, the Reichstag was dissolved on March 13, 1924. The elections were to take place in May. Ever since December 1923, there had been moves afoot to remove Stresemann from the foreign office. Participants in this conspiracy could be found in his own party as well as in the German National People's Party. Even some independent leaders were interested in his speedy removal.[11] The greatest immediate danger arose over the formation of a secessionist group within the People's Party. The "National-Liberal Association," led by some of the most prominent People's Party stalwarts, sought to give the party a more nationalistic program. Antisocialism also was part of the projected platform. All in all, the movement, which sought Stresemann's removal and which amounted to a virtual rebellion, promised to make it exceedingly difficult for him to pursue his foreign policy.[12] In addition, of course, an intraparty struggle just before an election, threatened to undermine the strength of the party at a crucial time. Stresemann's task, arising from these dangers, was to convince the country that his policy was the only acceptable and the only feasible one.

In the interest of his foreign policy, i.e., to let the Ruhr evacuation and the other demands await the findings of the reparation experts, it was now of paramount importance to stifle the cries of the nationalists, who demanded determined action. During his chancellorship, Stresemann had already made one move designed to appease the Right. He had permitted the ex-Crown Prince to return to Germany from exile.[13] By that move he had demonstrated to the Right that a success could be scored in the realm of foreign policy without resort to force. From time to time he had also launched protests in the direction of Paris, which had been designed to satisfy the nationalists' demands for militant action, especially for stronger diplomatic representations.[14] Replying to repeated demands by the nationalists that he follow a more consistent policy, that he should attempt to isolate France diplomatically, he patiently pointed out that the problem faced by Germany was a world problem and should be solved on that basis. Concerning the pressure exerted by nationalist circles toward a complete rejection of the Treaty of Versailles, he remarked: "Before the treaty is dealt with, the conditions prevailing under the treaty have to be attacked. The Ruhr invasion has to be nullified before anything else can be considered."[15] However, the most significant statement made by Stresemann, a statement summarizing his diplomatic intentions, was made at a campaign rally of the People's Party on March 9. There he remarked that the terms of the Treaty of Versailles would be fulfilled to the extent of Germany's capacity to fulfill them.[16] This stipulation was to become the keystone of his policy concerning the revision of the treaty.

While the foreign minister accelerated his campaign against resurgent nationalism and militarism at home, he took great pains to impress upon France and Great Britain the need for preventive measures against the rising tide of nationalism and radicalism, accusing these two powers of having failed to support the democratic elements in Germany.[17] In the same vein, he instructed the German Ambassador at Paris to emphasize the fact that French foreign policy had contributed to a strengthening of the radical Right in Germany.[18]

The opposition from the Right, including the rebellious faction within his own party, caused the minister to deliver an exhaustive reply to the most obnoxious accusations. In one address, making use of the best of his oratorical talents, he struck out against his opponents with telling force. Replying to the charge that he had failed to repudiate the war guilt accusation—a charge most frequently hurled at him—he noted that the world had begun to revise its estimate of the causes of the World War. He attributed this success to his policy of piecemeal propaganda through private channels, a policy which would be weakened by official support from the ministry. Next, he explained his alleged failure to "arouse the patriotic passions of the German people," a charge then advanced by Adolf Hitler. To arouse the passions of a people such as the Germans, he remarked, was an easy undertaking. However, the consequences of such foolishness would be disastrous. Finally, concerning the well-worn demand that the Treaty of Versailles be repudiated, he warned again that such repudiation would deprive Germany of her only legal armor against French intransigence.[19]

In an attempt to take the wind out of the sails of the nationalists in his own party and elsewhere, he went so far as to approve, publicly, the existence of a controversial factor: the so-called "patriotic organizations." "If they seek compensation for the lost opportunity of military service and wish to exercise their bodies by joining patriotic organizations," he remarked, "then we will not object."[20] Concerning an equally delicate issue, that of disarmament, he did not shy away from making another daring observation in the face of repeated Allied representations concerning alleged violations of the disarmament clauses by Germany. "We have nothing whatever to do," he observed on behalf of his party, "with those pacifists who are proud to be disarmed. To the contrary, we are ashamed of the enforced disarmament."[21] There is evidence that the candidate and party leader Stresemann, when it became necessary to win votes or to make inroads into the ranks of the opposition, or just to save a political gathering from turning against him and his conciliatory policy, was quite prepared to make off-the-record speeches which would have filled a Hugenberg or a Hitler with envy.

The conclusion is inescapable that Stresemann, in order to reach his objectives was prepared to temporize and to resort to tactical, political expediencies which were in many cases exceedingly distasteful to him personally. On one occasion, confronted by a hostile political gathering and taunted by the audience, he cast a prepared speech aside and, with the press excluded, delivered a patriotic oration of unequalled intensity. Casting all caution to the winds, he asserted that he had decided upon a policy of humiliation for the German people so that they would be hardened and conditioned for the coming struggle for freedom from foreign domination.[22] With such applications of tactical skill he succeeded in maintaining party unity to a certain extent and in maneuvering the opposition into untenable positions.[23]

As election day approached, the People's Party threatened to disintegrate.[24] To avoid a major landslide in favor of the German National People's Party, Stresemann had to campaign more vigorously than he had thought necessary. Moreover, he had to redouble his efforts to meet the attack against the Dawes Plan, in order to prevent misrepresentations of its purposes and scope as well as possible repercussions at Paris and at London.[25] He defended the proposed plan at major rallies in Berlin, Breslau, Magdeburg, and at numerous minor election gatherings. It seems that at one rally, at Magdeburg, he succeeded so well in pleasing the more nationalistic among his listeners that the leader of the Stahlhelm, rightist paramilitary organization, Franz Seldte, arose and offered three cheers for Stresemann.[26] If there was any doubt concerning the objectives of the election campaign of the People's Party, it was cleared up when the final election appeal was published. The party announced, "We were and we are opponents of the policy of fulfillment."[27]

Following the election, in which the nationalists had registered

TABLE I

Election Results for the Second Reichstag, May 4, 1924*

Parties	Total vote	Seats	Percent of total in 1924	Percent of total in 1920
DNVP[a]	5,696,368	95	19.5	15.1
DVP[b]	2,694,317	45	9.2	13.9
Splinter Parties	2,754,263	29	9.4	3.08
Center	4,860,027	81	16.6	18.1
DDP[c]	1,655,049	28	5.7	8.3
SPD[d]	6,008,713	100	20.5	39.55
NSDAP[e]	1,918,310	32	6.5	....
KPD[f]	3,693,139	62	12.6	2.08

* Source: Wilhelm Dittmann, *Das Politische Deutschland vor Hitler* (Zurich: Europa Verlag, 1945) (Plate II).
[a] German National People's Party.
[b] German People's Party (Stresemann's party).
[c] German Democratic Party.
[d] Social-Democratic Party of Germany.
[e] National-Socialist Workers' Party of Germany.
[f] Communist Party of Germany.

gains while the People's Party had lost, Lord D'Abernon observed in his diary that a desperate struggle was being waged concerning the future occupancy of the foreign ministry. The president, Friedrich Ebert, former Socialist leader, and the chancellor, member of the Center Party, were faithful to Stresemann. They reasoned that if the foreign policy was not to be changed, and all responsible leaders knew that Germany could not follow another policy at the time, then there was no point in changing the foreign minister. The Nationalists, however, replied that while they approved of the foreign policy heretofore pursued, to a certain extent, "they would make themselves ridiculous if they would join a government which contained Stresemann; their whole campaign had been based on abuse of him."[28] Since Stresemann continued in office, the German National People's Party remained in the opposition.

III. *The Dawes Plan and the Treaty of Versailles.* The first Committee of Experts had submitted its report, the Dawes Plan, on April 9, 1924.[29] It was now Stresemann's task to see the plan through parliament. He was certain, though, that parliamentary opposition to the plan could not be overcome unless France agreed to certain concessions. Consequently, he embarked upon a campaign on behalf of what he called the "prestige question." Foremost among these questions was of course the liberation of the Ruhr area from foreign occupation. "There are perhaps 500 persons in all of Germany," he told the American Ambassador, "who have read the experts' report.

However, there are millions of Germans who know that other Germans suffered imprisonment under French occupation."[30] The plan had to be sold to the German people, and the foreign minister wanted the help of the Allied and Associated Powers in that undertaking. He wanted "visible evidence of the intentions to evacuate the Ruhr." Among those questions which Stresemann considered to be of primary importance, there were, in addition to the expected evacuation, the return of all expellees, the return of German control over all of the Ruhr, and the return of all prisoners still in French hands.[31]

The political situation abroad seemed to be favorable to Stresemann. On May 11, 1924, Poincaré had to resign and the Radical-Socialist, Édouard Herriot, supported by the Socialists, became prime minister. In January of the same year, a similar change in Great Britain had brought to power a Labour government under James Ramsay MacDonald. Even though the Social-Democrats were not in the German government, Stresemann could nevertheless count on their support. Thus, the chances for an amicable settlement were good.[32] As long as Herriot was at the helm in France and MacDonald, prime minister of Great Britain, Stresemann had reason to hope for an understanding of his own struggle against reaction and nationalism in Germany.[33] However, the domestic scene was once again disturbed by attacks from the Right. They demanded stronger diplomatic representations, and a full-fledged and formal repudiation of the war guilt accusation as their conditions for acceptance of the Dawes Plan. At one point during the debate, a former member of the People's Party, Dr. Quaatz, now a Nationalist deputy, went so far as to insinuate that the foreign minister acted in the interests of France, rather than those of Germany.[34] However, a vote of no confidence failed to unseat the Marx-Stresemann cabinet. Instead, the Reichstag adopted a motion of support, sponsored by Stresemann's own party among others, stipulating that the government should attempt to obtain satisfaction concerning the so-called prestige questions, as a condition precedent to acceptance of the plan by parliament.[35]

In preparation for the coming conference, in the more deliberate and reasonable atmosphere of the Reichstag foreign affairs committee, Stresemann took a more cautious attitude than on the floor of the Reichstag. He warned the party leaders gathered to plan the agenda for the committee meeting that the desired evacuation of Allied troops could not be expected to take place in the near future. He told them, "I wish to avoid promising something which will in all probability not be obtained." "France," he warned, "sits at the longer arm of the lever; her security demands would be more likely heeded than German representations. We must seek the solution on a different basis."[36] The different basis was to be a gradual rather than a sudden evacuation. At the same time, while he warned the party leaders not to expect too much, he stepped up the diplomatic pressure for evacuation. He demanded a declaration on evacuation lest the Nationalists would refuse to vote for the Dawes Plan.[37]

The London Conference on the experts' report convened from July 16 to August 16, 1924. On July 26 there was a storm warning in the Reichstag when another no-confidence vote, sponsored by the National-Socialists, was barely defeated, with 81 members of the German National People's Party abstaining.[38] Dr. Hoetzsch, foreign policy expert of the latter party, presented a list of demands which, he insisted, had to be met before his party could support the government on the Dawes Plan. He demanded: a general amnesty of all political prisoners in the Ruhr and Rhineland; a guaranty against future incursions upon German territory by foreign troops; economic evacuation of the occupied areas; and, as *conditio sine qua non*, military evacuation of the Ruhr, Düsseldorf, Duisburg, Ruhrort, as well as of all other "illegally" occupied territories in the south of Germany.[39]

Before the London Conference met, all governments concerned had indicated their acceptance of the plan. Therefore, the conference was not required to discuss the contents of the plan; all it had to do was to consider the measures necessary to enact it. Among the questions discussed, the revision of the Treaty of Versailles and the Ruhr evacuation were most prominent. The matter of the war guilt accusation was merely a marginal issue.

The essential political problems involved in the projected negotiations were raised at two preparatory meetings between Herriot of France and MacDonald of Great Britain, the first on the occasion of Herriot's visit to London on June 22, and the second during MacDonald's return visit to Paris on July 8. The German foreign minister, not yet officially invited, noted with consternation that the communiqué issued on the two conferences said nothing about the desired military evacuation.[40] He learned subsequently that the two statesmen had agreed beforehand, apparently to spare Herriot the inevitable embarrassment in the Chamber of Deputies, to keep the Ruhr question entirely off the agenda of the London Conference. This was contrary to Stresemann's own plans. Therefore, as soon as he and Chancellor Marx arrived in London, he pushed the question to the fore. With encouragement from MacDonald, he succeeded in obtaining Herriot's qualified support following the latter's return from a

flying visit to the French capital.[41] According to one report, the negotiations between Herriot and Stresemann were so delicate that the
latter instructed his interpreter to talk to no one about the French
premier's concession, not even to the German chancellor.[42] There is
no certainty concerning any promises made by the German in return
for the support. Available evidence points to a promise to advance
once more Chancellor Cuno's offer of a peace and security pact for
the Rhine region.[43]

Following Herriot's return from a quick trip to Paris, the French
offer was extended to evacuation after one year had lapsed and after
military control, as provided by Articles 203 to 210 of the Treaty of
Versailles, had been terminated. Stresemann demanded that evacuation would begin at once. He informed Herriot that the German
government could no longer see the purpose for the Ruhr occupation,
since it had accepted the reparation settlement as proposed by the
experts. Moreover, he warned that certain of the Dawes provisions
would amount to mandatory constitutional changes in Germany and
would, in order to become law, require a two-thirds majority in the
Reichstag. If evacuation did not commence at once, he had grave
doubts whether the required majority could be obtained. By August 15, following a final spurt in the bargaining, the one-year evacuation had been agreed upon. French and Belgian troops were to leave
certain evacuation zones at specified dates, the whole process to be
completed within one year from the date of ratification of the
Dawes Plan.[44] Again, the German foreign minister had failed to
obtain full satisfaction. The legal principle of the application of
sanctions in retaliation for German reparation default had only been
dented. The Allies, especially France, were theoretically still in a
position to resort to military occupation in the event Germany proved
guilty of nonfulfillment of reparation or of other clauses of the Treaty
of Versailles. Apart from the legal and theoretical question, however, Stresemann had gained one important victory. From the time
the occupation had begun, to the London Conference, a diplomatic
front had emerged which promised strongest opposition to another
application of military sanctions by one power alone. Even though
he refused to take credit for it, it was nevertheless true that the United
States, Great Britain, and possibly Italy and Belgium had been won
over to his point of view. It seemed to be agreed that the application
of military sanctions on the basis of the treaty was, if not illegal, at
least immoral and politically inexpedient.[45] Furthermore, the British
prime minister, as a parting gesture, and acting upon the request of
the German delegation, dispatched a note to Herriot wherein he

charged that the unilateral action by France, in the case of the Ruhr occupation, had been "illegal."[46] In the future, then, the new diplomatic constellation promised to stand between French military designs and Germany's territorial integrity. To be sure, the note sent to Herriot had no legal or contractual force, but in the light of the new diplomatic alignment it could, potentially at least, assume major significance.

IV. *The Parliamentary Battle for Adoption of the Dawes Plan.* Following the termination of diplomatic negotiations abroad, Stresemann now had to face the nationalist opposition at home. The Dawes legislation reached the Reichstag on August 23. The Social-Democrats, the Center Party, the Democrats, and, so Stresemann hoped, his own party, the People's Party, could be counted in the "Yes" column. The German National People's Party had declared its rejection of the London agreements before the German delegation had returned to Berlin.[47] Since the proposed Railway Act required a two-thirds majority, and in view of the fact that Article XVII of the Dawes Plan stipulated that the experts' report was "one indivisible whole," the defection of one hundred deputies threatened to spell rejection of the entire plan.[48] There was an outside chance, however, that a sufficient proportion of the Nationalist deputies could be won over to the plan, thereby assuring passage of the key measure by the required constitutional majority. Stresemann addressed himself to that task with accustomed astuteness.

The debate commenced on August 23, with an attack by the Right on Stresemann's failure to obtain greater concessions at London. In his defense, the foreign minister pointed out that German insistence on immediate and total evacuation, in view of the parliamentary situation prevailing in France, could only lead to the downfall of Herriot and the return of Poincaré and the French Right to power. He also called attention to his success in placing the evacuation question on the London agenda in spite of the Herriot-MacDonald agreement to the contrary. The success of future negotiations, he maintained, depended upon acceptance of the agreements. Failure of the Reichstag to accept the Dawes Plan would most likely lead to the destruction of the diplomatic front, so laboriously constructed, and to the triumph of right-wing radicalism in neighboring France.[49]

The Hergt-Stresemann debate on the merits of the parliamentary system, especially on the need of German appreciation of French and British parliamentary problems, was indicative of the thorough change which Stresemann had undergone. Hergt, a monarchist, questioned the policy of "tying Germany's fate to foreign parliamentary coalitions and fluctuations."[50] Stresemann, on the other hand, was fully aware of the Poincaré-Herriot and Tory-Labourite struggles in France and Britain and appreciated the opportunity offered to Germany by the victorious Left in both countries to review the Treaty of Versailles. Himself an expert parliamentarian, he had decided to incorporate this consideration of other parliamentary problems into his foreign policy. The argument in defense of this point of view constituted his major effort on behalf of the passage of the Dawes Plan.[51]

In the final struggle, Stresemann the party leader came to the assistance of Stresemann the foreign minister. To influence the nationalists, he caused a letter to be addressed to the German National People's Party, on August 28, wherein he promised them representation in the cabinet in the event they should decide to vote for the Dawes Plan.[52] He also obtained support for the plan from General von Seeckt, Commander in Chief of the German *Reichswehr*. Von Seeckt sought to prevail upon the Nationalists to vote for the plan, for he feared increased military controls by the Allies in the event of rejection.[53] He, as well as members of the DNVP, feared dissolution of parliament if the Dawes Plan fell short of acceptance.[54] New elections at that time, it was believed, would have favored the Left and the middle parties. Furthermore, Stresemann promised a delegation of Nationalists that the government would address a declaration on the war guilt question to the Allied Powers. In return for this concession, he expressed his desire to see "as large a proportion of the gentlemen as was possible in the 'yes' column" when the Dawes Plan came up for a vote.[55] This maneuver led to a split in the ranks of the DNVP. Forty-eight Nationalist deputies kept the bargain and voted for acceptance of the Railway Act, thus assuring the measure the required two-thirds majority, and guaranteeing passage of the Dawes Plan as a whole.[56]

The long-range effects of the London negotiations and of the parliamentary victory could not at once be realized by the German people. There were some immediate, visible results, however. The French and Belgian troops were withdrawn from the Dortmund zone. The customs barrier erected between the Rhineland and the rest of Germany was removed. The railroads of the Ruhr reverted to their former status. The repatriation of refugees was begun. An eight hundred million mark loan was granted to Germany. The crucial political question concerning the interpretation of the sanction provisions of the Treaty of Versailles, while not entirely solved, had nevertheless undergone some change. The concept of sanctions remained, but the London agreement provided in detail for the settlement of all future frictions over reparation payments by appropriate arbitration methods. The

Reparation Commission, while continuing in existence, was substantially superseded. Germany's economic life could no longer be interfered with by arbitrary decisions made by one power alone. Instead, only the control organs provided for in the Dawes Plan and the Arbitration Tribunal of Interpretation between the Reparation Commission and the German government could render judgments. Paragraph 18 of Part VIII, Annex II of the Treaty of Versailles had been whittled down to a point where it was less of a detriment to German security than had originally been intended. The application of new reprisals, not already provided for in the treaty, had now been rendered most difficult if not altogether impossible. What remained to be done was to deprive France of existing holds, such as the other occupied territories.

The international trade policy followed by Germany while Stresemann was in office is beyond the intended scope of this study. It may be pointed out, however, that under that policy, as under the military policy pursued by the ministry of the armed forces, certain aspects of the Treaty of Versailles were almost imperceptibly altered in Germany's favor. Thus, provisions calling for economic sanctions were actually revised and abrogated.

It may be remembered that Paragraph 18 of Part VIII, Annex II of the treaty permitted the Allied and Associated Powers to take measures "which Germany agrees not to regard as acts of war," and which "may include economic and financial prohibitions and reprisals. . . ." On February 7, 1925, Stresemann announced to the Reichstag:

We all agree that the damaging provisions of the Treaty of Versailles will have to be revised and if we have the opportunity to expunge such articles from the treaty by our commercial policy, then we should do it. We have done it in all cases where we negotiated international trade agreements and treaties of commerce.[57]

The foreign policy supported by Stresemann between 1919 and 1923 was continued by him, in principle, after he became foreign minister. Adapted to the special conditions of the Ruhr invasion, his diplomatic strategy and foreign policy objectives remained, as before, primarily dedicated to the task of revising by peaceful means the most obstructive provisions of the Treaty of Versailles.

Acting upon the assumption that French moves were not alone motivated by a desire to enforce payment of reparations, but that certain long-range military plans of the French high command were also behind the Ruhr invasion, Stresemann endeavored to bring the latter motives out into the open. He sought to accomplish this by giving in to the reparation demands, while insisting simultaneously that the occupied areas be evacuated at once. Furthermore, in order to forestall future application of the penal clauses of the peace treaty, he was not satisfied to effect evacuation alone, but insisted also that military sanctions were to be considered illegal.

In the course of this campaign, Stresemann scored an important victory. Even though the legal principles underlaying the application of sanctions had only been weakened, a new diplomatic constellation had emerged which promised to stand in the way of any future application of additional sanctions under the penal clauses of the Treaty of Versailles. Through the establishment of a complex and cumbersome arbitration machinery, backed up by the new diplomatic front, the penal clauses were rendered ineffective if not, for all intents and purposes, inoperative. With that success, a breach of considerable dimensions had been opened in the legal fortification which originally had been erected to protect the victorious powers against German noncompliance and revisionism.

In order to foster and to maintain pro-German sentiments in Britain and France, Stresemann carefully avoided embarrassing friendly forces in the respective governments of the two countries. Knowing that the Left in France and the Labourites in Britain were faced with a nationalist opposition very similar to his own, he exercised utmost restraint and made repeated offers of a conciliatory nature. To a considerable extent, Stresemann's foreign policy during the Ruhr crisis was anchored on the Left in France and on the Labour government in Great Britain.

Such a policy, however, was most difficult to defend in Germany. Stresemann's long-range objectives, which no doubt would have pleased the German public had they become known, had to be carefully concealed and camouflaged, in order to protect the precariously established, relatively friendly and conciliatory governments of Britain and France. Thus, as far as the German public was concerned, Stresemann's policy spelled only further surrender of German sovereignty and further subjugation to foreign capital. To reduce the effectiveness of rightist propaganda while at the same time attempting not to upset the delicate international situation, Stresemann engaged in a dangerous political "tightrope act." From time to time, he declared his support of certain revisionist objectives, and made disarming gestures in the direction of the Right, while at the same time reassuring the Allies of his sincerity and determination to effect a *rapprochement*. In that connection, he never ceased to remonstrate with the Allied statesmen and ambassadors concerning the need for some concessions on their part in the interest of appeasement of the militant nationalists in Germany.

CHAPTER VIII

SECURITY VERSUS REVISION

I. *Prelude to Locarno.* The international situation in the winter of 1924–25 continued to be favorable for Stresemann's foreign policy. The London agreements and the acceptance of the Dawes Plan by the Reichstag promised to clear the atmosphere to the point where further progress in the revision of the Treaty of Versailles could be made. Of course, a number of obstacles had to be overcome.

As long as the British Empire faced difficulties in the Near East and in India, Great Britain could not afford to alienate her best and most reliable ally, France, over purely secondary issues. Thus, as a result of distant complications, Stresemann was temporarily deprived of Great Britain's support in the battle for revision of the treaty. Without Britain's active intervention, however, France was left in a position to continue her policy of attrition based upon punctilious execution of the treaty provisions by Germany. The German minister searched for a way out, to convince France that her security was not threatened, and that therefore she had no reason to resist peaceful change with regard to the peace terms. At the same time, he had to take steps to prevent renewed application of military sanctions in the event of another charge that Germany had been guilty of reparation default. This was to prove most difficult, however, in view of a new incident troubling the international horizon.

Under Articles 428 to 432 of the Treaty of Versailles the Allies had occupied three zones along the Rhine. According to Article 429, Paragraph 1, the first zone, Cologne and surrounding territory, was to be evacuated at the expiration of five years from the coming into force of the peace treaty, i.e., on January 10, 1925. On January 5, however, Great Britain, France, Italy, and Japan notified the German government that the scheduled evacuation could not take place because of certain violations by Germany of the disarmament provisions of the treaty.[1] Stresemann was determined to resist this renewed application of sanctions. As far as he was concerned, he had already presented an effective answer to this concept of Versailles. Bitterly, he suggested that all ministers who had associated their names with the acceptance of the Dawes Plan should resign at once.[2] In a press conference, he went even further: "I myself stood out against opposition when it was suggested that the Allies did not intend to fulfill their obligations. But today, I recognize with deep regret that the Cologne zone will not be evacuated on January 10, and that those were wrong who voted for the Dawes Plan in the hope that it would end the policy of sanctions."[3] His protestations were of no avail. The French policy of applying sanctions was once again triumphant, while Great Britain was engaged in diplomatic negotiations elsewhere. Stresemann noted in his diary: "Great Britain can only be attacked on one point and that is her nervousness over difficulties in Egypt and over the pending Mossul negotiations, as the result of which difficulties she will make concessions to France in the matter of the Cologne zone."[4]

Another opportunity to raise the question of partial revision of the treaty occurred in connection with Germany's entry into the League of Nations. The London negotiations had cleared the way for accession to the League inasmuch as Germany had demonstrated that she was willing and able to fulfill her obligations under international agreements. At any rate she had proved herself worthy of becoming once again an equal member of the community of nations. To prepare the way, Stresemann, on September 29, 1924, sent a note to the ten nations represented in the Council of the League of Nations.[5] This note summarized the conditions under which Germany would accede. The general tenor of the note was revision. It demanded immediate evacuation of the territories occupied "in violation of the treaty." With reference to Article 1 of the Covenant, it stated that Germany would not consider the qualifications regarding membership contained in that article as binding with regard to the war guilt accusation. Germany was to enter the League unhampered by restrictions or discriminations. The prerequisite for membership in the League, i.e., an assurance of "sincere intentions to observe its [Germany's] international obligations," was not to imply additional obligations derived from the alleged war guilt. In addition to the attempt to trade the very basis of the peace settlement for Germany's entry into the League, the note demanded that colonial mandates be given to Germany under Article 22 of the Covenant. Furthermore, it implied that the disarmament clauses of the peace treaty should be revised so that Germany could discharge her obligations under Article 16 of the Covenant with more assurance and effect. The German was now determined to press his demands to the limit. He sensed that Germany's absence from the League had now become an international problem of the greatest magnitude.

Moreover, the right-wing opposition could not be ignored. In return for co-operation on the Dawes Plan, the Nationalists had been promised participation in the government. Stresemann had personally recommended inclusion of the German National People's Party in the government coalition because without the nationalist vote, no reasonable foreign policy could be conducted.[6] The note to the League powers had been worded so as to satisfy possible Nationalist objections.[7] However, efforts to broaden the basis of the government failed, and the Reichstag was dissolved on October 20. During the ensuing election campaign, the issue of the Dawes Plan was submitted to the electorate. The People's Party, campaigning on Stresemann's record, registered a slight increase in voting strength and parliamentary seats. Since the German National People's Party also won additional seats, Stresemann decided to try again and to recommend inclusion of the Nationalists into the government, reasoning that the responsibility of cabinet posts would bring them to their senses. To be sure, a government oriented toward the Right would tend to disturb the delicate diplomatic situation, but it would also serve to educate the German people. "I see no better way to this," wrote Stresemann, "than to invite the Nationalists to assume their share of the responsibility."[8] This feeling of responsibility, so he hoped, would make them realize the limits of what was possible.[9] Moreover, a swing to the Right, on his own part, would serve as a warning to Great Britain and France that continued refusal to meet his demands would drive him into the arms of the militant extremists. There is evidence that he succeeded in disturbing his friend Lord D'Abernon who became concerned over what he called Stresemann's "unexpected bifurcation to the Right."[10] On one occasion, Stresemann went so far as to threaten the British with a Russo-German alliance in the event of another Allied move against Germany.[11] Thus, having met with continuous defeat at the hands of the Allies, the foreign minister threatened to trade the growing *rapprochement* with the Allies for what appeared to be a reconciliation with the nationalists at home. The primary reason for his insistence on inclusion of the Right in the government, however, was to become clear soon after January 15, the day when Dr. Hans Luther became chancellor, heading a cabinet which included four representatives of the German National People's Party.

II. *Security for Revision.* Between the resignation of the Marx cabinet and the formation of the new one, Stresemann had initiated a move designed to head off further difficulties with France. On December 31, 1922, the then Chancellor Cuno had made an offer to France and her Allies. According to that plan, Germany, along with

France and other powers interested in the Rhine frontier, and under
the guaranty of a disinterested power, was to enter into solemn agreement not to wage war for one generation without reference to special
authorization and without resort to a plebiscite.[12] Reverting to that
offer of 1922, Stresemann now risked his political fortunes by instructing his ambassadors at London and at Paris to sound out the
respective governments concerning their willingness to enter into a
security pact with Germany.[13] The move was most dangerous in the
light of Allied refusals to evacuate the Cologne zone on time, and in
view of the widespread resentment which that refusal had caused
among rightist elements in Germany. In all its ramifications, the proposal to stabilize Germany's western boundaries, advanced before the
government had obtained the approval of the newly elected Reichstag,
amounted to a virtual political *coup d'état*. But those who had been
disturbed over Stresemann's bifurcation to the Right, began to see
the purpose behind his move. With the Nationalists in the government, he could afford to be far more conciliatory than Herriot, who,
as a leftist, was encountering the most violent opposition from the
Right. Thus Stresemann had apparently concluded that a policy of
revisionism was more likely to succeed if advanced by a leader closely
identified with the political Right. He explained the situation as
follows:

It would be easier for Germany to make some agreement with Briand or
Loucheur, because neither of them would meet with the violent opposition
from the Right to which Herriot is exposed. It is an analogous case to that
of Germany where I am able, with the Nationalist members, to come to a
fair arrangement with the Allies, much better than the Socialists would
have done. No one believed that my object in bringing in [to the cabinet]
Nationalist members was to be conciliatory. Now they see . . . that I
can afford to be more conciliatory than the Socialists.[14]

Following some preliminary discussions, Stresemann's offer of
a security pact was first made by a secret tentative approach to the
British government on January 20, 1925.[15] Another offer was dispatched to the French government on February 9.[16] He proposed a
guaranty of peace on the Rhine and as many supplementary treaties
of arbitration as would be considered necessary to implement the
guaranty. The offer had been timed to counter the so-called Geneva
Protocol, a proposed agreement among members of the League of
Nations "to co-operate loyally and effectively and in resistance to any
act of aggression."[17] Stresemann had seen in the proposed protocol
an alliance directed against Germany, and had decided to substitute
an alliance scheme of his own. Moreover, the Geneva Protocol

amounted to a general agreement to uphold the status quo not only on the Rhine, but also concerning Germany's eastern boundaries with Poland and Lithuania. Stresemann knew that Great Britain was not ready to assume so vast a commitment. The Ruhr crisis had shown that she was not even prepared to assume responsibilities arising from French actions in the Ruhr and the Rhineland. Thus, when France demanded that Britain shoulder some responsibilities toward Poland, Czechoslovakia, and Lithuania, she found Sir Austen Chamberlain, British foreign secretary, unprepared to do so.[18]

With the acceptance of his Rhine pact, the German foreign minister sought to accomplish four major objectives. In the first place, the pact was to render another Ruhr occupation under whatever pretexts it should be attempted, absolutely impossible from the legal and diplomatic point of view. Second, the pact was to deprive France of any further justification to apply sanctions or to persist in her policy of retribution on the ground that her security was being threatened by Germany. Third, a wedge would be driven between the Western Allies and their Eastern associates, Poland and Czechoslovakia, leaving open the question of a future revision of the eastern boundaries. The fact that Great Britain had dropped a general guaranty against aggression anywhere in favor of a limited guaranty in the West seemed to indicate that Stresemann had succeeded on all three counts. Finally, by taking the initiative with a peace proposal, Stresemann had reason to hope, in the event that the proposal was rejected by France, that world opinion would be aligned in support of the German cause.[19]

The motives underlying the pact offer were clear to France. The French foreign office realized that Stresemann was seeking to prevent recurrence of the Ruhr occupation and to prepare a new attack on the Treaty of Versailles, on the ground that the new security guaranty would render the safeguards incorporated into the peace settlement obsolete.[20] For that reason the French government, in its reply to the Stresemann note of February 9, stipulated that the proposed pact "must not bring in its wake any changes of the peace treaties."[21] Furthermore, no changes were to take place "regarding the special conditions for the application of certain treaty provisions." In other words, sanctions, military occupation, and other measures taken in pursuance of the peace settlement were not to be ruled out. No revision was to take place.

The Franco-German conflict also centered on the proposed treaties of arbitration. France desired a type of treaty which would serve to maintain the status quo not only in the West but also in the East, while Stresemann preferred that a clear distinction be made between those two regions.[22]

In addition to French opposition, Stresemann was confronted by the usual extremist demands at home. The Right clamored for a *quid pro quo*. To satisfy these demands, but without identifying himself with them, he launched an anonymous article in the *Hamburger Fremdenblatt* on April 10. A few days before, he had assured the Nationalist ministers that the proposed pact would in reality amount to an Anglo-German alliance since Britain would be obliged to come to Germany's assistance in the event the latter was attacked by France.[23] To beat down any further arguments against the pending security pact, he now dangled the possibilities of far-reaching changes in the East before the eyes of the Nationalists.[24]

In further preparation for a renewed attempt to advance the cause of revisionism, Stresemann hinted to the British Ambassador that the pending pact constituted a potential threat to Russo-German relations. In spite of this threat, however, Germany was prepared to come to terms with the West, provided the latter was willing to reciprocate by granting him the desired concessions. The minimum demands to be met at this stage were reduction of the period of the Rhineland occupation and the granting of colonial mandates.[25]

Following delivery of the French reply on June 16, a cabinet crisis developed in Germany. The chancellor, fearing that he would be held responsible should the negotiations fail, sought to saddle his foreign minister with sole responsibility. Stresemann proved to be too strong to be sacrificed, however. He was still leader of a party which commanded a key position in any possible coalition. There was evidence that the Nationalists desired the ousting of Stresemann, but not the resignation of the entire cabinet.[26] Fully aware of the predicament, Stresemann forced an open debate of the entire issue on the floor of the Reichstag, thereby obliging the Nationalists to make a stand one way or the other.[27] Once again, the combination of foreign minister, deputy, and party leader proved to be of greatest value. Neither the Nationalists nor the leaders of the army were prepared to risk another major crisis. General von Seeckt, for example, feared most of all that a Stresemann driven into the opposition would represent a far greater obstacle to his own plans than a Stresemann in the cabinet.[28] Gustav Stresemann had become a veritable institution by virtue of his multiple parliamentary and political ties. He could not be dislodged without a general collapse of the government; and this in spite of the fact that the Allies had not yet given him a good cause to place before parliament in justification of his strong position.

On July 20 Stresemann sent another note to Paris and to London.[29] In it he stated under what conditions Germany would accede to the League of Nations and would agree to the security pact. He reiterated his claim that the proposed pact would establish a new set of facts, which would in turn have a profound effect upon the occupation question. The note denied that the Allies had a legal right to intervene militarily against Germany without previously examining a dispute objectively. This was to be true in the event of a German reparation default, as well as in the event Germany was once again charged with violation of the disarmament or the demilitarization provisions of the peace settlement. Finally, in the way of revisionist demands, the note stated that the possibility of adjusting existing treaties to changed circumstances through pacific settlement was not to be excluded. This was with reference to Article 19 of the League of Nations Covenant. If it had not been for Stresemann's restraining hand, many additional and less reasonable demands would have been presented. Chancellor Luther and the Nationalist members of the cabinet had insisted that the note should please all parties and that it should therefore include all of the conditions previously stated. Instead, Stresemann confined himself to the most essential points.[30] The major objective of the note had been the repudiation of the French position. At the same time, however, it was Stresemann's strategy not to endanger the coming negotiations by posing excessive demands and conditions.

The Locarno Conference lasted from October 4 to 16. In view of widespread intrigues against him, Stresemann insisted that the chancellor, Dr. Hans Luther, accompany him to the conference. This was to forestall another attempt to burden the foreign minister with sole responsibility for the negotiations. In spite of the chancellor's presence, however, the brunt of the German case fell upon the foreign minister's shoulders.[31]

Before arriving at the Locarno Conference, Stresemann followed this strategy. The security pact was to be the basis for far-reaching concessions on the part of the Allies in return for Germany's accession to the League and her demonstration of good will. The Treaty of Versailles had demanded that Germany fulfill her obligations. In the event of nonfulfillment, military and other sanctions were to be applied, and the scheduled evacuation of certain territories was to be delayed. Stresemann's plan was to reinterpret the concept of fulfillment. As long as Germany showed a willingness to fulfill her obligations, and even though she might fall short of the commonly expected minimum, the Allies would nevertheless be under obligation to consider the conditions of the treaty as having been fulfilled in principle.[32] He maintained that a complete fulfillment could not have been intended at the time the treaty had been signed, since the evacuation schedule provided for in Articles 428 to 432 was to see its completion by 1935, long before reparation payments could possibly be concluded. Thus the phrase of Article 431, "if before the expiration of the period of 15 years, Germany complies with all the undertakings," actually referred to Germany's good intentions to comply with the undertakings of the treaty. Because the security pact, initiated by Germany, as well as Germany's acceptance of the Dawes Plan, were sufficient evidence of her good intentions, the advanced evacuation called for in Article 431 should begin at once. In addition to this major principle, Stresemann demanded, in return for Germany's adherence to the pact and to the Covenant, fourteen minor concessions. These, termed *Rückwirkungen*, ranged from concessions in the matter of the Rhineland occupation, military investigation of Germany's state of armament, retention of the army's supreme command, and the training of troops, to the building of airports in occupied areas.[33]

The Locarno agreements consisted of a protocol, seven treaties, and a note.[34] The first of the seven treaties was a guaranty under which Britain, France, Belgium, Italy, and Germany, collectively and severally, guaranteed the western frontiers of Germany and the demilitarization of the Rhineland. This guaranty was based on Articles 42 and 43 of the Treaty of Versailles. France, Belgium, and Germany agreed "in no case to attack or to invade each other or to resort to war against each other," except in a flagrant breach of peace, or in fulfillment of League action against an aggressor state. The Treaty of Mutual Guarantee was to go into effect upon Germany's admission to the League of Nations. There followed four treaties of arbitration between Germany on the one hand and France, Belgium, Poland, and Czechoslovakia, severally, on the other. The significance of the latter treaties became more evident in Stresemann's Eastern policy. The treaties provided for disputes to be submitted to a conciliation commission and thence, if the need arose, to the World Court or to the League Council. The treaties of guaranty between France and Poland, and France and Czechoslovakia followed. The note was collectively addressed to Germany by the conferees in order to dispose of certain objections which Germany had raised against the applicability of Article 16 of the League Covenant to German conditions.

Once again, as in the case of the Dawes Plan, Stresemann had to go to the country to interpret the Locarno treaties to the public, and this in the face of violent opposition from the Right. The Nationalist group in parliament had decided, on October 22, not to support the treaty which, so they claimed, would deprive Germany permanently of the territories lost at the end of the World War. On October 25, one week after the treaties had been negotiated, the Nationalist cabinet members resigned. The task of selling the Locarno Pact to the country was made even more difficult by the Allied failure to make immediate, visible concessions.

In order to prepare the country for acceptance of the negotiated treaties, the foreign minister had to explain away several aspects of the agreement which, so it would seem to the public, were detrimental to Germany's best interests. At the conference itself, Stresemann had refused even to take notice of the separate treaties of guaranty concluded between France and her Eastern allies. Now, addressing himself to the country, he pointed out that his refusal to take cognizance of the treaties prevented any future claim by the Allies to the effect that he had guaranteed the Polish or Czechoslovak borders.[35] Next, he turned to the controversial guaranty of the territorial status quo of Germany's boundaries with Belgium and France contained in Article 1 of the Treaty of Mutual Guarantee, popularly known as the Rhineland Pact. The Nationalists saw in that guaranty a renunciation of all moral rights, on Germany's part, to recover lost territories like Alsace-Lorraine and Eupen-Malmédy. In reply, Stresemann asserted that a guaranty of the status quo, instead of amounting to a recognition of existing boundaries for all times, was merely a renunciation of aggressive action; moral rights to recover lost territories had not been forfeited.[36] In a subsequent reply to an interpellation on the floor of the Reichstag, he stated: "The effect of Article 19 of the Covenant (concerning the *clausula rebus sic stantibus*) is not abrogated by Article 1 of Locarno."[37]

Concerning the arbitration treaties concluded at Locarno, he pointed out that under these treaties, disputes arising from the entire Versailles settlement, as well as from the Locarno Treaty of Mutual Guarantee, were now subject to pacific settlement and that unilateral, arbitrary action by one power was now ruled out. France, so he told a radio audience, had declared an end to her policy of applying military sanctions under the Treaty of Versailles, and Great Britain, her former ally, was now pledged to defend Germany's western frontier against any aggression from whatever source.[38] Not even Article 6 of the Treaty of Mutual Guarantee, which sought to safeguard the rights and obligations of the contracting parties, under the Versailles settlement, could serve to freeze the peace settlement. Germany, he declared, had concluded a series of postwar treaties with Hungary, Czechoslovakia, and with Austria, wherein a provision of the Treaty of Versailles had been specifically declared to be inoperative.[39]

While the edge of Versailles had been blunted, and considerable long-range effects had been obtained, Stresemann still faced the problem of obtaining visible concessions from the Allies. The fact that he succeeded in pushing the Locarno treaties through parliament before such evidence of Allied good will was available, and in spite of opposition by the Nationalists, is highly indicative of his political acumen. The vote in the Reichstag was 292 against 174, with the German National People's Party, the Communists, and the National-Socialists voting in the negative. Even his own party had declared that the Reichstag could not accept the Locarno treaties unless the Allies came through with some concessions. With the acceptance of the Locarno treaties by the Reichstag, he had convinced a majority of parliament, and presumably of the country, that in spite of the Allied refusal to grant concessions, the agreements still amounted to a success of German foreign policy.

Prior to the signing of the Locarno treaties at London, on December 1, Stresemann made one more attempt to obtain the desired visible evidence of Allied good will. He called for what he termed "a package announcement by the Allies about relief in the occupied areas," or "some announcement to the effect that new consequences would accrue to Germany under Article 431 of the Treaty of Versailles."[40] Since Germany had fulfilled her treaty obligations in principle, she could therefore expect immediate withdrawal of the occupation forces. His efforts were of no avail. Instead, the continued silence from across the Rhine raised havoc with his political position at home. The Nationalists, sensing a dilemma, charged him with having played Germany into the hands of the reluctant Western powers, while a friendly Soviet Union had been spurned. The latter, so they reasoned, was Germany's only real ace against the Treaty of Versailles.[41] If the Soviets shared the suspicions of the Nationalists, and there was evidence that they did, then Germany would be cut off completely from her only support and would be utterly at the mercy of France and Britain. To strengthen himself against such a contingency, Stresemann assured the Soviets that Germany would not depart from a policy of strict neutrality between East and West, and would never wage war or permit herself to be drawn into a combination against the Soviet Union.[42] As a further safeguard, he had already insisted, at Locarno and during the preceding diplomatic exchanges, that Germany be exempt from participating in military sanctions against an aggressor under Article 16 of the League Covenant, and had also made it clear at the time that he considered that article to be directed against the Soviet Union.[43] To remove any remaining doubts, he had finally influenced the cabinet to permit the signing of a long-pending treaty of commerce between Germany and the Soviet Union. The treaty was not ratified until 1926, but the preliminary signing subject to later correction and adjustment was nevertheless a victory for the pro-Russian forces in the German government. They had pressed Stresemann for the longest time to make a friendly gesture in the direction of the great power in the East.[44] The fruits of this policy, so Stresemann hoped, would be redoubled efforts on the part of the Allies to evacuate the occupied areas and to speed admission of Germany to the League of Nations.

The only visible result, however, was the evacuation of the Cologne zone, which commenced on the day the Locarno treaties were signed at London and was completed on January 31, 1926, one year after the date scheduled for evacuation under Article 429 of the Treaty of Versailles.[45]

The diplomatic victory won by Stresemann at the end of the Ruhr conflict had been a limited one. While it could be assumed that no additional sanctions would be applied, there remained, however, the possibility that the Allies would delay liquidation of sanctions already in existence.

It had become clear to Stresemann that no existing diplomatic combination, however impressive it might have been, could oblige France to surrender what she considered vital guaranties of her security. Addressing himself to that fact, Stresemann embarked upon a plan to abolish the apparent *raison d'être* for French aggressiveness by launching a far-reaching peace and security proposal designed to guarantee the territorial status quo on the Rhine against armed aggression from any direction. Aside from results not directly related to the Treaty of Versailles, the proposal had as its objectives: (1) the permanent abandonment of additional military sanctions; (2) while Germany would renounce all intentions to regain the districts lost in the West by force of arms, a general adjustment of existing treaties to changing conditions, under observance of the rules of pacific settlement, was not to be excluded; (3) the emphasis of German revisionism was to be shifted to the East with the corollary effect of driving a wedge between the Western and Eastern powers;

(4) world public opinion was to be convinced of Germany's peaceful intentions and was to be won over to the cause of peaceful change.

Stresemann's diplomatic strategy during the preliminary negotiations consisted of the following elements: (1) in return for Germany's conciliatory gestures, i.e., her adherence to the proposed peace pact and accession to the League of Nations, the Allies were to grant her certain, enumerated concessions; (2) because the proposed pact with the Western Powers would tend to endanger Russo-German relations, Germany was doubly entitled to compensations; (3) above all, Germany's willingness to guarantee the territorial status quo at France's western boundary, was to be considered a satisfactory measure of fulfillment in principle of her treaty obligations. Consequently, all sanctions already in effect, and all future sanctions were to be ruled out and evacuation of foreign troops from German soil was to begin at once.

With the signing of the Locarno agreements, Stresemann accomplished in fact what he had set out to do. While Eupen-Malmédy could not be regained by force of arms, that district could theoretically be regained by resort to the machinery of pacific settlement of international disputes. Second, a repetition of the Ruhr invasion by France would find Great Britain, Italy, and Belgium pledged to come to the assistance of Germany. This would be the case even if France should seek to justify her acts by reference to the Treaty of Versailles. Thus, by effectively blocking direct resort to armed force in pursuance of the penal provisions of Versailles, Stresemann had in effect rendered the enforcement of the treaty provisions by the Allies highly problematic, if not altogether impossible. Finally, the pact left the door open to future revisions of the territorial status in the East. All of these achievements had of course the dual purpose of assisting Stresemann in his battle against nationalist reaction at home.

In order to prepare the country for the planned move, Stresemann had strengthened his relations with the German National People's Party prior to Locarno. Bringing the Nationalists into the cabinet, he had sought to accomplish two things: first, a cabinet oriented to the Right would enable him to follow a more daring foreign policy than would have been possible if the Nationalists had remained in opposition. In particular, there was reason to hope that the Nationalists would vote for the peace pact if they had shared part of the responsibility for the negotiations. Second, the inclusion of the Nationalists in the government coalition promised to make them more responsive to a reasonable foreign policy in general. This meant, paradoxically, that Stresemann had come to the conclusion that the support of the Nationalists was needed to carry out a conciliatory foreign policy. Finally, he believed that his own "bifurcation" to the Right would serve to cause alarm in the camp of the Allied Powers, and that it would tend to bring them to the realization that concessions had to be granted to the democratic forces in Germany, lest the whole democratic structure be threatened with collapse.

However, the domestic effects of the Locarno agreements came to naught when the Allies failed to grant the expected visible concessions. The long-range effects of Locarno were not sufficient to assure the continued co-operation of the Nationalists, and the resultant dissatisfaction contributed considerably to the ultimate failure of the Stresemann policy.

CHAPTER IX

LIMITED SUCCESS

I. *Economic Collaboration for Revision.* Stresemann's foreign policy concerning the Treaty of Versailles had, in its initial phases, been designed to effect substantial changes in the treaty structure. After the signing of the Locarno treaties, however, the effort to revise certain provisions of the peace settlement was slowed down to a piecemeal attack, a whittling away rather than a sweeping revision. The evacuation of the Cologne zone had not served to satisfy the nationalist opposition in Germany because it had been delayed beyond the scheduled date. The long-range effects of Locarno, the possible future revision of Germany's eastern frontiers, the return of lost districts, and additional removals of repressive devices such as disarmament control, were not sufficiently visible to serve the foreign minister of a nation intent on rapid political changes. The attacks on his person became more vicious with every passing month. Efforts were made to draw the People's Party away from him.[1] His own party's parliamentary leadership became suspicious of him, fearing that he did not properly appreciate the need for strong political arguments against the Nationalists who were sapping the strength of the People's Party. They feared that he was oblivious to the party's desperate need for concrete political achievements in the field of foreign policy.[2]

As a result of the withdrawal of the Nationalist ministers from the cabinet, Stresemann had to co-operate more closely with the Socialists, whose 132 votes were of crucial importance in the Reichstag. Such co-operation, of course, was bound to find expression in domestic politics with unavoidable adverse effects on Stresemann's own position in the relatively right-of-center People's Party.[3]

The year 1926 witnessed two significant developments: Germany's entry into the League and an abortive conference between Gustav Stresemann and Aristide Briand of France. The ramifications of Germany's accession to the League do not have a direct bearing upon Stresemann's policy of revisionism. Suffice it to say that his failure to gain admittance for Germany at the March session of the League of Nations Council did not enhance his prestige at home.[4]

In order to prevent a resurgence of nationalism at home, a development which would have endangered the Locarno policy and the results expected to accrue from it, Stresemann was now fighting to reduce the number of foreign troops in the remaining two zones of occupation. Once again he appealed to Britain and France for ammunition against the ever growing ranks of dissatisfaction and radicalism at home, against the growing clamor for a new policy of revenge, revision by force, and for a new, Eastern orientation. He asked for grand gestures on the part of the Allies to save the "spirit of Locarno." The latter, so he declared before the Reichstag, could not be reconciled with continued occupation of the remaining zones.[5] Mutual confidence could not be established as long as foreign troops, symbolizing the very aggressiveness thought to have been abolished at Locarno, remained on German soil.

While he advanced his demands, he was perfectly aware of the fact that the expected grand gestures would not and could not materialize for some time to come. His realism had taught him that a nation must have armies to force the settlement of political issues. In the absence of a power potential necessary to back up demands, diplomacy remained the sole means to achieve political ends.[6] In spite of this realization, however, he refused to follow the example of the *Reichswehr* and draw upon the power potential of the Soviet Union to achieve foreign policy successes in the West. Reference has already been made to his opposition to other than tentative diplomatic collaboration with the Soviets.[7]

The next opportunity to raise the entire complex of revision and to translate the "Locarno spirit" into concrete terms, arose, indirectly, as a result of Germany's final entry into the League of Nations on September 10, 1926. With that event, and on the strength of the preceding London and Locarno conferences, Germany was once more admitted to the concert of nations as an equal partner. But it was neither at the Council's table nor on the floor of the Assembly that the major move was made. Instead, it was at an exclusive and most secret meeting with Briand, in the village of Thoiry in France, that Stresemann made his most determined effort to settle all major questions between France and Germany. Animated by the magnificent reception given him on the floor of the Assembly in Geneva, and especially by the moving oratory of Aristide Briand, the German foreign minister felt inclined to resort to personal diplomacy to obtain results denied him by other, more orthodox methods. In doing so, he fell back upon a favorite idea of his, namely, that the economic interdependence of France and Germany was bound to bring the two nations together again.

At Locarno, his strategy had been to give France the desired security in return for which he had expected some revision of the treaty conditions shackling Germany. This strategy had produced some potential, long-range advantages, but nothing that could be used to bolster his position at home. There had been no effective, visible results. Now he offered Briand a way out of France's economic difficulties. By a convincing gesture of reconciliation based on the firm grounds of what he considered economic reality, faced by all European countries after the war, Stresemann hoped to pave the way for a peaceful change of the treaty terms imposed upon vanquished Germany.

In preparation for this move, he dropped a number of hints on several occasions, all of which pointed to a concerted effort to solve Europe's economic ills.[8] In return for what he regarded as feasible economic sacrifices, France was expected to promote the revision of some of the most obstructive and untenable provisions of the Versailles settlement. Without going too deeply into the highly complex financial aspects of the Briand-Stresemann scheme, the idea was for Germany to make a capital payment to France, the amount to be deducted from reparations, the payment to be effected through the marketing of a block of German railway bonds. Since France was at the time engaged in negotiations with the United States over war debts, the former had experienced an economic slump, and her currency was badly in need of stabilization.[9] Prior to Thoiry, Briand had informed Stresemann that he would support the lifting of the entire Rhineland occupation, the return of the Saar to Germany, and the lifting of military controls in return for German assumption of France's financial obligations. At the meeting itself, Stresemann demanded not a gradual lifting of the occupation, as Briand envisaged, but immediate evacuation because of certain difficulties he had encountered in presenting the proposed financial scheme to the cabinet.[10] In other words, the more difficult it was for him to have the scheme accepted in Germany, the higher would be the price.

The financial experts of both countries, however, raised a number of objections. Cabinet Minister Julius Curtius and Hjalmar Schacht, Germany's foremost financial expert, objected to what they called "the purchase of the Rhineland." Furthermore, Washington, reacting to misgivings of Wall Street, also refused to support the deal.[11]

Franco-German relations, and especially Stresemann's hopes for

an early revision of the treaty, received another blow from an unexpected direction. At Thoiry, Briand had informed the German
foreign minister that certain circles in France looked with apprehension upon the growth of paramilitary organizations in Germany.[12]
Stresemann had belittled the charges. Upon his return from Thoiry,
however, he undertook at once the curbing of certain illegal activities
by the *Reichswehr*. General von Seeckt was forced out of his position as Chief of the Army Command in October.[13] Shortly afterwards, on December 16, a Social-Democrat accused the *Reichswehr*
on the floor of parliament of fraternization with certain "patriotic
organizations," and of receiving ammunition and other military items
from the Soviet Union.[14] The results of the ensuing uproar were another cabinet crisis and the fall of the government. With an eye on
the United States and Great Britain, the two powers in a position to
assure the realization of the dreams of Thoiry, Stresemann now
fought to keep the Nationalists out of the cabinet. He declared his
readiness to resign unless the Nationalists, as a condition of participation in the government, were made to agree to support the Dawes-
Locarno-Thoiry policy. Contrary to his pre-Locarno attitude, he now
held that the German National People's Party in the government
would be a direct affront against Briand. For it was that party,
more than any other, which was identified with the very paramilitary
organizations to which the French statesmen had objected at Thoiry.
In spite of Stresemann's efforts to the contrary, however, the Nationalists were included in the new cabinet.[15] The Socialists continued
their "silent" support of his foreign policy, outside the government.
One minor cabinet change was made subsequently, in order to soften
the impact of a rightest cabinet on the outside world: the Minister of
the Armed Forces was sacrificed upon recommendation by Stresemann. To be sure, the power of the Nationalists to prevent the passage of foreign policy measures in the Reichstag had been weakened
considerably, primarily because of Stresemann's personal power and
political influence. On the other hand, and in spite of Stresemann's
efforts to the contrary, the die had been cast, and Briand's own political position had been damaged beyond repair. The Right in France
had been given ammunition to destroy the delicate fabric of Thoiry.
They were now able to point out that Briand's attempts to effect a
rapprochement had failed to stem the rising tide of nationalism in
Germany.

II. *The Home Front.* The consequence of Germany's entry into
the League of Nations, as far as Great Britain and France were concerned, had been the establishment of a more permanent forum for

discussion of mutual problems with the loser of the World War. The League was to be a medium for regular conferences between the Great Powers and Germany. Thus there developed, within the League Council, what one scholar called "a Cabal of Great Powers," or a supreme council of great powers. The council consisted of Briand, Chamberlain, and Stresemann. At first, the principal subject of discussion was the evacuation of the Rhineland.

It soon became apparent that no argument advanced by the German minister and no tactics applied by him, could bring the conflict nearer to a solution. The German, pointing to Article 431 and referring to his country's evident willingness to abide by her treaty obligations, demanded a speedy end to military occupation.[16] Germany, so he pointed out, had waived her claims to Alsace-Lorraine by signing the Locarno Pact; she had put her signature to an agreement which provided for permanent demilitarization of the Rhineland; and she had undertaken not to use force to change her eastern boundaries. "In the light of these solemn undertakings," Stresemann asked, "was there any further justification for military occupation?"[17] Once again he threatened to resign, but all the old arguments, and all the new ones, did not bring evacuation any closer. France was no longer impressed, if she ever had been, by his appeals for support against the enemies of reconciliation in Germany. Briand had his own difficulties with the French general staff, and Sir Austen Chamberlain was not prepared to hurt Briand. Moreover, Poincaré had again become Premier and had succeeded in stabilizing the franc, thus eliminating the need for implementation of the Thoiry agreements. Even though Briand remained as foreign minister, he could no longer afford to be identified with a revisionist policy.[18]

Before the Reichstag, as well as elsewhere, Stresemann pointed to a promissory note addressed to the German government by the Conference of Ambassadors in November 1925, a note which he contended had served as a basis for Germany's adherence to the Locarno agreements.[19] Aside from that, he pointed to Germany's membership in the League of Nations and questioned the use of arms by some member nations in the control and occupation of another. This was the opening move, indicative of further demands to come, and designed to announce to the world that with Germany's entry into the League, an era had come to an end.

In spite of the evident Allied procrastinations in the evacuation question, Stresemann fought on, and continued to defend the Locarno policy in the face of constant attacks from the Right. In the course of the election campaign for the fourth Reichstag, he lashed out against impatience and misrepresentation. He advised the nationalists again to note the preponderance of power on the opposing side, and asked them not to mislead the country by reference to an alternative which did not exist. Germany's foreign policy had to be based on diplomacy alone, the kind of diplomacy carried out by a nation without arms.[20] During this election, the foreign policy platform of the People's Party stated, among other things, that "it might be necessary, because of exaggerated French demands, to alter the tactics heretofore applied," and to await the legal termination of the Rhineland occupation as provided for in the Treaty of Versailles. It quoted Stresemann as having assured the people in the East that Germany would never permit an "Eastern Locarno," and stated, "The People's Party has tried for a long time to turn the eyes of the German people . . . to the East."[21]

TABLE II

ELECTION RESULTS FOR THE FOURTH REICHSTAG, MAY 20, 1928*

Parties	Total vote	Seats	Percent of total in 1928	Percent of total in 1924 (December 7)
DNVP[a]	4,381,563	73	14.2	20.5
DVP[b]	2,679,703	45	8.7	10.1
Splinter Parties	4,326,912	51	14.1	7.72
Center	4,657,796	78	15.2	17.34
DDP[c]	1,479,374	25	4.8	6.3
SPD[d]	9,152,979	153	29.8	26.0
NSDAP[e]	810,127	12	2.6	3.0
KPD[f]	3,264,793	54	10.6	9.0

* Source: Wilhelm Dittmann, *Das Politische Deutschland vor Hitler* (Zurich: Europa Verlag, 1945) (Plate II).
[a] German National People's Party.
[b] German People's Party.
[c] German Democratic Party.
[d] Social-Democratic Party of Germany.
[e] National-Socialist Workers' Party of Germany.
[f] Communist Party of Germany.

The election took place May 20, 1928, and indicated a swing to the Left. The People's Party and the Nationalists lost six and thirty seats, respectively, while the Socialists gained twenty-two, to become by far the largest party in the new parliament. Stresemann, as party leader, was displeased, but as foreign minister he was most satisfied with the outcome. Once again he could base his foreign policy on the so-called Great Coalition. A parliamentary basis, ranging from the Socialists to the Democrats, promised to be more acceptable to the treaty powers than a rightest cabinet would have been. On these premises, of course, he had to risk another revolt within his own party, a considerable segment of which was opposed to a Left orientation. On the other hand, the party leadership was fully aware of its dependence upon the party chairman. Thus the latter's views prevailed once again: Stresemann and Julius Curtius represented the party in a cabinet of the Great Coalition.

III. *Collective Security for Revision.* Stresemann's next opportunity to attack the status quo came with the negotiations and the signing of the Peace Pact of Paris in the year 1928.[22] In his reply to the American note of April 13, which invited Germany to participate with the United States and other nations in "an unqualified renunciation of war," Stresemann made the following statement of German objectives:

. . . this new guarantee for the maintenance of peace must give a real impulse to the efforts for carrying out general disarmament, and further still, the renunciation of war must, as a necessary complement, enlarge the possibilities of settling in a peaceful way the existing and potential conflicts of national interests.[23]

Uppermost in the German's mind was of course the conflict over the occupation of the Rhineland and the interpretation to be given to Article 431 of the Treaty of Versailles, coupled with a rectification of Germany's western frontiers. Revisionism in the East was not yet a matter subject to direct negotiations. Traveling to Paris to sign the Peace Pact, under a severe physical handicap, he raised the question once more in conversation with Briand and Poincaré, as well as in a statement to the French press.[24] However, the attempt to obtain satisfaction through personal contact with the French statesmen brought no results. Poincaré sought to tie the evacuation question once again to reparations and debts, while Stresemann, pointing to the American refusal to co-operate in any financial undertaking, maintained that the former question would have to be settled in order to avoid grave repercussions in Germany.[25] The Kellogg Pact became history, and Allied troops remained on German soil.

Following the signing of the Pact of Paris on August 27, 1928, it became increasingly apparent that Stresemann was rapidly losing his patience. There is reason to believe that a conversation with the American financial expert and general reparation agent, Parker S. Gilbert, on November 13, 1928, convinced Stresemann that no revision of the Treaty of Versailles could take place without prior settlement of the reparation question, and that the United States was not prepared to assist in the solution of the problem in the sense of Thoiry.[26] He now announced that the time had come to take the matter out of the sphere of unofficial and confidential talks and to press Germany's claims formally. These claims, so he maintained, were justified in spite of constant attempts on the part of Allied statesmen to deny that Germany had fulfilled her obligations in the sense of Article 431 of Versailles. Again, he insisted that "compliance with all undertakings," did not mean complete fulfillment, but referred instead to evidence of good intentions to fulfill existing obligations.[27] In spite of his determination to forego future private conferences, however, Stresemann wisely did not close all doors. When the Kellogg Pact came before the Reichstag, he defended its high principles vigorously. Of course, he availed himself of the opportunity to demand once more that "a conclusion of a development in international law" must be more than "only a promise and a basis for further development of the international legal order." As in the case of Locarno, he considered it Germany's moral right to expect concrete results from her international undertakings.[28]

IV. *Fulfillment for Revision.* On September 16, 1928, the representatives of Germany, Belgium, France, Great Britain, Italy, and Japan, in attendance at Geneva at the ninth ordinary session of the Assembly of the League of Nations, announced agreement upon the following points: (1) The opening of negotiations for complete evacuation of the Rhineland; (2) the establishment of a committee of financial experts for a new settlement of the reparation problem; (3) the establishment of a committee of verification and conciliation.[29] In the course of the negotiations on the projected revision of the Dawes Plan, in pursuance of the announcement of September 16, Stresemann encountered renewed difficulties with his party. Party leaders began to feel the burden of having to choose between loyal support of their chairman and, as an alternative, a decided move to the Right and into the opposition. While the foreign minister still moved on the plane of international understanding and supported the proposed reparations plan in principle, the party leadership was now determined to swing to the Right and to oppose further acceptance of financial burdens by Germany.[30]

Stresemann's strategy was to support the readjustment of reparations on condition that the two related aspects of the peace settlement, reparations and guaranties for their payment by Germany, were to be considered separately. As long as the two aspects were treated together, he feared that a stalemate on reparations would adversely affect the talks on evacuation. To press his point, he returned to the matter of an early settlement of the Saar dispute.[31]

At The Hague Conference on the Young Plan, meeting from August 6 to 31, Stresemann participated in the deliberations of the political commissions. Fortified by a majority decision in the cabinet, and with his back to the wall—a failure to obtain substantial concessions meant resignation for him—he took the offensive once more. Acting swiftly upon the first signs of disunity in the camp of Germany's creditors, he impressed Briand with the need for concessions in a secret, personal letter. The contents of that letter were not known to any member of the German delegation except the interpreter.[32] At last, the almost insolvable problem of evacuation approached the stage of agreement. On August 29, Stresemann was informed that June 30, 1930, would be the date on which the last Allied soldiers would leave German soil. Belgium and British troops were to move out first, with the French to follow as rapidly as possible. The entire operation was to be completed by June 1930. The evacuation of the third occupation zone was to begin with the date of ratification of the Young Plan by the French and German parliaments.[33] An attempt to establish a conciliation commission to settle disputes arising over Articles 42 and 43 of Versailles, concerning the demilitarization of the Rhineland, was successfully warded off by the German foreign minister.[34]

The struggle begun in 1923 had been fought to a successful conclusion. In his report to the nation, Stresemann could proudly point to these political achievements: the fifteen-year period of occupation, provided for in Article 428 of the Treaty of Versailles, had been reduced, and the decision on the interpretation of Article 431 had been made in favor of Germany. Second, the idea of a control commission, to substitute for the withdrawal of military forces from German soil, had been rejected. Above all, the cause of revisionism, as pursued by Stresemann, had been advanced to a point where even the Allies had to admit that Germany had fulfilled her obligations in good faith. With this breach in the armament of the status quo powers, the way was clear to further, more substantial changes.

One condition for peaceful change in Central Europe, as Stresemann had seen it, was the reconciliation of Germany and France. In spite of his success at The Hague, however, the concessions granted to him by the Allies had been too little and too late. A nationalist bloc, composed of the German National People's Party and the more radical National-Socialists had begun an all-out attack against the policy of fulfillment and of revision through conciliation.[35] In September of 1929, the newly formed "National Union" initiated a plebiscite which demanded, among other things, that those responsible for the Dawes and Young policies should be subjected to prosecution for treason.[36] To be sure, the plebiscite, voted upon after Stresemann's death, fell short of the required 50 percent. Yet, it was clear to all who cared to see, that the long battle waged by Gustav Stresemann against renascent nationalism had been lost, that a wave was threatening to wash away the beginnings of reconciliation, and that the era where peaceful change had been possible had come to an end.

In spite of the Locarno agreements, Stresemann had been unable to bring his policy of conciliation to fruition. The direly needed concessions from the Allies had not materialized. To be sure, Locarno had brought a number of long-range results, but that was not what was needed to stem the nationalist tide sweeping over Germany at the time.

In order to obtain "visible" concessions in time for an energetic counterattack against nationalist claims and charges, Stresemann attempted once more to reach the desired understanding with France. Falling back upon a favorite device, he sought to solve all existing political questions separating France and Germany by resort to highly imaginative and sweeping financial arrangements. However, he was unaware of all the ramifications of a complex financial situation and had to see his magnificent scheme of a grand understanding come to naught.

After Thoiry, it became clear to Stresemann that the time for great, decisive foreign policy moves had not yet come. The international situation, and above all Germany's position, were not susceptible to fundamental changes suddenly arrived at. Instead, he became convinced that for some time to come he would have to apply himself to the task of chipping away at the peace structure instead of removing large chunks. He had to wait until Germany had grown strong enough, by her own efforts, to assert her rights and to enforce her legitimate demands.

In keeping with his policy of seeking concessions from the Allies in return for German co-operation in international undertakings, Stresemann now tried to attach conditions to German adherence to the Kellogg Peace Pact. His position was, that a collective attempt to denounce war would have to be followed by a collective effort to remove existing injustices and threats to the peace. The presence of foreign troops on German soil, so he reasoned, was incompatible with the high purposes of the Kellogg Pact. However, neither Lo-

carno nor the Kellogg Peace Pact brought any changes in the peace
structure erected at Versailles. The fallacy of Stresemann's reasoning consisted in an overestimation of the appeal of the Kellogg Pact
to the French with their excessive security-consciousness. As far as
France was concerned, the presence of her troops on German soil
was a real guaranty against German aggression, while the Peace Pact
was merely a hypothetical one.

The next opportunity to bring the evacuation question, i.e., the
penal and guaranty clauses of the Treaty of Versailles, to the fore,
arose when it was decided to prepare a new reparation schedule, the
Young Plan.

The Young Plan, however, brought a modest measure of success.
Here Stresemann succeeded in separating two principles which had
always been connected by the Allies. He separated the principle that
Germany should pay reparations from the principle that she should
pay all of her reparations, and fulfill all of her obligations, before
Allied troops would leave German soil. Now, it was admitted that
Germany had proven her willingness to fulfill the treaty obligations,
and that therefore the need for application of sanctions on those
grounds had ceased to exist. The Allies agreed to evacuate all of their
troops five years earlier than had originally been anticipated. However, even though Stresemann had fought long and hard to obtain
that important concession, the victory was hollow when it came.

Because of widespread dissatisfaction at home, Stresemann had
been unable to keep the Nationalists in the government. Consequently,
and because of the Socialist victory at the polls, he returned once
more to an alliance with the Social-Democrats and to a government
of the Great Coalition. Hoping to realize some of his foreign policy
projects, he was now determined to keep the Nationalists out of the
government, primarily in order to reassure foreign capitals aroused
over scandals involving the German armed forces. However, the very
situation which he had sought to avoid before, when he had made his
unexpected move to the Right, materialized now. The nationalist
opposition to his policy and to an understanding with the Versailles
powers in general, grew to the point where neither Britain nor France
was willing to trust German intentions any longer. Every move on
Stresemann's part which was intended to appease the Right tended to
undermine his reputation abroad. It was a tragic, hopeless situation
which saw Stresemann's policy denounced as treasonable in Germany
and as cunning and untrustworthy in France and Britain.

CHAPTER X

TERRITORIAL REVISION IN THE WEST

The foregoing discussion of revisionism in the West was confined, almost exclusively, to the question of sanctions and the evacuation of foreign troops from German soil. In addition to the problems arising from the application of sanctions, however, Stresemann's revisionist policy also addressed itself to the eventual return of areas and districts which had been detached from Germany as a result of the peace settlement. Since the latter objective was continuously overshadowed by events connected with sanctions and the resultant occupation, it did not reach the degree of intensity of the former phase of Stresemann's policy. As the preceding part of this study has attempted to show, Stresemann's Western policy very often served merely as a steppingstone for his Eastern policy. However, in view of existing alliances and traditional ties between France and countries to the east and southeast of Germany, it was necessary to come to terms with the West before dealing with the East. Thus the diplomatic strategy called for a solution of the sanction problem before other, more direct revisionist moves could be made in the West. Actual territorial revision in the East had to wait until all problems in the West had been solved and the Western Allies had been pacified and reassured that no further territorial problems stood between them and Germany.

I. *The Saar.* The Saar, or more specifically, the Saar Basin, as defined in the Treaty of Versailles, was located between France and Germany, to the north of Alsace-Lorraine. It contained valuable coal deposits and mining facilities, claimed by France in compensation for the destruction of French mining properties by the Germans in the last days of the war. However, the Saar territory had not been permanently detached from Germany. On the other hand, in recognition of the French claims to compensation, the coal mines of the Saar had been assigned to France, to be repurchased by Germany when the territory itself was returned to German administration. Article 49 of the treaty stipulated a renunciation of sovereign powers over the Saar territory by Germany. The renunciation was to be in favor of the League of Nations. After fifteen years from the coming into force of the peace treaty, the inhabitants of the Saar were to "indicate the sovereignty under which they desire to be placed," by a plebiscite.

Stresemann's objective was to advance the date on which the plebiscite was to be held. This appeared to be particularly advisable in view of the fact that French troops were in occupation of the Saar and were in a position to influence the inhabitants by their mere presence.

As early as 1919, Stresemann had gone on record as favoring a foreign policy designed to accomplish the return of all lost territories to the motherland.[1] However, since the government of the Saar was in the hands of a League commission, he did not seriously address himself to that problem until Germany had entered the League in 1926. He had raised the question of advancing the plebiscite at the Locarno Conference but nothing had come of that. In fact, one of the reasons why Stresemann had worked toward Germany's entry the agency charged with responsibility for a number of problems into the League had been the prospect of working more directly with which had arisen from the peace settlement. In particular, the question of minority rights and the Saar problem were the points of attraction which led Stresemann to appreciate the work of the League of Nations.[2]

It was only shortly after his triumphal entry into the hall of the League Assembly that Stresemann, in an unguarded moment, announced his intention to obtain a speedy reduction in the number of French troops in the Saar in preparation for an early return of that district to Germany.[3] This announcement coincided with an unofficial attempt to raise the question of the return of the Saar at the Thoiry luncheon with Aristide Briand.[4] On that occasion, Stresemann proposed that Germany repurchase the mines from France by assisting in the stabilization of the French franc. However, the complexity of the proposed financial arrangement condemned the scheme to failure before it was officially considered. The failure to solve the problem by direct negotiations with France led Stresemann to rely even more on the League of Nations.

The first official move, then, was a complaint to the effect that France was maintaining an excessive military force in the Saar Basin. After protracted discussions before the Council of the League, a resolution was adopted on March 12, 1927, establishing a limited protective force in the Saar to replace the several French military formations.[5] Reporting to the Reichstag on this matter, Stresemann declared:

Because the League of Nations, in addition to its major tasks, has also been made the executor of a number of provisions of the Treaty of Versailles, questions concerning Germany are in the forefront of its activities. There we appear as trustees of our own affairs.[6]

As on similar occasions, Stresemann was again accused of having been satisfied with too little. In reply, he told the Reichstag that a major attack on the Saar question could not be launched until a major issue had presented itself.[7] This contingency never did arise in Stresemann's lifetime. While he kept the general issue alive in press interviews, parliamentary addresses, and by other public pronouncements, no real attempt to achieve a revision of the status of the Saar was made until the summer of 1929.

The last effort to settle the Saar problem, i.e., to advance the plebiscite and to remove all vestiges of military occupation from that area, was made in connection with the negotiations for the revision of the Dawes Plan. By that time, the evacuation of the Rhineland had approached the stage of liquidation, and the reintroduction of another Franco-German dispute did not appear to be too dangerous. Since the negotiations on reparations promised to lead to a satisfactory arrangement, Stresemann devised the following strategy. The occupation of the Saar and its temporary detachment had been decided upon at Versailles primarily because of French claims for compensation based on the destruction of French mining facilities by German troops. Thus, it stood to reason that the Saar could be considered as a reparation province, similar to the occupied territories in Germany proper.[8] If the Saar question could be successfully tied to the question of reparations, there was hope that a settlement of the latter could bring a settlement of the former problem in its wake. Following acceptance of the Young Plan at The Hague Conference in 1929, Briand was persuaded to agree to a reopening of the question. The discussions were expected to result in an earlier return of the Saar without resort to a plebiscite.[9] However, the negotiations did not produce the desired results. The year of the plebiscite continued to be 1935.

The final reference to that thorny question was made in Stresemann's last address before the League Assembly. Once more, he appealed for a total settlement of all questions which had arisen from the war. Referring to the Saar, he pleaded:

If this barrier is broken down, the way will be cleared for that close and fruitful collaboration between Germany and her former adversaries which is necessary in the interest of all nations and consequently of the League itself.[10]

The intention was clear. Collective security was to give way to individual security as a basis for revisionism.

II. *Eupen-Malmédy.* The districts of Eupen and Malmédy, situated directly to the east of the sixth lateral and north of the fiftieth parallel, between Germany and Belgium, had been ceded to Belgium as a result of the peace settlement. Following extraordinary plebiscite procedure, heavily weighted in favor of Belgium, a resolution by the Council of the League of Nations had transferred the two districts to Belgium, on September 16, 1920.[11] As in the case of the Saar, the return of Eupen-Malmédy was first demanded in connection with Germany's acceptance of the instruments of Locarno.[12] When this failed, and again in keeping with the strategy applied to the Saar question, Stresemann sought to come to terms directly with the Belgians. In return for financial concessions on the part of Germany, the Belgians were expected to return the districts to the former owners.[13] Prior to Germany's entry into the League, Stresemann sought to obtain Briand's support for the proposed transaction, but found the latter opposed to any bilateral deals between Germany, the vanquished, and one individual victor state.[14] Once again, Stresemann was reminded that Germany was confronted by a hostile group and not by individual opponents. Either he came to terms with all of the Versailles powers or he had to content himself with a recognition of the status quo. Briand based his argument on the contention that the proposed arrangement would constitute a modification of the Treaty of Versailles and was therefore subject to approval by all powers who had signed the treaty. To this Stresemann replied that the arrangement was a peaceful one, executed through ordinary diplomatic channels, and would thus obviate the consent of the other powers.[15]

Briand's second argument against the proposed deal concerned the Locarno Pact. He claimed that the return of Eupen-Malmédy to Germany would be a violation of the Locarno agreements, inasmuch as it would serve to change the territorial status of Germany's western boundaries. Stresemann countered, with "amazement," that Locarno could hardly have meant the permanent freezing of conditions in the West. All that it did mean was that no treaty power would resort to hostile action to effect territorial changes. Peaceful changes could not be precluded by any legal or political action or arrangements for any length of time. Moreover, there was Article 19 of the League of Nations Covenant, and if Briand's argument was correct, then it stood in direct contradiction to the spirit and the letter of that article which addressed itself to the "self-evident need" for periodic reconsideration of conditions which had become unbearable.[16]

The Committee of Experts which worked out the new (Young) plan in 1929 included in its provisions the liquidation of Belgian claims to reimbursement for currency losses incurred as a result of the German occupation during World War I. It was agreed by the committee that negotiations on that question should be concluded before the new reparation plan came into force. In the course of the discussions in the committee, the German experts attempted, in keeping with Stresemann's policy, to connect the compensation question with the desired adjustment of the Eupen-Malmédy situation.[17] This maneuver failed, however, primarily because of American objections. A letter by the German members assured the American experts that "no territorial questions will be raised in these negotiations."[18] As a result, Stresemann was unable to raise the point at The Hague Conference. As the Saar case had indicated, the time was not yet ripe for a reopening of territorial questions in the West.

As in the matter of the evacuation and sanction questions, Stresemann hoped that the Saar and Eupen-Malmédy issues could be translated into foreign policy successes which would serve to stem the nationalist tide rising in Germany. He constantly beseeched Allied statesmen to give him the foreign policy successes needed to prove to the German people that a peaceful policy, with full regard of democratic procedures, could achieve results. However, the application of sanctions and the resultant presence of foreign troops on German soil had a far greater psychological impact upon the German people than the Saar and Eupen-Malmédy issues could produce. Therefore the element of urgency did not apply in the latter cases as much as in the former. The nationalists were more likely to gather strength against the foreign minister and his party over the continued presence of foreign troops on German soil than over the failure to return the lost territories.[19]

Territorial revisionism in the West was restricted to two objectives. The largest area lost as a result of the Treaty of Versailles, Alsace-Lorraine, was not considered redeemable by Stresemann. Only the Saar and Eupen-Malmédy played a role in his revisionist endeavors.

As far as the Saar was concerned, it was merely a question of advancing the date when the territory was to be returned to Germany, and of creating the most favorable condition for the scheduled plebiscite. The major phase of the Saar policy, as limited as it was, was enacted in and around the League of Nations. Because the League had been assigned the function of administering and governing the Saar, Stresemann hoped, through Germany's membership in the Council, to exercise ever increasing influence over that area; Germany was to participate in the task of preparing the Saar for the coming plebiscite as a trustee acting in her own behalf. The primary tactical objective in this regard was the reduction of French troops in the Saar to the point where the population could no longer be intimidated or alienated.

One brief, unsuccessful attempt was made by Stresemann to accelerate the return of the Saar by direct negotiations with France. Advancing the argument that the territory had been temporarily detached from Germany as a reparation measure, he claimed that Germany's apparent willingness to pay reparations had obviated the need for further retention of the Saar as collateral.

Concerning Eupen-Malmédy, Stresemann was just as unsuccessful as in the case of the Saar. He attempted to achieve his objective by direct negotiation with Belgium, only to discover that the remaining status quo powers would not permit a breach of their front by bilateral negotiations and arrangements. In view of this unassailable fact, Stresemann enlarged the scope of his argument by reference to questions of international peace and co-operation. He maintained that neither Versailles nor Locarno had precluded peaceful change. It appears that in advancing this argument in connection with Eupen-Malmédy, Stresemann sought to establish a precedent. If the Allies had permitted the return of the districts, a considerable breach would have been opened in the legal armor of the status quo powers; Article 19 of the League of Nations Covenant would have been interpreted as a basis for further revisions of the Treaty of Versailles.

It appears also that while domestic considerations played some part in Stresemann's Saar and Eupen-Malmédy policies, the issues were relatively too insignificant, and disturbing to other plans, to permit extensive concentration on the task of facilitating their return to the homeland. Revision in the East and the corollary, conciliation with the West, were too important to be sacrificed, or even endangered, by insistence on the relatively minor issues concerning the two disputed areas.

CHAPTER XI

TERRITORIAL REVISION IN THE EAST

Previous chapters have pointed out that Stresemann's policy of revisionism had more of an Eastern than a Western orientation. Here an attempt will be made to analyze the Eastern phase and to establish its relationship to his over-all foreign policy concerning the Treaty of Versailles. Even though, in a historical sense, Eastern and Western revisionism were well integrated and supplementary to one another, it is considered worth while to study the two phases separately. Concerning the diplomatic methods and foreign policy concepts applied, Stresemann's Eastern policy was considerably different from his approach to the West.

Revision in the East addressed itself to Articles 87 to 108 (Part III) of the Treaty of Versailles, dealing with Germany's losses to Poland, the separation of East Prussia from the homeland, the transfer of Memel to Lithuania, and the establishment of the Free City of Danzig.[1] There is no evidence that Stresemann was interested in any revision of Germany's frontier with Czechoslovakia or that he addressed himself seriously to the problem posed by the transfer of Memel to Lithuania.

I. *The Initial Phase.* Soon after the Treaty of Versailles had been ratified, and before Stresemann's political ascendancy, he complained bitterly about the separation of East Prussia from the German motherland.[2] Of all the territorial changes wrought by the treaty, this separation affected Stresemann's Eastern policy more than anything else. The loss of a part of Upper Silesia, while regretted by him, did not stir him into action once he had become foreign minister.[3] In 1924 he voiced a demand for the reincorporation of Danzig.[4] But this too was not subject to active revisionist steps in later years.

Yet, while he did not overtly seek the immediate return of Danzig and the lost districts of Upper Silesia, he used these points nevertheless as planks in his foreign policy. The audience for whose benefit the demands for Danzig and Silesia were voiced from time to time consisted of the Soviet Union on the one hand and of the Ger-

116

man nationalists on the other. A third group, the German minorities abroad, while no doubt encouraged by such demands, attached greater value to Stresemann's minority policy proper. When the question of Germany's entry into the League of Nations became acute, Stresemann sought to allay Soviet fears by assuring the latter that Germany had no intention of recognizing the eastern frontier with Poland.[5] He stressed this point with the Russians because he knew that the one development most feared by the Soviet government was a coming to terms of Germany with the Western Allies. As long as the revision in the East stood between Germany and the West as an unresolved conflict, an anti-Soviet coalition was unlikely to be formed. The Nationalists, strongly influenced by the army, were seeking sympathy for their cause by declaring themselves guardians of the lost territories in the East.[6] To avoid giving them campaign material against the People's Party, Stresemann had to refer to the Eastern question from time to time, even though he did not harbor any urgent sentiments in that direction.[7]

Locarno was a case in point. Stresemann's policy called for the conclusion of a security pact designed to allay French fears of renewed German aggression. On the other hand, the German army and the Nationalists clamored for revision in the East, an endeavor which stood in direct contradiction to French treaty commitments in the eastern European region. The Soviets, highly suspicious of the pact, exerted themselves to discover the true meaning of the agreements, and attempted to bring them to naught.[8]

Prior to Locarno, Stresemann had already indicated the approach which he intended to take, when he told the Reichstag:

Germany does not have the power to force through an alteration of her frontiers nor does she have the desire to do so. Since Article 19 of the Covenant of the League of Nations, however, states expressly that treaties which have become inapplicable can be altered, no one can expect Germany to renounce, for all time, her right to take peaceful advantage of this principle and to reopen the question at some future date.[9]

The passage indicated clearly that he was not thinking in terms of aggressive acts, nor in terms of immediate action, but that he was merely attempting to raise the question and to prepare the ground for future action by establishing the principle of the legitimacy of peaceful change. On April 10, 1925, he registered his claims in the form of an anonymous article. Alluding to Sir Austen Chamberlain's failure to object, in the course of the pre-Locarno negotiations, to his revisionist plans concerning the East, Stresemann noted:

". . . Doubt has been cast upon the validity of the Treaty of Versailles as far as the eastern frontier is concerned." Of greatest significance, however, was the following statement contained in the same article:

Poland finds herself in the same position towards Germany as she is towards Russia, because Russia also does not recognize her frontiers with Poland. Affairs in the East are by no means settled. As soon as Russia decides whether she is prepared to remain permanently within these frontiers or not, and when she raises the question of Poland and the Baltic states, then a new era will open up in European history.[10]

It is interesting to note that when the Russians actually attempted to have him join them in a secret pact "to push Poland back to her ethnographic limits," he showed no inclination to accept. Chicherin's and Krestinsky's efforts to stay the development in the West on the eve of Stresemann's departure for Locarno found the German adamant in his refusal to embark upon military adventures with the Russians. Furthermore, to keep the record clear, Stresemann checked the files and then proceeded to refute Chicherin's allegations that the initiative for a secret pact had come from the German side.[11] It was one thing for Stresemann to conjure up the picture of a Russo-German alliance and quite another to actually embark upon such an adventure.

On the other hand, not to press his anti-Communist inclinations too far and in order to allay the apprehensions of the nationalists that Germany was being deprived of a reliable ally, Stresemann made a number of reassuring gestures in the direction of Moscow. In conversations with Litvinov and Krestinsky, he even pointed out that the projected security pact could not possibly be directed against the Soviet Union since Germany had reserved her freedom of action concerning the eastern boundaries.[12] With that he wished to convey to the Soviets that a German alliance with France against the Soviet Union would of course bring in its wake a German-Polish understanding, since Poland and France were firmly allied already. Since Germany intended to deprive Poland of some of her newly won possessions, it stood to reason that she could not well afford to tie her hands by such an alliance with Poland's treaty partner. Therefore, there was no reason to fear an anti-Soviet move on the part of Germany.

With the Locarno Conference in mind, and after having prepared the ground thoroughly, Stresemann embarked upon a twofold strategy. In the first place he reminded his treaty partners that the benefits of the concept of *rebus sic stantibus*, as implied in Article 19 of the League Covenant, had to accrue to Germany somehow; if Germany was to renounce all claims in the West, then changes had to be permitted in the East.[13] Second, as an insurance against the contingency that the Allies were not prepared to grant the first point, Stresemann saw to it that nothing was incorporated in the treaties to be signed which would tend to stand permanently in the way of future changes in the East.[14] In particular, he was anxious to arrive at a clear definition of the term "aggression." This was to prevent French military support of Poland in the event that the latter state should refuse to abide by the decisions of the arbitration tribunal provided for in the treaties of arbitration, and should seek to invoke the defensive clauses of her alliance with France. For similar reasons, he objected to France's assuming the role of a guarantor since: "no state which is allied with another (i.e., France with Poland) can guarantee impartial execution of a treaty of arbitration affecting one of the allies."[15]

Under the treaties of arbitration, concluded at Locarno between Germany on the one hand, and Poland and Czechoslovakia severally on the other, the following was agreed upon: all disputes "of every kind" (i.e., justiciable and nonjusticiable questions), between the contracting parties concerning their respective rights and "which it may not be possible to settle amicably by the normal methods of diplomacy, shall be submitted for decision either to an arbitral tribunal or the Permanent Court of International Justice."[16] It had been Stresemann's desire to see judicial and political questions treated separately. He had proposed that judicial questions be subject to arbitration without exception whereas political questions should only be subject to conciliation. In the latter case, the decision to accept or to reject the recommendations of the tribunal would be left to the governments concerned.[17] The French government, on the other hand, had demanded that the treaties should be all-inclusive, i.e., all disputes, regardless of their nature and regardless of whether they pertained to East or West, would be subject to decisions by an arbitration tribunal.[18] The result of Locarno was a compromise. The arbitration treaties left it to the several parties to bring an issue to the League Council "if the two parties have not reached an agreement within a month from the termination of the labour of the Permanent Conciliation Commission."[19]

Thus, while Germany was not obliged to accept the decision of the arbitration tribunal, she could bring up a multitude of political claims and charges and submit them to the League Council, if she so desired.

In order to pacify her Eastern allies and to counterbalance the apparent advantage obtained by Stresemann through the arbitration treaties with Poland and Czechoslovakia (nowhere did these treaties recognize the inviolability of Germany's eastern boundaries), France concluded treaties of mutual guaranty with these two countries.[20] This was particularly necessary because Stresemann had refused to conclude similar treaties with them. He had even gone beyond that by instructing his delegation at Locarno to ignore completely the instruments of mutual guaranty concluded between France and her allies, and to take no official cognizance of them.[21] This had been done to avoid leaving the impression that Germany recognized the boundaries which had been guaranteed in those treaties. Addressing himself particularly to the *casus foederis* provided for in Article 1 of the treaties between France and her allies, Stresemann made a most ominous observation: he stated that it would be very difficult to establish when the *casus foederis* would apply. Since France was only to come to the assistance of Poland upon the finding of "an unprovoked recourse to arms (by Germany)," Stresemann believed that it would only remain Germany's task to make aggression appear "unprovoked."[22] This he believed would be possible unless Germany once again committed as serious a blunder as on August 4, 1914, when Chancellor Bethmann-Hollweg had termed the neutrality of Belgium "a scrap of paper."[23] There is no reason to believe, however, that pacific revisionism had been dropped in favor of a more militant type. The whole argument was advanced to allay fears, current among some Germans, that Germany had once for all renounced her claims to changes in the East and that Stresemann had permitted Germany to be encircled by France. The end result, as far as Stresemann was concerned, was that nothing had been undertaken which would have tended to deny Germany the right to achieve an eventual peaceful revision of the eastern boundaries. During all of the preceding negotiations and diplomatic maneuvers, there was no mention of specific revisionist demands. The battle had centered only upon the clarification of pertinent principles.

A corollary of the Treaty of Mutual Guarantee with the Western Powers was an agreement with the Soviet Union. It was clear to Stresemann that any attempts on his part, or on the part of future German governments, to change any boundaries in the East, would at once lead to charges of aggression. Furthermore, the Nationalists continued to demand that he take precautions against a possible alienation of the Soviets over the Locarno policy. In particular, the Soviets feared that Germany's entry into the League would oblige her to participate in League actions against the Soviet Union in the event that Article 16, the sanctions clause, was invoked.[24] For these reasons, Stresemann accepted the conclusion of a treaty of friendship and mutual guaranty with the Union of Soviet Socialist Republics.[25] As far as Stresemann's over-all revisionist policy was concerned, the Treaty of Berlin, as the pact became known, assured Soviet neutrality in the event that Germany was subjected to sanctions under the League Covenant. This was to apply especially to an embroilment of Germany with Poland's Western Allies over charges of aggression in the East. At the same time, of course, Germany pledged neutrality in the event that the Western Allies would make war upon the Soviet Union. Article 3 of the additional notes exchanged on the occasion of the signing of the treaty left it to Germany to decide when the Soviet Union should be termed "an aggressor" in the sense of Article 16 of the League Covenant. Yet, from the Soviet point of view, the foreign minister remained a menace and it appears that they preferred to lend support to right-wing nationalists in Germany in order to check Stresemann and to hasten the day when a more co-operative minister would take his place. "As long as Stresemann is at the wheel," wrote Krestinsky, "Germany will remain on the side of the Soviet Union's enemies."[26]

II. *The Advanced Stage.* Stresemann had voiced opposition to the eastern boundary settlement made at Versailles at the earliest opportunity. However, he studiously avoided making specific demands until after Germany had joined the League of Nations in September 1926. It became clear from then on what course his revisionist policy was to take with regard to Germany's eastern boundaries. It was to be a policy of peaceful, gradual, almost imperceptible assertion of German influence over the lost areas, through channels available in the League Council, the Assembly, and the several committees.

It soon became apparent that Stresemann planned to prepare the stage for boundary revisions, if not the return of entire districts, by a process of questioning the underlying bases of existing relevant treaties. He sought to establish the principle that decisions made by the League Council before Germany had become a member, and which concerned the interpretation and application of existing treaties—such as agreements and treaties between Poland and the Free City of Danzig—did not constitute "irrevocable legal doctrine."[27] On that premise, he proceeded to cast doubts upon the validity of a long string of League decisions and recommendations concerning Danzig and other areas under the protection of the League, all of which had been handed down before Germany had joined the League, i.e., before Stresemann had been in a position to exercise his veto in the Council.[28] In other words, Stresemann tried to "put the clock back" to the time when the idea of League sponsorship and supervision of treaty arrangement had been in its infancy, i.e., when it had scarcely emerged from the parent instrument, the Treaty of Versailles. Once this maneuver was successful, it stood to reason that an attack on the pertinent provisions of the Treaty of Versailles would be less hazardous. Above all, things would be returned to where they had been at the very beginning; thus the head start gained by the status quo powers would be reduced to the point where Germany was no longer under the handicap of a late-comer.

As the German foreign minister identified himself more and more with a policy of revisionism, and as it became ever more apparent that Germany would not accept the views of the status quo powers, Poland redoubled her efforts to halt what threatened to become a dangerous situation. At the anniversary of Germany's entrance into the League of Nations, Stresemann was thus confronted by a Polish move designed to stop the indirect attacks upon the integrity of her western boundaries. The Polish move took the form of a proposed resolution, to be adopted by the League Council, and which was to have the effect of an international nonaggression pact, an "eastern Locarno."[29] Stresemann at once undertook to weaken the resolution to the point where it could not stand in the way of his policy.[30] The result was that the original Locarno agreements remained the governing instruments for the Eastern European situation. The advantage gained at Locarno, when only limited treaties of arbitration had been signed, was safeguarded and the political basis for revisionism in the East was as strong as before. In fact, the Western Allies, Great Britain and France, assisted Stresemann in the attempt to water down the Polish resolution.[31] It was now as it had been at Locarno: Great Britain was not prepared to extend her commitments to a guaranty of Poland's boundaries against Germany, and France was not willing to part company with Great Britain on that issue. As a result, German revisionism remained unchecked and Stresemann could score another diplomatic triumph. On the other hand, the fact that Stresemann was not averse to supporting a general nonaggression pact as long as such a pact did not single out Poland's western boundaries, shows that his policy was essentially pacific.[32]

Concerning proposals to assist Poland financially and thus prepare the way for a compromise solution of the boundary problem, Stresemann maintained a negative attitude.[33] He was convinced that such a solution would turn out to be unsatisfactory and that it would tend to prejudice future claims by Germany. The German-Polish question, as far as he was concerned, was a central point not only in German but also in European politics, and he preferred that the economic recovery of Poland be postponed until Germany was in a position to exact a more favorable price for her aid.[34] Yet, it was too dangerous to go too far in this respect and something had to be done to show Germany's good will.

Thus, in order to avoid serious diplomatic setbacks, Stresemann forced the cabinet to agree to the signing of a Treaty of Commerce with Poland. When it appeared that nationalist circles demanded a *quid pro quo* before they would consent to the signing of the treaty (the German National People's Party had been represented in the cabinet since January 1927), Stresemann resorted to a favorite device: he threatened to resign.[35] Furthermore, to clear the diplomatic atmosphere, he informed the German public that revision by force was out of the question. Revision could only be achieved if it was treated as a matter of European rather than of purely regional significance.[36] In other words, Poland was to be "stimulated" into a co-operative attitude because Locarno and subsequent developments had brought Berlin, Paris, and London closer together, and Poland could no longer rely on French diplomatic support. Partly to offset nationalist propaganda to the effect that he had forsaken East Prussia by his Locarno policy, and partly in explanation of his evident preoccupation with Eastern affairs, he publicly proclaimed that the Locarno policy had in reality been an Eastern policy. He assured the people of East Prussia, and the rest of Germany, that Locarno had merely been the prelude to Eastern revisionism and that the hour for a reunion of East Prussia with the motherland was close at hand.[37]

In May of 1928, however, Stresemann was confronted with a domestic political shift of considerable magnitude. As a result of the elections to the fourth Reichstag, the need for an appeasement of the Nationalists was no longer urgent. The Social-Democrats had replaced the German National People's Party as the largest party in parliament.[38] Once again, it was possible for Stresemann to base his foreign policy upon a "Great Coalition" extending from the Socialist Left to the middle-of-the-road Bavarian People's Party.[39] With the new cabinet, formed in June 1928, there came, of course, a shift of emphasis as far as the relative importance of East and West was concerned. The once urgent question of a reunion of East Prussia with the motherland (largely based on the fact that East Prussia was a nationalist stronghold) was replaced by renewed

efforts to come to terms with the West.[40] Almost abruptly, Stresemann departed from the policy of diplomatic aggression against
Poland and turned to more peaceful pursuits. As he addressed himself to the policy which was to lead to total evacuation of foreign
troops from the Rhineland, to the Young Plan, and the Kellogg Peace
Pact, the eastern boundaries remained exactly as they had been determined at Versailles. Only in one respect did he continue to prepare the ground for future revision in the East: he did not abandon
the policy designed to assure an ever extending control by Germany
over her minorities in Poland.

Stresemann's revisionist policy as far as the eastern boundary
settlement was concerned, was tactically subordinated to his Western
policy and addressed itself to the following objectives. East Prussia was to be reunited with the motherland by elimination of the
so-called "Polish Corridor." This was to be accomplished in one of
two ways. Either the Free City of Danzig was to be returned to
German sovereignty or the "Corridor" was to be abolished, with
Danzig remaining independent. In either case, Poland's access to the
Baltic Sea would have been blocked and some compensation would
have been necessary to give her the desired access elsewhere.

Stresemann's strategy followed these general lines: in the first
place, he carefully avoided giving the Allies, and Poland in particular, cause to maintain that Germany, by her own free will, had recognized the eastern frontier settlement. This was accomplished by a
policy designed to prevent the conclusion of any pacts, treaties, or
agreements which would have amounted to a *de jure* or *de facto* recognition of the finality of the Versailles settlement. Second, he followed
the policy of coming to terms with the French, the Belgians, and with
Great Britain over questions concerning Germany's western frontiers, while at the same time strengthening diplomatic ties with the
Soviet Union, the other great power interested in changes in the
Polish area. In order to avoid leaving the impression that Germany
was an enemy of the peace, he consented to the conclusion of a treaty
of arbitration with Poland. However, nothing in this treaty precluded recourse to diplomatic or other action over "nonjusticiable"
questions.

The major political and legal argument advanced by Stresemann
with respect to the legitimacy of German claims to boundary revisions in the East was based on the concept of peaceful change necessitated by conditions which had become "unbearable." This was in
particular reference to Article 19 of the League of Nations Covenant.

The League entered into his strategy on the strength of its role as a guarantor of the status of the Free City of Danzig. It was clear that no changes could be effected in that regard unless Germany was a member of the League of Nations. Second, the treaty of arbitration stipulated that nonjusticiable disputes with Poland, and that included disputes over Danzig as far as Stresemann was concerned, were to be submitted to the League Council, where the principle of unanimity ruled. It seemed to be certain that no actions detrimental to German interests would be taken there. In order to place Germany in the strongest possible position in the League, Stresemann insisted that no actions taken by that body prior to Germany's entry should have the air of finality.

If one considers the limitations to which a German foreign policy was subjected at the time, one cannot be surprised that a German foreign minister rejected violence as a means of recovering lost territories. What is noteworthy, however—and it speaks well for Stresemann— is his steadfast refusal to consider a proffered partnership with the Soviet Union and to harness the latter's malcontent and revolutionary aspirations to Germany's chariot. Even though territorial revision in the East seems to have been a high priority goal of his foreign policy, Stresemann preferred to attain that goal by the more circuitous but more peaceful approach through an understanding with the West.

CHAPTER XII

THE PROBLEM OF MINORITIES AND THE
TREATY REVISION

As a result of the boundary settlement of the Treaty of Versailles, considerable numbers of Germans of ethnic stock had come under foreign rule.[1] By far the largest number were transferred from five German provinces to the Republic of Poland, occupying thereafter what became known as the "Polish Corridor." As early as the Paris Peace Conference, the Germans had demanded the right of their minorities to support and to frequent German schools and churches and to publish German newspapers.[2] An attempt was even made to achieve complete cultural autonomy for the minorities. In reply to that proposal, the Allied leaders stipulated that while they were prepared to accord guaranties for the educational, religious, and cultural rights of German minorities, such guaranties would be established by reference to the League of Nations only.[3] Subsequent treaties and conventions between Germany, the Allied and Associated Powers, and the states which had received minorities, stipulated that the treatment of persons belonging to racial, religious, or linguistic minorities constituted obligations of international concern. The entire matter was to be placed under the guaranty of the League of Nations. The obligations were not to be modified without the assent of a majority of the Council of the League of Nations.[4] It was because of this development that Stresemann's policy with respect to the German minorities came almost exclusively under the aegis of German membership in the League of Nations. It was on the floor of the League Assembly, at the Council table, and at the several League committees dealing with that question, that Stresemann unfolded his strategy.

I. *The Preparatory Stage.* When it appeared that the victor nations were seriously considering Germany's entry into the League of Nations, Stresemann at once saw the opportunity to develop his strategy.[5] The protection of German minorities, as far as he was concerned, was one of three foreign policy objectives which he believed could be realized within a relatively short period of time. The other two objectives, a reunion of Austria and Germany and the revision of Germany's eastern boundaries depended upon the successful conclusion of the campaign for control of the minorities, i.e., for the right of self-determination.[6] There was reason to expect strong opposition from the group of nations which had received German minorities. The only effective way open to Germany was to pursue the policy of maintaining and extending her influence over the minorities by reference to the League of Nations.[7] If Germany's role was to be that of a guardian over the minorities, and as long as she was disarmed and weak, the League and its machinery could achieve what only strong armies could otherwise have accomplished.[8] When some nationalist circles expressed fears that membership in the League of Nations would bring unpleasant and cumbersome obligations for Germany, Stresemann pointed out that greater fears were harbored by Czechoslovakia and Poland. He quoted the Czechoslovak foreign minister as having warned his country that as soon as Germany was firmly installed in the League, Czech policy with regard to German minorities would no longer be controlled by Prague but by Berlin.[9] In connection with the campaign for acceptance of the Locarno agreements in 1925, he again cited the remarks of a Czech parliamentarian in support of his thesis:

Herr Virasmatch, leader of the Czech Nationalists, has come very close to the truth, when he stated in the Czech parliament, that Germany's membership in the League could have the result that the vanquished will control the minority policy of the victors, and will interfere with their affairs of state. I consider that the most fruitful task which a German delegation at the League could assign to itself.[10]

It was for the above reasons that Stresemann evinced a keen interest in the League's machinery for the consideration of minority questions. As early as October 23, 1925, one year before Germany actually joined the League, he noted, with apprehension, that the Allies were trying to alter the procedural rules of the Committee of Three on Minority Questions, by deciding to exclude any nation from its hearings if that nation was ethnically related to a complaining minority group. However, several other factors militated in Germany's favor. The treaty between the principal Allied and Associated Powers and Poland, stipulated, among other things, that differences of opinion as to questions of law or fact between Poland and any other power were to be considered disputes of an international character. If the "other power" was a member of the League Council, the Covenant and the machinery of the World Court were at its disposal. The same treaty gave any member of the Council the right to bring to the attention of the Council any infraction or any danger of infraction of contracted obligations. As mentioned above, Poland had to assent to any modifications of the minority provisions of the treaty if such modifications met with the approval of a majority in the Council. Then there were the provisions of the Covenant itself which promised Germany ample opportunity to attack Poland's minority policy under the heading of peaceful settlement of international disputes.

Thus, on the basis of the treaty between the Allies and Poland, and in the light of the provisions of the League Covenant itself, it was necessary for Germany to take the following steps in order to assure herself a position from where German minorities could be controlled. (1) She had to become a member of the Council of the League of Nations; (2) Poland, the principal ruler of German minorities, had to be kept out of the Council, or at least had to be prevented from becoming a permanent member of that crucial body; (3) Germany had to convince a majority in the Council, and the Assembly, that disputes between German minorities and their rulers were not matters of domestic jurisdiction and thus beyond reach, but that they constituted disputes of an international character subject to discussion and settlement in the League of Nations. There is evidence that Stresemann was fully aware of all of these implications before he embarked upon his League policy.[11]

Prior to Germany's entry into the League, the question of German minorities in the district of South Tirol led to a clash with the Italians. Shortly afterwards, the Polish policy of attempting to liquidate the property of former German nationals in Poland led to diplomatic complications with that country. Consequently, Stresemann told the German press that he was most anxious to speed Germany's entry into the League, "because a number of questions will come up in the next few months (before the League Council) which are of greatest interest to us."[12]

Even though South Tirol had been detached from Austria, and not from Germany, Stresemann apparently felt that mistreatment of ethnic Germans in that region, or anywhere else for that matter, was of greatest concern to Germany. Replying to a particularly belligerent speech by Benito Mussolini, chief of the Italian government, Stresemann attacked the peace settlement, its disregard of the right of self-determination, and in particular, the Italian assertion that Germany had no right to interest herself in the fate of Germans transferred to Italy under the peace terms. Indicating what he thought of Mussolini's latter point, Stresemann made it clear that if Germany were a member of the League, the dispute would certainly be brought before the Council.[13]

Whatever Stresemann's objectives were, at the time, he succeeded in disarming any group in Germany which stood to oppose Germany's entry into the League by reference to the minority problem. He told the British Ambassador, with a great deal of satisfaction, that "the curious effect of the [minority] controversy has been to make public opinion, particularly German nationalist opinion, alive to the advantage of Germany's being a member of the League."[14]

Before Germany became a full-fledged member of the League, Stresemann had to experience a great disappointment. The major League powers had decided to enlarge the Council by the addition of three permanent seats. One of these seats was to be assigned to Poland. Since Poland, however, was a major recipient of former German nationals, Germany could not afford to tolerate that country on the League Council. Under such circumstances, the entire *raison d'être* for Germany's membership in the League, at least as far as Stresemann was concerned, would have been nullified.[15] The danger was that Poland's "veto" could serve to sidetrack any considerations of complaints by minorities or to reduce considerations to dilatory matters, if that state was given the preferential status of Council membership. Furthermore, Poland could then, under Article 15, Paragraph 5, do great harm to Stresemann's projected propaganda campaign by filling the Council's agenda with countercomplaints which would tend to reduce the effectiveness of German charges.

When Germany failed to gain admittance to the League during the March session, Stresemann was upset.[16] However, aware of the great values inherent in a League membership, he refused to let that incident stand in his way and continued his battle unabated. To overcome the wave of hostility that swept the country when he returned from Geneva empty-handed, he pointed out that the reason Germany had not been admitted had been the fear on the part of the Versailles powers that German membership would tend to change the old construction of the League as an instrument to perpetuate the status quo. With this argument, he soon succeeded in overcoming the opposition.[17]

II. *The League Phase.* Germany entered the League officially on September 8, 1926. With that event, Stresemann's policy with respect to the minorities entered upon a more active phase.

To prepare the ground for a complete unfolding of his campaign, Stresemann requested of the Nationalist leadership that their foreign policy expert, Professor Dr. Otto Hoetzsch, be delegated to accompany him to Geneva. This request was not met. For similar reasons, he then sought to have the principle accepted that the matter of the composition of the German delegation to all meetings of the League of Nations be removed from partisan politics. The sole criterion for a delegate's fitness for the post was to be his professional qualification and judicious temperament. As foreign minister, he demanded the co-operation of parties not in the government "to enable us to prove to the outside world that Germany, in matters of foreign policy, presented a united front."[18] There is reason to believe that Stresemann, in order to obtain the support of the Nationalists for his League policy, made certain concessions to the military.[19] In addition to placating the League powers and the world press, he announced that he would represent Germany at Geneva in person as much and as often as his health and his duties would permit.[20] Whatever he really expected in the way of results, it was clear then that the minority question was to be the primary objective to be pursued in the League, and that this was to be done in an atmosphere of harmony on the national as well as on the international level.

Germany was to regain some control over the minorities through her membership in the League of Nations, especially through the Council.[21] Among the several minority problems to be considered, the Polish problem loomed larger than that of the German minorities in Czechoslovakia, Lithuania, and Italy. Danzig, the Saar, Denmark, and Belgium were lesser problems, as far as German minorities were concerned.

Danzig did not represent a minority problem in the real sense because the city had been granted a semi-independent status under the protectorate of the League of Nations. As has been shown above, Stresemann considered Danzig primarily a vital steppingstone to East Prussia. As far as the fate of the Sudeten Germans was concerned, the German foreign minister did not evidence any appreciable concern during his years in office. Immediately following Germany's entry into the League he made it clear to the expectant Sudeten Germans that he was not inclined to look for trouble with Prague since he regarded the issues between Berlin and Warsaw as the more pressing ones.[22]

The first clash occurred on September 20, 1926, over a question of principle. The point raised concerned the right of members of the League to bring complaints initiated by minorities before the Council "whenever it considered it opportune to do so."[23] This represented the opening shot in the campaign to breach the wall of argumentations erected by the treaty powers against a German renascense and against an attempt on her part to exert any influence over German minorities in order to facilitate territorial changes. The defensive argument centered on two points. On the one hand, an attempt was made to have all questions concerning the status and rights of minorities considered as matters of domestic jurisdiction and thus really outside the scope of the League of Nations. This argument was based on Article 15, Paragraph 8 of the Covenant. Second, it was claimed that German sponsorship of complaints by German minorities constituted a violation of Article 10 of the League Covenant. This article made it incumbent upon League members to respect and preserve as against external aggression, the territorial integrity and existing political independence of all members of the League. In reply to the latter point, Stresemann called attention to Article 19, which allowed for reconsideration of treaties "which had become inapplicable," and which provided for "consideration of international conditions whose continuance might endanger the peace of the world." He stated that it could not have been the purpose of the League Covenant, especially not that of Article 10, to freeze, forever, all human relationships and to command a halt to all developments favoring better international relations.[24]

Stresemann's argument, however, especially in the light of his refusal to sign unconditional treaties of arbitration with Poland, left him open to the charge of wanting to flout the machinery provided in the Covenant and in the Statute of the Permanent Court of International Justice to facilitate pacific settlement of international disputes. In order to protect himself against this charge ("to protect my back"), he promoted German adherence to the Optional Clause of the World Court Statute.[25] The clause provided for compulsory jurisdiction of the World Court in certain cases. Germany's signature, while it did not in any way restrict her freedom of action, tended to counteract the ill effects of her refusal to come to terms with Poland. Moreover, because it was more likely that Germany, rather than Poland, would be a plaintiff in disputes concerning minority rights, the Optional Clause promised to become a vehicle for the advancement of German claims without forcing Germany to give further recognition to the eastern frontier settlement.

As the number of disputes before the League Council increased, Stresemann exerted himself to establish the Council's incontestable jurisdiction in minority questions. On every occasion, he opposed attempts by the powers which had received German minorities to deny jurisdiction to the League on the grounds that petitions of complaint against them were more properly subject to domestic jurisdiction of the powers in question. It soon became apparent that

Gustav Stresemann was not prepared to abandon the strategic principles which had led him to promote Germany's entry into the League. It was very significant that one of the few incidents which saw him lose his composure occurred in connection with a dispute over minority rights. When the Polish delegate to the Council charged that the ever increasing flood of complaints and petitions by certain German groups in Poland "endangered the peace," Stresemann slammed his fist down on the Council table.

Count Zaleski, the Polish delegate, had accused the German *Volksbund* (German Minority Association in Poland) of stirring the minorities up against their country of citizenship, of engaging in political agitation, and of being guilty of subversive activities. Organized efforts by the *Volksbund*, he charged, tended to sap the strength of the Polish state and were calculated to endanger the peace. Stresemann became so agitated because Zaleski's contentions touched upon the very core of Germany's League policy, i.e., to use the League in order to keep the minority question constantly before the world. When the Polish delegate added that "there is no evidence either of a serious social dispute or of any decline in the general level of culture in Silesia," Stresemann could no longer contain himself. He asked point-blank:

I should like to know as from when the minorities will no longer be allowed to exercise their right to form associations and to bring petitions before the Council of the League? . . . I may say quite definitely that, were the League to indorse this opinion and were it to cease dealing with the rights of minorities, it would be losing one of the reasons for its existence and would cease to represent for some States the ideal which induced them to join it.[26]

In March 1929, the last year of his life, Stresemann considered the fight for minority rights (or, stated differently, the fight for extension of Germany's control over the minorities) the main reason for his continuance in office. Addressing himself to a friend, he wrote:

I feel that I am obliged to remain in office until the last phase of the minority question has been fought out. I would consider myself a deserter, if I would leave the question, which I have begun before the world, or if I would leave it to my successor.[27]

The March session of the League Council was primarily devoted to consideration of the minority rights. At the session of March 6, Stresemann laid down what he believed to be the guiding principles to be followed by the Council in the consideration of minority rights. His four-point program suggested the following approach. (1) A careful study was to be made of the existing possibilities for an improvement of the procedure for the consideration of minority petitions; (2) the participation of certain interested nations should be considered instead of their exclusion; (3) a study should be made of the ways in which the League could better exercise its function in the fulfillment of its duties as a guarantor of minority rights outside the sphere of petitions; and finally, (4) the principle of a guaranty of minority rights by the League of Nations should be interpreted in favor of the minorities and not, as had been the case, in favor of the states having minorities. Addressing himself to the contention that sponsorship of minority rights by Germany constituted interference with the domestic jurisdiction of the receiving states, he stated his position as follows:

The provisions for the protection of minorities imply a duty which is neither impossible nor beneath the dignity of a sovereign state to fulfill. The fact of belonging to a minority and the social position resulting from that fact, are certainly in no way incompatible with the accomplishments of the duties of a loyal citizen toward the State. This being so, it equally follows that the interest taken by a country in the minorities of another country, an interest which may take the form of an appeal to the guaranty of the League of Nations, cannot be regarded as an inadmissable political interference with the domestic affairs of a foreign power.

Developing this point further, he advanced the contention that German sponsorship of minority rights would not be in contradiction of the principles guiding the League of Nations, even if this sponsorship were to lead to irredentist movements. "Frankly," he observed, "I do not think that we have in the present century established a state of affairs which is eternal, and that idea is very clearly expressed in the Covenant of the League of Nations."[28] Here was the clearest statement of Stresemann's policy. Here he attempted to link the concept of change with respect to the status of minorities to that of general change. It was an unconcealed announcement to the effect that irredentism was to lead to territorial revision. However, an Allied reaction set in at once. Replying to Stresemann's allusion that "finality was not human," Sir Austen Chamberlain of Great Britain warned that "to cite Article 19 [of the Covenant] in connection with the minority treaties can only make trouble. The Council will expect the minorities to show that they have behaved loyally to the country of which they are a part."[29] Even though Stresemann made an effort, during the subsequent meeting of the Council, and following Chamberlain's reply, to set the record straight and to soften the impression of concealed rebellion against the status quo, the damage had been done. Article 19 of the Covenant had been definitely linked with the minority question. Germany had gone on record with an announcement that the minority treaties, and all that went with them in the way of political and legal implications, were subject to change.

In keeping with his basic concept, namely, that the whole campaign over minority rights was being waged to facilitate the ultimate return of the "lost population" to the German mother country, Stresemann turned next to the question of duration. He noted that an attitude had taken root which tended to consider the provisions guaranteeing the rights of the minorities as being provisional in nature. There was a notion, he observed, to view these provisions as covering "a kind of transition period before the final disappearance of minorities as such, that is to say, to cover the period up to the time when the minorities would be absorbed by the majority of the populations of the states to which they belong."[30]

In addition to laying down the above principles, Stresemann also made another attempt to weaken the preferred position held by the Committee of Three on Petitions of Minorities. At the June meeting of the Council, which was entirely devoted to the minority question, he noted that Germany was intentionally prevented from participating in the committee's deliberations. He asserted that while the committee had followed a practice of excluding all "interested" states from its meetings, this practice had "curiously enough" not been extended to those states which had received the minorities. It appeared to him that only those states were being excluded which had "legitimate" interests in the minorities of other countries.[31]

III. *The Final Phase.* When the Committee of Three, at the Madrid session of the Council, submitted its recommendations to the Council, Stresemann opposed them bitterly. He opposed the recommendation which suggested that the inclusion of a country like Germany in the committee "was contrary to the idea of equality which should underlie all work performed by the League." However, there was nothing that he could do about that at the time. Second, he objected to the proposed creation of a permanent committee on minorities on the grounds that the proposed committee would assume the character and function of a permanent executive organization. All he wanted was a committee to supervise the minority situation, not one which would tend to supervise the minorities themselves. In spite of Briand's admonition to agree to the tendered report, Stresemann, feeling that it did not do justice to Germany and to what he considered her legitimate aspirations, recommended that the points at issue be submitted to the World Court for an advisory opinion. In so doing, he succeeded in setting up himself, and Germany, as a defender of the minorities, making it appear as though anyone accepting the report would want to persecute these groups. Finally, Stresemann reiterated his previous position by asserting the rights of the minorities to maintain their special characteristics of race, culture, and language. Nothing should be allowed which would tend to lead to the absorption or assimilation of the minority groups by the countries of which they were nationals.[32] To dispel any doubts concerning the reasons for his insistence on minority rights, he even admitted that his minority policy was not only a matter of maintaining cultural relations, but that it had "an unusual significance with respect to Germany's political relations with neighboring countries."[33]

Stresemann's last appearance before the League Assembly on September 9, 1929, brought the minority question once more before the international forum. Following a recapitulation of the results, and of disagreements at previous Council meetings, Stresemann closed with this admonition:

I am convinced that [in the matter of the assumed guarantee of minority rights] the League ought not merely to give effect to the various petitions submitted to it; [but] under the terms of the minority law in force, it ought to keep itself constantly and generally informed of the position of minorities under the system set up by the treaties in force.

In conclusion, he recommended that a special organization be set up to deal with minority questions in a manner similar to the machinery already in operation for the consideration of economic questions and colonial mandates.[34] It was clear, of course, that such an organization was to include Germany as a member.

Having encountered determined resistance to proposed territorial revisions, Stresemann, especially after 1926, concentrated on the task of safeguarding the bases for German claims to certain lost districts and territories in the East. These bases were demographic in nature; they included the former German nationals who had now minority status in areas which he wished to reclaim. He wished to safeguard the rights of these minorities so that the territories which they inhabited could be returned some day, even if the return was made subject to plebiscites. Because the largest single minority was under Polish rule, and because the Polish Corridor represented the primary revisionist objective, Stresemann's major effort with respect to minority rights was concentrated at that point.

The question of the rights and duties of minorities in states having become responsible for such groups as a result of the peace treaties, was subject to supervision and control by the appropriate organs of the League of Nations. For that reason, Stresemann enacted most of his policy in that regard on the stage of the League; it was because of the crucial role of the League in the minority question that he had pressed for accession to the League in the first place.

His diplomatic strategy followed these lines: the minorities were to be encouraged to safeguard their characteristics and to insist upon their rights. If violations of their status occurred, they were to be encouraged to address petitions to the League of Nations. To guarantee effective representation by a friendly power, Germany was to occupy the seat of a permanent member in the League Council. Any attempts by the status quo powers, or "host" nations, to treat the petitions as matters of domestic jurisdiction were to be frustrated by Germany acting in the Council. If no petitions were received by the League, or if they were being suppressed, Germany was to endeavor to bring the complaints to the attention of the world through the Council. In order to make maximum use of the privileged position as a Council member, it was necessary to keep the greatest "host" nation and the potentially greatest adversary off the Council; if that was not possible, that state was to be at least denied the status of a permanent member of the Council.

In particular, Stresemann fought to establish these points. (1) Germany was to be recognized as a party to the disputes between the German minorities and their respective governments. As such, she was to be entitled to participation in the meetings of the crucial committee of the League concerned with minority questions. The result of this policy, if successful, was to be the removal of disputes between minorities and their respective governments from the sphere of domestic affairs. Instead of being mere disputes of an intrastate character, settled under the supervision of the League, questions of minority rights were to be magnified to become matters of international concern. (2) As an interested party, and for the above mentioned reasons, Germany was to have the right to bring any dispute to the attention of the Council. (3) German sponsorship of the petitions or disputes in the League of Nations was not to be considered an infringement of other states' sovereign rights or of their domestic jurisdiction, nor acts of aggression or threats against the territorial integrity or political independence of a state. (4) Changes in the status of German minorities were not to be precluded. This point was based on Article 19 of the League Covenant. By the same token, the entire matter of minorities, their status, their rights, and the accompanying guaranties, were not to be considered as provisional in character. There was to be no absorption or assimilation of minorities by the "host" nations. The issue was to be kept alive until the territories which they inhabited were returned to Germany.

There can be no doubt that Stresemann's minority policy was largely a deliberate attempt to encourage and to foster irredentism in Polish lands. Here was the link between territorial revisionism and his minority policy. Since there were other factors preventing territorial revision at the time, a vigorous minority policy was the most effective long-range measure to assure the return of the lost territories at some future date. However, even though Stresemann's minority policy appeared to be aggressive, his approach to the problem and the execution of the policy tend to indicate the essentially pacific nature of his revisionism.

CHAPTER XIII

DISARMAMENT AND REVISION

In order to render Germany militarily impotent, the Allied Powers had provided, through the Treaty of Versailles, that substantial disarmament was to be undertaken by Germany with regard to armed forces on land, in the air, and on the sea.[1] Germany's armed strength was fixed at 100,000 men. Restrictions were imposed upon her concerning the number and type of weapons which she was permitted to have and the quantity of ammunition which she was allowed to use and to store. Weapons which could be used for modern aggressive warfare were forbidden. A demilitarized zone was established along the Rhine, and elsewhere existing fortifications and military installations were ordered to be destroyed. The naval forces were reduced and replacements of ship bottoms were carefully restricted. Germany was not permitted to operate an air force nor to train military aviation personnel. Inter-Allied commissions of control were established to supervise the disarmament and demilitarization provisions.

The preamble to the disarmament clauses turned out to be a primary source for bitter recriminations on the part of Germany, and was to assume greatest international significance in later years. When Gustav Stresemann attempted later on to promote an early revision of Germany's state of armament as provided in the peace treaty, he was to make frequent reference to that preamble. Based on Point Four of President Wilson's Fourteen Point Program, the preamble read as follows:

In order to render possible the initiation of a general limitation of the armaments of all nations, Germany undertakes strictly to observe the military, naval, and air clauses which follow.[2]

I. *The Initial Moves.* A critic of the Weimar Republic has stated that, as far as Germany's rearmament was concerned, there was less difference between Adolf Hitler, General von Schleicher, and Stresemann than one would suspect by examining their records.[3] A close examination of Stresemann's record on this score, however, will establish that he was less of a nationalist and militarist than his critics would suspect.

Toward the close of World War I, as has been pointed out, Stresemann was indeed a most active militarist. Addressing himself to the kind of peace which Germany needed to guarantee her own security after the war, he showed no faith in any international contracts or agreements unless those were based upon the existence of strong military forces. Following the Armistice, he expressed bitter disappointment over the destruction of Germany's armed might, especially in the light of unsettled conditions arising from military defeat. He was particularly apprehensive over the lack of armed forces to stem revolutionary movements in Germany's eastern provinces. In an article published one day after the signing of the Treaty of Versailles, Stresemann wrote:

We call for the sword but not even God can return it to us. We wielded it once, and it was the most precious ever given to a people. But we deliberately broke it ourselves, and are therefore now a people and a nation faced with a future of sorrow and shame.[4]

It was the danger of a Bolshevik penetration of Germany's eastern provinces, and the accompanying danger of insurrection, which caused Stresemann to demand an easing of the disarmament restrictions. Referring to Allied protests against the citizens' militia which had sprung into existence everywhere in Germany, he addressed this warning to the West:

If the path is cleared for a victorious advance of bolshevism by [Allied insistence upon complete disarmament of Germany], then bolshevism will not halt at the Rhine, nor at the Channel, unless it is stopped in Germany.[5]

There was no doubt that Stresemann, relatively early, sought to utilize the revolutionary unrest in Germany and its ties with the Soviet Union, to secure the removal of some restrictions imposed upon Germany's armed forces. In this endeavor, he based his argument on a sympathetic understanding on Britain's part, castigating, at the same time, the "hysterical fears on the part of France," which led that country to oppose any increases in Germany's military potential. In the same vein, he asked how it was possible for Germany to be as neutral as had been envisaged by the Allies if she lacked the strength to resist infiltration by forces supported by the Soviets.[6]

II. *The Disarmament Policy Takes Shape.* When Stresemann

became chancellor and foreign minister, the disarmament phase of the peace settlement had been somewhat clarified at the several Allied conferences of Spa, Boulogne-sur-Mer, and San Remo. Three political questions had emerged: the question of internal security control in Germany, the problem of Allied supervision and control, and the duration of the unilateral disarmament of Germany. The first question centered on the number, type, and control of the police forces permitted to function in Germany. The second question was primarily concerned with the rights and privileges, and the jurisdiction of the Military Inter-Allied Commission of Control in Germany. The third question addressed itself to the state of armament, or disarmament, of the several Allied and Associated Powers.

As foreign minister, Stresemann continued to belittle the alleged state of rearmament of Germany and termed all accusations in that respect as nonsense. The first official action with which Stresemann was directly concerned was the dispatch of a reply to an Allied note on disarmament control in Germany.[7] The tenor of that note was conciliatory. Germany was prepared to permit general inspection of her armed forces and of her military facilities. However, Germany's disarmament was to be identified with and closely related to universal disarmament and international conciliation. In that connection, he proposed that military control, now that Germany had been disarmed, should revert from the individual Allied nations to the League of Nations, as envisaged in the Treaty of Versailles. This was an attempt designed to change the nature of the control machinery from that of enforcement to one of mere supervision. At this time a new reparation schedule was under discussion, and the international situation seemed to be favorable to permit changes in the disarmament clauses. After all, Germany showed her compliance by consenting to a review of reparations.

Another opportunity to remind the Allies of German disarmament arose with Germany's imminent accession to the League of Nations. On that occasion, Stresemann advanced the following argument against German acceptance of the implications of Article 16 of the League Covenant:

> As long as the present inequality of armaments, caused by the disarmament of Germany, persists, Germany will be unable, unlike other members of the League of Nations, to participate in any League action under Article 16. A disarmed people surrounded by well armed neighbors . . . and which does not have the means to defend its borders against these forces, cannot afford to give up its neutrality without further consideration.[8]

In a letter to the Secretary General of the League, Sir Eric Drummond, Stresemann made it doubly clear that Germany could only consider participation in sanctions, or advance commitments in that regard, if she were militarily in a position to do so. Under the circumstances, Germany could not defend herself against retaliatory acts by the state, or states, against whom the League actions were being taken. His point was that foreign troops, under the sponsorship of the League of Nations, could never be an effective substitute for German troops fighting to defend German soil. A combined military undertaking of the Western Powers would only be acceptable to Germany if it would mean that Germany's eastern borders were protected by German troops and planes.

On December 17, 1924, the Allied Military Committee at Versailles was asked to ascertain the state of German disarmament and to see whether she had fulfilled her treaty obligations under Part V of the Treaty of Versailles. This was done to establish whether the evacuation of the Cologne zone, as scheduled in Article 429 (1), was justified or not. On January 5, 1925, the German government was informed that a series of violations had come to the attention of the Allied Powers.[9] Stresemann's response was one of sarcasm. While he did not deny the allegations, he attempted nevertheless to make them appear ridiculously insignificant and irrelevant. He did not care to deny the alleged violations because he was only too aware of the truth of the Allied charges.[10]

In view of the fact that the peace and security pact had been launched on February 9, Stresemann now attempted to apply the spirit of conciliation to the disarmament question. Once more he returned to the question of German acceptance of the obligations inherent in Article 16 of the League Covenant. To be sure, he did not specifically demand an increase in Germany's armed strength. On the other hand, however, he made it quite clear that Germany could only accept the obligations if she had the military strength to protect herself against repercussions.[11] As long as Germany was not equipped to take an effective part in the execution of League sanctions, he demanded that the principle *ultra posse nemo obligatur* be applied to her. Addressing himself to the proponents of an immediate accession to the League on Germany's part, and obliquely to German elements working toward international conciliation, he pointed out that not even the "veto" in the League Council could protect Germany from being drawn into a League war, for use of the veto against the League sanctions would lead to the identification of Germany with the aggressor state against whom the League machinery was being brought into operation. Simultaneously, he stressed the fact that in spite of the preamble to the disarmament clauses, universal disarmament had not yet begun. As long as this was the case, he denied the Allies the right to insist upon strict maintenance of controls and restrictions of German armaments. With the then pending negotiations for a security pact in mind, he stated, "A permanent international order is unthinkable as long as individual nations, or groups of states, are enabled, by their preponderance of arms, to realize their political aspirations without the risk of effective resistance."[12] This meant that international peace could only be obtained if Germany was allowed to arm to the level prevailing among her neighbors, or, as implied in the preamble to Part V of the Treaty of Versailles, if her neighbors disarmed to conform with Germany's level. In the same vein, he made the point that the Allies had only to blame themselves if Germany was unable to pledge her support for an effective application of sanctions against aggressor states.

In particular, Stresemann's argument concerning the state of German armament in conjunction with concerted international action, ran as follows. As long as the *Reichswehr* was not permitted to be more than a police force, it could not be expected to participate in the execution of League-sponsored sanctions against aggressor states. Second, in the event that the aggressor was the Soviet Union, and everything pointed to that at the time, 100,000 German soldiers would probably be just enough to quell internal riots caused by procommunist elements in Germany.[13]

Following Germany's entry into the League of Nations, Stresemann accelerated his attempts to achieve a change in the disarmament situation. There were two major objectives which he hoped to reach in this regard through Germany's membership in the League. In his maiden speech before the League Assembly, he demanded that Germany's capacity to resist disadvantageous interpretations of the Treaty of Versailles was to be improved by a universal paring down of arms to Germany's level.[14] On the other hand, Allied military control over Germany was to be terminated as soon as possible. The latter point was pursued with reference to Germany's "established willingness to fulfill her international obligations."[15] Similar to the strategy employed in connection with the evacuation question, he again hinted that he would be forced to resign if the gestures of good will evidenced by Germany at Locarno and at Geneva did not soon lead to reciprocal actions by the Allies, and hence to the termination of military controls.[16] In the event that the Allies persisted in their attitude, he warned that the controls of German foreign policy would inevitably gravitate into the hands of extremists. The forces which had long been dormant in Germany were drawing strength and comfort from the continuous existence of foreign control commissions upon German soil. Here it was significant that Stresemann vigorously defended his authorship of the disarmament policy in the face of nationalist contentions that it had only been because of their insistence that he had come around to a policy of limited resistance to Allied restrictions. The reason he maintained that he and not the Right had originated the policy was a concern for his own party and a fear of losing votes to the German National People's Party.[17]

III. *Domestic Implications of the Disarmament Policy.* While Stresemann was working on the conclusion of the Locarno agreements, he caused a conciliatory note to be sent to the Conference of Ambassadors at Paris, wherein he promised that the majority of Allied demands concerning disarmament would be fulfilled before the end of 1925.[18] Five demands, so the note stated, involved "special difficulties," however. The items on that list were: (1) the strength of the German police, the titles of higher officials, questions of personal administration, and the type and nature of police barracks; (2) the nature of the army high command; (3) the problem created by the prohibition of training with certain weapons; (4) the question of artillery at the fortress of Königsberg; and (5) the problem created by the existence of paramilitary organizations.

As far as the domestic political situation was concerned, point two presented the greatest problem to Stresemann. General von Seeckt, the Chief of Staff of the Army, had for a very long time aroused the suspicion of the Allies. To the German foreign minister, engaged in a policy of reconciliation with the Allies, the problem posed by the continuous presence of Von Seeckt in high office was anathema. Whether Stresemann was directly involved in the dismissal of Von Seeckt is not clear. At any rate, the obstruction to a better understanding with the Allies was removed on October 14, 1926, over a matter of military discipline. With this problem out of the way, there remained the general behavior of the army.

Ever since 1920, military circles in Germany had been engaged in a circumvention of the disarmament provisions through the utilization of training grounds and production facilities in the Soviet Union. Camouflaged front organizations had been established to facilitate these clandestine operations. Stresemann had been aware of some of these activities since 1923, if not earlier. At the time of his ascent to the chancellorship he had been informed that a certain sum of money had to be paid to the Soviet Union for ammunition and for military equipment. He had agreed, at the time, to live up to the obligations contracted by the previous government with the understanding that the illicit transactions were to be terminated as soon as possible. However, the army contrived instead to expand the scope of the operations, attempting at the same time to implicate the foreign office. It was alleged that the foreign office had been in agreement all along and that nothing was being done without its knowledge and approval. Stresemann denied these allegations vigorously and repeatedly.[19] His relationship with the army was further strained when he was informed that the *Reichswehr* ministry was tapping his telephone line and that copies of all incoming and outgoing foreign office communications were received by military intelligence.[20] Under these circumstances, it became increasingly difficult for him to pursue his policy objectives independent from the influential *Reichswehr*. Yet, exercising the utmost caution, he succeeded in remaining aloof from the entire conspiracy.[21] There is no doubt that he was well aware of the Soviet government's long-range plans and aspirations and that he did not wish to endanger his foreign policy in the vain pursuit of conspiratorial schemes in the company of professional revolutionaries.

IV. *The League Phase.* The December meeting of the League Council produced the agreement on dissolution of the Inter-Allied Military Commission of Control.[22] While the Socialists, at home, publicized the army's violations of the disarmament provisions of the peace treaty, Stresemann succeeded in reaching a satisfactory solution of the question at Geneva. Two days before Philipp Scheidemann, Socialist leader, revealed the army's secret plans and operations to the public, the German foreign minister was able to announce that the Control Commission was to be withdrawn on January 31, 1927.[23] The agreement of greatest political and diplomatic significance, however, was the stipulation that as soon as the Allies relinquished their control over Germany's armament, the League was to take over. This was in accordance with Article 213 of the treaty.

Having achieved the withdrawal of the Allied control organs and the transfer of investigatory powers to the Council of the League of Nations, Stresemann had successfully revised the substance, if not the letter, of the disarmament clauses of the Treaty of Versailles. He could rightfully say, on December 20, 1926, that the agreement signified universal recognition of German contentions that the disarmament process had been concluded, and that the need for control organs had therefore been obviated.[24] As far as the investigatory powers of the League Council were concerned, Stresemann had no fears.

Few, if any, of the member nations would risk losing the friendship of Germany in the Council or elsewhere in the League by casting their votes in favor of continued investigatory expeditions into Germany. Simultaneous with the agreement on the Control Commission, the League launched the Preparatory Commission for the Disarmament Conference, which Stresemann hoped to utilize toward further revision of Germany's armament status.

The year 1927, while seeing no substantial changes or revisions in the armament picture, witnessed nevertheless what might be called the quiet burial of controls and investigatory rights. By May, Von Seeckt was back in unofficial government service and was attached, in an advisory capacity, to the president and the foreign minister. It is very significant to note Von Seeckt's comments on his first encounter with the foreign minister following his re-employment: "Stresemann was most cordial and I shall try, of course, to get along with him in the foreign office, *in the interest of the cause*."[25] This remark would tend to further discount suspicions that Stresemann was a coconspirator in the illegal activities of the army.

With the direct threat of Allied or League investigations of the German armament industry and the military establishment safely warded off, Stresemann turned more and more to the question of universal disarmament. He knew of the secret rearmament conducted by the army and was well aware of the armament capacity of German industry. There was hope, however, if his campaign for universal disarmament succeeded, that the German public could be persuaded to embrace international conciliation, and that the nationalists would lose ground in Germany. With that objective in mind, he proceeded to hammer away at the hypothesis of German disarmament, namely, that the rest of the world would disarm to the same extent as Germany. Appealing to international morality and pointing out that morality and the desire for security should be more closely linked together than had been the case in European international relations, he declared himself as being in favor of a general declaration "to abjure all that leads to violence."[26] This was in anticipation of the Kellogg-Briand Pact. The desire for security, justified as it was, was not necessarily met by increased armaments. Germany's state of armament, he declared, had placed her in a position where she could well afford the complete removal of force from international relations.[27] Germany could achieve her diplomatic objectives without recourse to force, provided that the Versailles powers reciprocated and reduced their armaments to a level approximating that of Germany.[28]

While Stresemann was impressing the League of Nations and the world with Germany's peaceful intentions and was maintaining that Germany had been "completely" disarmed, the situation concerning the army's secret machinations had not improved. The German government, on October 18, 1928, had been informed by Admiral Raeder, chief of the naval high command, and by General Heye, chief of the army command, that secret measures designed to circumvent the disarmament clauses of the peace treaty had continued in many respects.[29] At that time, General Gröner, minister of the armed forces, aware of the implications of the events of 1926, had decided to present the entire matter to the rest of the Müller-Severing-Stresemann Cabinet. After a full account of the state of the armed forces had been given by the responsible officers, the government absolved the minister of all responsibility, and declared itself ready to face the consequences whatever they would turn out to be.[30] It cannot be established with certainty whether or not Stresemann attended this meeting.[31]

Whether Stresemann was directly involved in the violations and breaches of the peace treaty or not, and recently uncovered evidence would indicate that he was not, it is clear that he emphasized universal disarmament rather than increased reliance upon Germany's own potential strength. The nationalists, of course, evidently aware of the growing strength of the German legal and illegal armies, demanded that the "army-in-being" concept be applied to German foreign policy. In reply to that argument, Stresemann stated that his policy, designed to achieve universal disarmament, was the only policy which Germany could follow. Under general disarmament the demands of one's opponents could be resisted far more effectively and one's own demands could be prosecuted more successfully than would be the case if Germany, whatever her state of armament, were facing a united world, well armed and determined to resist her revisionist demands.[32]

The final move in the disarmament question, as far as Stresemann's endeavors were concerned, came with the negotiations on the revision of the Dawes Plan in the course of the discussions on the Young Plan. The French position was that the existing controls of Germany's military potential through the League of Nations were insufficient. Briand considered it necessary to establish a special organ which was to be called the Committee of Verification and Conciliation. Stresemann countered that the combination of Article 213 of the Treaty of Versailles and the conciliation commission to be established under the treaties of arbitration concluded at Locarno were entirely sufficient to guarantee German observance of the disarmament provisions of the peace treaty.[33] He was opposed to the introduction of new controls because it had become all too evident that the old ones had lent considerable force to the nationalist argument that Germany was being "governed" by the Allies.

Stresemann would have given his consent to the Briand solution provided that the unpleasant consequences of additional controls would be balanced by some notable concessions by the Allies. If he had to return to Germany with additional controls as the only positive result of his trip to The Hague, he would find it very difficult to maintain himself against the inevitable nationalist onslaught. To avoid adverse domestic reaction at home, the Allies would have to make a conciliatory gesture having the magnitude of a total evacuation of all occupied territories.

In the end, he secured the desired evacuation of the Rhineland without additional controls. On September 11, 1929, he was able to announce to the press that the idea of a new control commission was dead, and that the machinery set up at Locarno remained the only means by which the Allies could hold Germany responsible and by which complaints against Germany could be aired.[34]

When Gustav Stresemann appeared before the League Assembly for the last time in his life, on September 9, 1929, he could truthfully say that the disarmament clauses of the Treaty of Versailles had been modified for all practical purposes. To be sure, there had been no formal revision; the pertinent clauses of the peace treaty had not been changed. However, of all the controls provided for in the treaty, only the investigatory powers of the Council of the League of Nations remained. By virtue of her return to the position of an equal power, Germany could prevent the Council from exercising its prerogatives. While the principle of unanimity did not necessarily apply if the Council wished to investigate the state of the German army or to inspect armament facilities, it stood to reason that no majority could be marshaled in support of an investigation into the domestic affairs of a League member, and of a powerful and influential one at that. As far as the arbitration machinery set up at Locarno was concerned, there could hardly be any disputes submitted if there was no effective way to discover violations. Thus, all that was necessary for Germany was to avoid flagrant violations which would be clearly recognizable. From the tenor and contents of his last address before the League, it was clear that Stresemann, had he been permitted to live, would have concentrated on the theme of universal disarmament, permitting the disarmament clauses of the peace treaty to remain dead letters.[35]

Stresemann was dissatisfied with German disarmament for a number of reasons. Immediately following the war, he expressed fears that a disarmed Germany might fall prey to Communist insurrections or invasion by Soviet-supported revolutionary bands. To impress the Allies with the need for partial rearmament, or at least a strengthening of the militia or police forces, he repeatedly warned against a general inundation of European defenses by the "bolshevik flood." In the same vein, he stressed the need for armament to back up German neutrality in the event that the Soviets should try to win her over to their side under pressure. Coupled with the matter of border and internal security, Stresemann also desired some degree of rearmament in order to gain a more effective backing for German foreign policy in general. He considered this necessary as long as the Versailles powers showed no inclination to fulfill their obligations toward the advancement of universal disarmament.

His diplomatic strategy concerning the revision of the disarmament clauses of the Treaty of Versailles was as follows. He recognized that the sanction clauses of the League Covenant could quite conceivably be applied against the Soviet Union. In that event, the Western Allies could not readily undertake effective military action without the utilization of German soil. On that basis, he demanded that Germany be rearmed before she be expected to subscribe—in advance—to the principle of collective action against aggressor states, i.e., before she declared herself willing to permit Allied troops to march through Germany. His point was this: Germany could not subscribe to the sanction obligations unless she was assured effective protection against possible retaliatory measures by the presumed aggressor. Anticipating the Allied argument to the effect that Allied troops would furnish the desired protection, he stated categorically that Allied troops were no effective guaranty. Only German troops guarding Germany's eastern frontier in strength would be considered as sufficient protection; and the restricted military force of 100,000 men, as prescribed in the treaty, was barely enough to quell internal riots to be expected if the collective action was directed against the Soviet Union.

The main point of attack against armament restrictions was the matter of inter-Allied controls. The first step in Stresemann's revisionist strategy, as far as concrete modifications of the peace arrangement were concerned, was the transfer of controls and investigatory rights from Allied organs to the League of Nations before the assigned tasks of the several Allied commissions had been completed. While this was only a modification within the general framework of the Treaty of Versailles, it actually amounted to a *de facto* revision, since the control powers of the League were never put into force as far as Germany was concerned. The available evidence points to the conclusion that he sought to weaken the control and inspection phase of the disarmament clauses for the following reasons: (1) foreign controls over Germany's military establishment tended to strengthen the Nationalist forces at home; (2) since the Allies, although obliged to do so, had shown no intention to proceed with universal disarmament, Germany would be in a more favorable diplomatic bargaining position if the Allies—and especially Poland—had no effective way to ascertain the true state of Germany's military potential.

The available evidence also points to the conclusion that Stresemann, while doing everything to weaken and to remove Allied and League controls, was not directly involved in the actual rearmament of Germany by clandestine means. However, it stands to reason that he was not displeased with the efforts to give Germany better military protection. As long as universal disarmament had not become a fact, his views of the bases for the conduct of international relations and power politics led him to support the concept of an "army-in-being." In the last analysis, however, Stresemann was too convinced of Germany's economic potential to rely exclusively upon armed force as a means to achieve foreign policy objectives. To the contrary, when the machinations of the German army became too brazen, he attempted to put an end to its illegal activities.

SUMMARY AND CONCLUSION

Gustav Stresemann became foreign minister of a country which had lost a major war and which had subsequently been subjected to one of the most far-reaching peace settlements of all times. Partly because of his own political background, partly as a result of political pressure at home, and for economic reasons, he dedicated his ministerial career to the revision of certain parts of the Treaty of Versailles. Circumstances forced him to operate under most adverse conditions. At war's end, Germany was an outcast and was surrounded by hostile nations intent upon preventing a too rapid military, economic, and political recovery of the vanquished land. By force of necessity, a German foreign policy had to be peaceful, bare of all reference to the use of arms. On the other hand, the peace settlement had created enough dissatisfaction among the German masses to render a rational and moderate foreign policy highly impractical from the point of view of domestic politics.

In spite of his monarchistic background, Stresemann accepted the Weimar Republic in principle and remained faithful to its constitution. As a parliamentarian of long standing he was neither dismayed nor discouraged by the comparatively more complex nature of politics and the conduct of foreign policy in a democratic frame of reference. Preferring to follow British practice in the conduct of foreign policy, he nevertheless bowed to the demands of a republican form of government. His parliamentary experience permitted him to engage in compromises with the several political parties without losing sight of his over-all objectives. Of greatest importance, however, was the fact that he combined parliamentary experience and a firm grasp of the essentials of statecraft with the role of leadership in a strategically placed political party. In spite of all domestic difficulties, Stresemann succeeded in securing majority support for his policy in a politically divided parliament, which was constantly in need of forming coalitions. Although his own party, the German People's Party, was relatively small, and even though it was itself badly divided, Stresemann never permitted the larger parties to relegate it to the political side lines. At all times between 1923 and 1929, and by virtue of the strategic position into which Stresemann had maneuvered his party, he remained virtually indispensable to the formation of workable government coalitions. But it was not only his expert use of parliamentary tactics which permitted him to weather constant political storms. Addressing himself to the existence of a strong Socialist movement in Germany and an equally strong Nationalist bloc, he carefully avoided being drawn into purely domestic conflicts between the two extremes. Instead, he confined himself to the propagation of foreign policy issues, seeking all the time to make his foreign policy palatable to both, the Left and the Right. Whatever the foreign policy issue was, Stresemann knew how to present it to the people. He did this at one time in a manner which pleased the Left; at another, in almost the same words which the militant Nationalists used to attack him. When it came to the vote in the Reichstag, it always seemed that neither the Left nor the Right could well afford to cause the defeat of foreign policy measures proposed by the foreign minister.

In recognition of the adverse circumstances confronting postwar Germany, he based his over-all diplomatic strategy upon these premises: (1) the exploitation of any evidence of Allied disunity; (2) the utilization of any conflicts between East and West; (3) the utilization of Germany's economic potential.

Stresemann's foreign policy was almost exclusively concerned with the revision or modification of the Treaty of Versailles. Because this treaty had become an inseparable part of the new legal and political order in postwar Europe, he soon realized that an attack upon the treaty could only succeed if it was conducted in a piecemeal fashion. The pattern which he applied in his revisionist efforts, through the years, may be summarized as follows:

1. In the beginning, a propaganda attack was launched against the legal, political, and moral concepts upon which the peace settlement was based. His technique consisted of repeated critical references to the war record and the motives of the Allied Powers. Instead of criticizing the treaty, he criticized its origins, its background, and its foundation. The war guilt question played a considerable role in this respect. Even though he had to exercise some restraint in the raising of this delicate question in an official manner, Stresemann left no doubt concerning his views on the matter. His occasional diplomatic sorties against the war guilt accusation had the purpose of weakening the Allied case against Germany. In principle, it was immaterial to Stresemann whether the Allies repudiated the accusation in a formal manner, or whether a repudiation would come about

gradually and imperceptibly as a result of Germany's propaganda campaign.

2. As far as specific provisions of the treaty were concerned, Stresemann's revisionism addressed itself, in the first instance, to the penal clauses of the Treaty of Versailles. He believed that if the penal clauses could be rendered ineffective by diplomatic action, a major obstacle to further revision would be eliminated. If the Allies were unable to punish Germany for nonfulfillment of her treaty obligations because the power to apply military sanctions had been wrested from their hands, Germany's bargaining position would be considerably enhanced. The attack upon the penal clauses was executed in two stages: first, Stresemann worked for the removal of foreign troops from German soil, and second, he sought to prevent, by diplomatic action, the future application of military sanctions by the Allies. This diplomatic campaign centered on the arguments that sanctions tended to disrupt the economies of Germany and of Europe in general, and that they were detrimental to the cause of peace and collective security. The most effective diplomatic success was won when, at Locarno, the principle of the inviolability of Germany's western boundaries became an accepted principle of European politics. From then on, the Allies had, if not in a legal sense, then at least in a practical, political sense, surrendered the weapon needed to enforce fulfillment of the treaty terms by Germany. What Stresemann preferred to call the "Spirit of Locarno," was in reality the end of sanctions. All that remained to be done was the total evacuation of foreign troops still on German soil.

3. The phase of Stresemann's policy designed to achieve territorial revisions of the treaty was governed by the following considerations: Stresemann's sanction policy required that Germany, as well as the Allies, accept the principle of the inviolability of western boundaries. Once the Western Allies were convinced that he entertained no serious thoughts on the revision of the western boundaries—with the exception of the Saar question—he could hope to proceed with a policy designed to achieve changes in the East. The fact that close ties existed between France and Poland, played a considerable role in this reasoning. A France reassured of Germany's peaceful intentions toward her was less likely to object to boundary changes in the East. The strategy followed with regard to territorial revision in the East followed these lines: (a) Stresemann categorically refused to recognize the finality of the territorial boundary settlement. The concept *rebus sic stantibus*, of dynamic change in international relations, was consistently applied by him in support of territorial claims. While

the principle of peaceful change was applied to the Western situation, i.e., to Eupen-Malmédy and the Saar, in a limited sense only, it was vigorously asserted with regard to the Polish-German frontier settlement. (b) A corollary of the assertion that no treaty settlement could be final—and because this was so, change could not be arbitrarily delayed or prevented—was a studied refusal to recognize the finality of the German-Polish frontier in any formal manner above and beyond the initial signature of the Treaty of Versailles. (c) There were two alternate methods used to advance territorial revisionism. First, Stresemann attempted to make boundary changes and to achieve the return of lost territories by direct negotiations with the countries concerned. When this failed, he resorted to the League of Nations. The balance of power, heavily weighted against Germany in ordinary European politics, was somewhat different in the framework of international organization. Here, Germany was not alone. Moreover, in the League, the treaty was only one of many problems, while in ordinary Franco-German relations, for example, the peace settlement was the sole governing instrument. As it became more and more evident to Stresemann that the balance of power in European politics was definitely and unalterably in favor of the status quo powers, his faith in the utilitarian functions of the League grew in direct proportion. However, the extent to which the League could advance the cause of revisionism spelled the limits of Stresemann's adherence to the basic principles upon which that international organization was based.

4. As it became increasingly clear that the prevailing international situation did not favor boundary changes, Stresemann placed more and more weight upon the minority question. Future territorial revision was to be assured by the promotion of irredentism in the countries contiguous to Germany. Stresemann's minority policy consisted of the following strategic elements: (a) Germany was to play the role of a guardian of the rights of German minorities in states which had been singled out as targets for territorial revisionism. (b) Because the minority question and the League Covenant were closely related to one another, Germany was to join the League, and was to secure a position of influence which would permit the pursuit of an aggressive minority policy. (c) Germany was to make certain that irredentism was kept alive, and that world public opinion was constantly aware of the problems created by the peace settlement in that regard. (d) In view of the ultimate purposes of his minority policy, Stresemann resisted all attempts by the status quo powers to have the minority question considered as though it were a temporary,

domestic problem. Instead he fought to have it considered as an international question—a situation threatening the peace—and as a question which could only be solved if the areas concerned would be returned to Germany. There was to be no "absorption" or "assimilation" of the minorities.

5. The success or failure of Stresemann's revisionism, although peaceful in its inception, was necessarily dependent upon an equalization of armaments among the European powers, i.e., among the protagonists in the struggle for revision. As long as Germany was unilaterally disarmed, her foreign policy was bound to be ineffective, and greater objectives were unlikely to be attained. For that reason, Stresemann insisted upon a redemption of Allied pledges to proceed with universal disarmament as implied in the preamble to the disarmament clauses. As long as the Allies showed no inclination to redeem their pledges, however, he demanded a limited rearmament of Germany. He advanced two major arguments in favor of rearmament: (a) a disarmed Germany was incapable of defending herself, and Europe, against Russian Communism; (b) Germany could not be expected to participate in League action under the sanction clauses unless she was permitted to strengthen her armed forces. The substitution of Allied troops for German contingents was rejected. To create the basis for a conditional rearmament of Germany, which was to be limited, to be sure, Stresemann endeavored to remove all vestiges of inter-Allied control over Germany's military establishment and over her armament industry. In this respect, he was eminently successful.

It can be said that the fate of Stresemann's revisionism depended among other things upon the extent to which he could weaken the arguments advanced by the nationalists by pointing to foreign policy successes. He wished to attain a minimum of revision only. If the Allies would have granted him some visible concessions, they would have found him more conciliatory on other matters. His failure to obtain the desired concessions in time permitted the nationalist opposition to swell to the point where pacifism and democracy were swept aside. If Stresemann appeared to be belligerent at times, it was primarily because it was necessary to appease the extremists at home. Stresemann's hesitation to alienate the Allies by unnecessary insistence upon repudiation of the war guilt clause, his readiness to renounce Alsace-Lorraine and Eupen-Malmédy, his failure to pursue the matter of the Austrian *Anschluss*, and the abstention from any interference in the affairs of Czechoslovakia over the Sudeten-German question, would indicate that he would have been content with limited concessions.

The over-all pattern of Stresemann's revisionism may be summarized as follows: 1. He commenced with an attack against the legal, political, and moral premises upon which the peace settlement was based. This attack accompanied diplomatic actions throughout the campaign. 2. Next, he concentrated on the task of weakening the penal clauses of the peace treaty. 3. With varying degrees of intensity, Stresemann then proceeded to work for the return of lost territories and for an advance of the date when the Saar was to be returned to Germany. 4. Failing in the attempted territorial revisions, he placed ever increasing emphasis upon the promotion of irredentism. 5. In order to enhance Germany's diplomatic bargaining power, he sought to obtain an early cessation of Allied controls over Germany's armaments. This, like the propaganda attack upon the treaty, was a continuous effort.

The degree of success in this struggle for revision was not at all in proportion to the efforts invested. Stresemann was successful, however, in creating conditions favorable for future revision. By obtaining limited modifications of the treaty, he succeeded in casting doubt upon the applicability of the doctrine *pacta sunt servanda* as far as the Treaty of Versailles was concerned. At the time of his death, the treaty was no longer the inflexible instrument which it had been at the beginning. By rendering the penal clauses virtually ineffective and by eliminating all effective Allied controls over German armaments, Stresemann had established that the fulfillment of treaty obligations by Germany was no longer to be considered as a foregone conclusion. Furthermore, by transferring the debate over minorities from the sphere of domestic affairs to the diplomatic sphere and thence to the League of Nations, he made certain that the stage was set for the territorial revisions in the East, which he had not been able to obtain in his lifetime.

When Gustav Stresemann was first placed in charge of German foreign policy, defeated Germany was unable to offer anything but passive resistance to the policy of strict enforcement of the peace terms by France and her Allies. The Treaty of Versailles, backed by the combined military might of the victor states, loomed as an insurmountable barrier preventing a return of Germany to a position of power and equality. When Stresemann left the political scene, Germany was once again an equal member of the community of nations, and the Treaty of Versailles was but a hollow shell.

Stresemann had proven that a militarily weak and defeated nation could arise from under a severe peace settlement without resorting to armed force. The pattern which he followed in his revisionism may be considered his primary contribution to international politics and diplomacy. As for the charge that his policies prepared the way for World War II, one might ask: Is it reasonable to evaluate a foreign policy in terms of subsequent developments which cannot be linked to it either by reliable documentary evidence or by logical inference? There is little need to contest the observation that Stresemann was an astute politician as well as a highly skilled diplomat. It would likewise be idle to deny that Stresemann wished to see Germany rise again to a position of power and influence. It is denied, however, that Stresemann had the slightest intention of resorting to force in order to achieve his revisionist objectives. Gustav Streseman died in a fight against the then existing international order. But his was a fight for reason.

APPENDIXES

APPENDIX A

FUNDS AVAILABLE TO THE FOREIGN OFFICE FOR PRESS AND PUBLIC
RELATIONS FOR THE YEAR 1927*

Budget Item	Sum Appropriated (in Reichsmarks)
Advancement of the German news service abroad†	2,760,000
Advancement of the German news service at home†	446,000
Commercial news service abroad	500,000
Secret expenditures‡	7,000,000
Advancement of cultural, humanitarian, and scientific relations to foreign countries	6,000,000
Support and assistance for Germans abro. ‡†	1,330,000
Total	18,036,000
Total government expenditures for 1927	62,507,440

* Source: Reichshaushaltsplan für das Jahr, 1928; *Reichstag, Anlagen*, 1928, Bd. 433, No. 697.

† The sum was transferable and at the exclusive disposal of the foreign minister.

‡ The expenditures were not subject to the ordinary auditing processes of the Court of Accounts.

APPENDIX B

FUNDS AVAILABLE TO THE FOREIGN OFFICE FOR PRESS AND PUBLIC
RELATIONS FOR THE YEAR 1928*

Budget Item	Sum Appropriated (in Reichsmarks)
Advancement of the German news service abroad†	2,400,000
Advancement of the German news service at home†	416,000
Commercial news service abroad	500,000
Secret expenditures‡	6,000,000
Advancement of cultural, humanitarian, and scientific relations to foreign countries†	6,000,000
Advancement of German schools abroad†	2,600,000
Support and assistance for Germans abroad†	2,300,000
Total	20,216,000
Total government expenditures for 1928..............	64,507,900

* Source: Reichshaushaltsplan für das Jahr, 1928; *Reichstag, Anlagen,* 1928, Bd. 433, No. 697.

† The sum was transferable and at the exclusive disposal of the foreign minister.

‡ The expenditures were not subject to the ordinary auditing processes of the Court of Accounts.

APPENDIX C

FUNDS AVAILABLE TO THE FOREIGN OFFICE FOR PRESS AND PUBLIC
RELATIONS FOR THE YEAR 1929*

Budget Item	Sum Appropriated (in Reichsmarks)
Joint press department of the Reichschancellery and the foreign office	3,644,200
Advancement of the German news service abroad†	2,650,000
Advancement of the German news service at home†	3,066,000
Commercial news service abroad	450,000
Secret expenditures‡	6,000,000
Advancement of cultural, humanitarian, and scientific relations with foreign countries	4,700,000
Advancement of German schools abroad†	3,550,000
Support and assistance for Germans abroad	2,000,000
Total	26,060,200
Total government expenditures for 1929	68,812,000

* Source: Reichshaushaltsplan für das Jahr, 1929; *Reichstag, Anlagen,* 1928, Bd. 434, II.

† The sum was transferable and at the exclusive disposal of the foreign minister.

‡ The expenditures were not subject to the ordinary auditing processes of the Court of Accounts.

APPENDIX D

CRITICAL VOTES ON FOREIGN POLICY ISSUES IN THE GERMAN REICHSTAG FROM 1923 TO 1929*

Date	Issue	Government Parties†	DVP Strength in Terms of Total Reichstag Membership	Government Majority in Terms of Total Reichstag Membership		Opposition Vote, Including Abstentions	Major Parties Supporting the Government†	Major Parties Opposing the Government†
V, 14, '23	Vote of confidence in the Stresemann cabinet	DVP SPD DDP Z	13.9%	239	52.0%	101	DVP SPD DDP Z	DNVP BVP
XI, 23, '23	No-confidence vote against Stresemann cabinet	DVP SPD DDP Z	13.9%	156	50.3%	231	DVP DDP Z	SPD DNVP BVP
VIII, 29, '24	Vote on the Dawes Plan (Railway Act)	DVP DDP Z DNVP (1)	9.2%	311	65.3%	127	DVP DNVP SPD	DNVP KPD BVP
XI, 27, '25	Final vote on Locarno treaties and Germany's entry into League of Nations	DVP DNVP DDP Z	10.1%	292	59.0%	177	DVP SPD DDP BVP Z	DNVP NSDAP BVP KPD

III, 23, '26	No-confidence vote over failure to enter League of Nations	DVP DDP Z	10.1%	260	52.8%	141	DVP SPD Z DDP	DNVP NSDAP KPD
XI, 20, '28	No-confidence vote against Stresemann	DVP SPD DDP Z	8.7%	216	43.0%	100	DVP SPD DDP BVP Z	DNVP NSDAP KPD
II, 6, '29	Vote on the Kellogg Peace Pact	DVP SPD DDP Z	8.7%	288	58.6%	127	DVP SPD DDP BVP	DNVP NSDAP KPD

* Source: *Reichstag, Verhandlungen,* 1923–29, Bd. 361–426.
† Abbreviations:
BVP = Bavarian People's Party.
DVP = German People's Party.
DDP = German Democratic Party.
DNVP = German National People's Party.
KPD = Communist Party of Germany.
NSDAP = National-Socialist Workers' Party of Germany.
SPD = Social-Democratic Party of Germany.
Z = Center Party.

APPENDIX E

DISTRIBUTION OF INDUSTRIALISTS AND PARLIAMENTARIANS CLOSELY
ASSOCIATED WITH INDUSTRY IN THE GERMAN REICHSTAG
AND PRUSSIAN LANDTAG, 1928*

Parties	Reichstag		Landtag	
	A†	B‡	A†	B‡
German People's Party	15	8	4	7
German National People's Party.........	9	9	3	7
Center Party	3	6	4	8
German Democratic Party	8	3	1	8
Bavarian People's Party	1	1	..	..
Economic Party	1	12	1	10

* Source: *Mitteilungen der Vereinigung der Deutschen Arbeitgeberverbände,* July 31, 1928, as reprinted in Richard Lewinsohn (Morus), *Das Geld in der Politik* (Berlin: S. Fischer Verlag, 1930), p. 93.
† Deputies close to industry.
‡ Deputies, close, in a wider sense.

NOTES

NOTES

A few select works, frequently cited throughout the study, or in several chapters, have been abbreviated and are cited as follows:

D'Abernon
> D'Abernon, Viscount Edgar Vincent. *An Ambassador of Peace: Pages from the Diary of Viscount D'Abernon* (Berlin: 1920–26). 3 vols. London: Hodder and Stoughton, Ltd., 1929–30.

Die Ursachen des Deutschen Zusammenbruchs
> Germany, Reichstag. *Das Werk des Untersuchungsausschusses der Verfassunggebenden Deutschen Nationalversammlung und des Deutschen Reichstags, 1919–1928: Die Ursachen des Deutschen Zusammenbruchs im Jahre 1918.* Vierte Reihe, Vols. VI, VII (Parts 1 and 2), and VIII. Siebente Reihe, Vol. II. Berlin: Deutsche Verlagsgesellschaft für Politik und Geschichte, G.m.b.H., 1928.

Nachlass
> Germany, Auswärtiges Amt, Politisches Archiv. *Nachlass des Reichsministers Dr. Gustav Stresemann.* Microfilm. German War Documents Project. National Archives. Washington, D.C.

Nationalversammlung, Verhandlungen
> Germany, Verfassunggebende Deutsche Nationalversammlung. *Verhandlungen der Verfassunggebenden Deutschen Nationalversammlung, Stenographische Berichte und Anlagen zu den Stenographischen Berichten.* Vols. 326–43 (February 6, 1919—May 1920). Berlin: Norddeutsche Buchdruckerei-Anstalt, 1920–21.

Reden und Schriften
> Stresemann, Gustav. *Reden und Schriften: Politik, Geschichte, Literatur, 1897–1926.* 2 vols. Dresden: Carl Reissner Verlag, 1926.

Reichstag, Verhandlungen
> Germany, Reichstag. *Verhandlungen des Reichstags, Stenographische Berichte und Anlagen zu den Stenographischen Berichten.* Vols. 344–430 (June 1920–July 1930). Berlin: Reichsdruckerei, 1920–30.

United States, Foreign Relations
> United States, Department of State. *Papers Relating to the Foreign Relations of the United States* (1919–29). Washington: Government Printing Office, 1938–43.

Vermächtnis
> Bernhard, Henry (ed.). *Gustav Stresemann; Vermächtnis: Der Nachlass in drei Bänden.* 3 vols. Berlin: Verlag Ullstein, 1932.

Versailles and After
    United States, Department of State. *The Treaty of Versailles and After,
    Annotations of the Text of the Treaty.* Washington: Government
    Printing Office, 1947. Pp. xiv + 1018.

CHAPTER I

[1] For the best biographies on Gustav Stresemann, see Dr. Heinrich Bauer, *Stresemann: Ein Deutscher Staatsmann* (Berlin: Georg Stilke, 1930); Walter Görlitz, *Gustav Stresemann* (Heidelberg: Ähren Verlag, 1947); Rudolf Olden, *Stresemann* (New York: E. P. Dutton & Co., Inc., 1930); Baron Rochus von Rheinbaben, *Stresemann, The Man and the Statesman* (New York: D. Appleton and Co., 1929); Edgar Stern-Rubarth, *Three Men Tried . . . Austen Chamberlain, Stresemann, and Briand and Their Fight for a New Europe* (London: Duckworth, 1939); Antonina Vallentin, *Stresemann* (London: Constable and Co., Ltd., 1931).

[2] See Ralph H. Lutz, *The Causes of the German Collapse in 1918* (Stanford: Stanford University Press, 1934), pp. 8–11; and Lutz, *Fall of the German Empire, 1914–1918* (Stanford: Stanford University Press, 1932), I, 305.

[3] See *Handbuch des Alldeutschen Verbandes* (14 ed. München: Verlag J. F. Lehmann, 1915), chap. VI. A brief summary of the activities of the Pan-German League is given in S. Grumbach, *Das Annexionistische Deutschland* (Lausanne: Verlag Payot and Co., 1919), pp. 123–32. For selected war aims of political parties in Germany see Lutz, *Fall of the German Empire*, pp. 305–91.

[4] Ludwig Stein, *Aus dem Leben eines Optimisten* (Berlin: Brückenverlag, 1930), pp. 225 ff.

[5] Lutz, *Causes of the German Collapse*, p. 218.

[6] *Die Ursachen des Deutschen Zusammenbruchs, 7.* Reihe, II, 220.

[7] *Ibid.,* 4. Reihe, VIII, Part II, 303–4.

[8] Lutz, *Causes of the German Collapse*, p. 192.

[9] Konrad Hausmann, *Schlaglichter* (Frankfurt: Frankfurter Sozietätsdruckerei, 1924), p. 231.

[10] *Die Entstehung der Deutschen Volkspartei* (Berlin: Staatspolitischer Verlag, G.m.b.H., 1920), p. 8.

[11] Accounts of the merger negotiations may be found in: *Die Entstehung der DVP,* p. 8, and A. Kempkes (ed.), *Deutscher Aufbau* (Berlin: Staatspolitischer Verlag, G.m.b.H., 1927), pp. 7–15. The negotiations considered from the point of view of an erstwhile opponent of Stresemann may be found in Theodor Wolff, *Through Two Decades* (London: William Heinemann, Ltd., 1936), pp. 142–43. See also Hermann Pachnicke, *Führende Männer im Alten und im Neuen Reich* (Berlin: Reimar Hobbing, 1930), pp. 196 ff.

[12] Dr. Eugen Leidig in *Deutsche Stimmen,* 31. Jhrg. (February 23, 1919), pp. 117–20.

[13] *Reichstag, Verhandlungen,* Bd. 344 (July 3, 1920), 184.

[14] See Appendix D.

[15] See *Vermächtnis,* I, 75.

[16] Reference is made to Lord Edgar Vincent D'Abernon, British Ambassador to Germany from 1920 to 1926. For the ambassador's appraisal of Stresemann, see *D'Abernon,* I, 177.

[17] *Reichstag, Verhandlungen,* Bd. 361 (November 23, 1923), 12294. Also, *Vermächtnis,* I, 245.

CHAPTER II

[1] Herbert von Dirksen, *Moskau, Tokio, London* (Stuttgart: W. Kohlhammer Verlag, 1949), p. 57.

[2] Antonina Vallentin, *Stresemann,* pp. 158–59.

[3] See Paul Schmidt, *Statist Auf Diplomatischer Bühne, 1923–1945* (Bonn: Athenaeum Verlag, 1949), pp. 56 and 61.

[4] See Edgar Stern-Rubarth, *Three Men Tried . . . Austen Chamberlain, Stresemann, and Briand and Their Fight for a New Europe.*

[5] Vallentin, *op. cit.,* p. 220.

[6] Eric Sutton (ed.), *Gustav Stresemann* (New York: The Macmillan Co., 1935), III, 179.

[7] *Ibid.,* p. 500.

CHAPTER III

[1] Gustav Stresemann, *Warum Müssen Wir Durchhalten* (Berlin: Kriegspresseamt, 1917), p. 25. See also the following books by Stresemann: *Deutsches Ringen, Deutsches Hoffen* (Berlin: Reichsverlag Hermann Kalkoff, 1914); *Das Deutsche Wirtschaftsleben im Kriege* (Leipzig: S. Hirzel, 1915); *Michel Horch, der Seewind Pfeift* (Berlin: Hermann Kalkoff, 1916); *Industrie und Krieg* (Berlin: Selbstverlag des Bundes der Industriellen, 1916); *Deutsche Gegenwart und Zukunft* (Stuttgart: Julius Hoffmann, 1917); and *Macht und Freiheit* (Halle: Carl Marhold, 1918).

[2] Stresemann, *Warum Müssen Wir Durchhalten,* p. 25.

[3] *Ibid.* For a representative exposition of German war aims, see Ralph H. Lutz, *Fall of the German Empire, 1914–1918,* Vol. I, chap. VII.

[4] Stresemann, *Warum Müssen Wir Durchhalten,* p. 27. Also, *Deutsche Stimmen,* 29. Jhrg. (January 10, 1917), p. 718.

[5] Stresemann, *op. cit.,* pp. 17–18.

[6] *Ibid.,* p. 6. In an article written on July 25, 1917, he denied ever having speculated on the duration of Great Britain's resistance. Stresemann, "Gedanken zur Krise," *Deutsche Stimmen,* 29. Jhrg. (July 1917), p. 422.

[7] See Stresemann, *Michel Horch* and *Macht und Freiheit,* pp. 21 ff.

[8] *Die Ursachen des Deutschen Zusammenbruchs,* 4. Reihe, VIII, 299 and 305, and VII, Part II, 309. At the outset of the war, Stresemann had envisaged a Greater Germany, from Kronstadt in the Baltic to the British Channel: "The possession of the continental coast means nothing else but the opportunity to develop one's strength across the seas and in the final analysis it means the

opportunity to extend continental politics into the world arena." Stresemann, *Michel Horch*, p. 19. Freedom of the seas for Germany's merchant marine was another of his war aims. See Dr. Paul Luther, *Stresemann Buch* (Berlin: Staatspolitischer Verlag, G.m.b.H., 1923), p. 47. For reasons of political strategy, to create a favorable basis for eventual peace talks, he proposed further that Germany hold on to Alsace-Lorraine, Poland, and Belgium. January 30, 1918, *Deutsche Stimmen*, 30. Jhrg. (February 3, 1918), p. 78.

[9] February 20, 1918, *Deutsche Stimmen*, 30. Jhrg. (February 24, 1918), p. 126. See also *Die Ursachen des Deutschen Zusammenbruchs*, 4. Reihe, VIII, 336; March 10, 1918, address before the central executive committee of the National-Liberal Party, *Deutscher Geschichtskalender*, VIII (January–March 1918), 519 ff.

[10] March 19, 1918, address before the Reichstag, Lutz, *The Fall of the German Empire*, I, 786.

[11] July 9, 1917, Ausschuss für den Reichshaushalt, *Die Ursachen des Deutschen Zusammenbruchs*, 4. Reihe, VIII, 130.

[12] Stresemann, "Gedanken zur Krise," *Deutsche Stimmen*, 29. Jhrg. (July 25, 1917), p. 430.

[13] Stresemann, *Warum Müssen Wir Durchhalten*, p. 20.

[14] July 16, 1918, *Deutsche Stimmen*, 30. Jhrg. (July 21, 1918), pp. 482–83.

[15] *Deutsche Stimmen*, 30. Jhrg. (August 11, 1918), p. 530; also, *ibid.* (August 25, 1918), p. 561.

[16] *Ibid.* (June 16, 1918), p. 401.

[17] *Die Ursachen des Deutschen Zusammenbruchs*, 7. Reihe, II, 236.

[18] Konrad Hausmann, *Schlaglichter*, p. 231.

[19] Major General Hoffmann wrote in his diary under October 2, 1918: "Hertling and Hintze go, probably some others too, in order to make room for parliamentarians. Chancellor, probably Fehrenbach, Foreign Office—Stresemann." General-Major Max von Hoffmann, *Die Aufzeichnungen des General-Major Max von Hoffmann* (Berlin: Verlag für Kulturpolitik, 1929), I, 213.

[20] Prince Max of Baden, *The Memoirs of Prince Max of Baden* (London: Constable and Co., Ltd., 1928), II, 12; see also Philipp Scheidemann, *The Making of the New Germany: The Memoirs of Philipp Scheidemann* (New York: D. Appleton and Co., 1929), II, 167.

[21] October 10, 1918, Prince Max of Baden, *op. cit.*, p. 73.

[22] October 31, 1918, Stresemann, "Ludendorffs Abschied," *Reden und Schriften*, I, 20.

[23] Stresemann to Friedberg, October 26, 1918, *Vermächtnis*, I, 12–13.

[24] *Reden und Schriften*, I, 215.

[25] *Nationalversammlung, Verhandlungen*, Bd. 326 (February 10, 1919), 167. As late as 1924, Stresemann was not ready to forgive Wilson for 1918 and 1919. On the occasion of the President's death, he ordered the German Ambassador at Washington to express his regrets over the latter's failure to lower the flag but not because of a slight to Wilson's memory but out of respect for the national mourning of the American people. February 6, 1924, *Vermächtnis*, I, 291.

[26] February 22, 1919, address at a rally of the German People's Party, *Deutsche Stimmen*, 30. Jhrg. (March 2, 1919), pp. 137–38.

[27] Stresemann, "Politische Umschau," *Deutsche Stimmen*, 31. Jhrg. (May 4, 1919), pp. 393–94.

[28] *Nationalversammlung, Verhandlungen,* Bd. 327 (May 12, 1919), 1100–1102.

[29] May 14, 1919, *Deutsche Stimmen,* 31. Jhrg. (May 18, 1919), p. 349.

[30] *Ibid.*

[31] *Nationalversammlung, Verhandlungen,* Bd. 327 (June 22, 1919), 1138.

[32] Luther, *op. cit.,* p. 36.

[33] Gustav Stresemann, "Kriegsschuldlüge und Versailler Vertrag," *Reden und Schriften,* I, 333.

[34] Luther, *op. cit.,* pp. 37–38.

[35] Edgar Stern-Rubarth, *Three Men Tried . . . Austen Chamberlain, Stresemann, and Briand and Their Fight for a New Europe,* pp. 276–77.

[36] *Nationalversammlung, Verhandlungen,* Bd. 330 (October 8, 1919), 2917–18.

[37] Stresemann, "Zum Jahrestag der Revolution," *Von der Revolution bis zum Frieden von Versailles* (Berlin: Staatspolitischer Verlag, G.m.b.H., 1919), p. 195.

[38] *Reichstag, Verhandlungen,* Bd. 344 (July 28, 1920), Part II, 311.

[39] December 3, 1920, Stresemann, *Deutsche Volkspartei und Regierungspolitik* (Berlin: Staatspolitischer Verlag, G.m.b.H., 1921), p. 12.

[40] Scheidemann, *op. cit.,* I, 248.

[41] April 6, 1916, Stresemann, *Michel Horch,* p. 100.

[42] Stresemann, *Deutsche Gegenwart und Zukunft,* p. 16.

[43] Article 4 read: "The generally recognized rules of international law are valid as binding portions of the German national law." *Reichsgesetzblatt* (Hrsg. vom Reichsministerium des Innern. Berlin: Verlag des Gesetzsammlungsamts, 1918–1932), 1919, No. 152, p. 1383.

[44] *Nationalversammlung, Verhandlungen,* Bd. 326 (March 4, 1919), 495.

[45] February 19, 1924, *Vermächtnis,* I, 314.

[46] September 12, 1924, *ibid.,* II, 569.

[47] *Ibid.,* pp. 568–69.

[48] Stresemann, *Das Werk von Locarno* (Berlin: Staatspolitischer Verlag, G.m.b.H., 1925), pp. 9–10.

CHAPTER IV

[1] See Ludwig Bergsträsser, *Die Geschichte der Politischen Parteien in Deutschland* (5 ed.; Mannheim: J. Bensheimer, 1928), pp. 191–93.

[2] *Reden und Schriften,* I, 133. It is interesting to note that it was not only the National-Liberal influence which served to formulate Stresemann's concept of the role of parliament in the state, but his thoughts on that subject were also stimulated by such men as Friedrich Naumann, Walther Rathenau, Ludwig Stein, Count Ulrich von Brockdorff-Rantzau, Albert Ballin, Albert Südekum, Otto Hoetzsch, and Georg Bernhard, all of whom belonged with Stresemann to the so-called Wednesday Society. Naumann's influence becomes apparent if one compares Stresemann's wartime speeches and writings on the subject of parliament and state, and parliament versus monarchy, with Naumann's literary efforts. See Friedrich Naumann, *Der Kaiser im Volkstaat* (Berlin: Fort-

schritt, G.m.b.H., 1917), pp. 38–40; also, Ludwig Stein, *Aus dem Leben eines Optimisten,* pp. 255 ff.

[3] See Bergsträsser, *op. cit.,* p. 160.

[4] Prince Max of Baden, *The Memoirs of Prince Max of Baden,* I, 160–61.

[5] Stresemann, *Deutsche Stimmen,* 30. Jhrg. (July 3, 1918), p. 445.

[6] Ralph H. Lutz, *Fall of the German Empire, 1914–1918,* I, 388.

[7] *Die Ursachen des Deutschen Zusammenbruchs,* 4. Reihe, VII, Part I, 11, 63.

[8] The *Nachlass* shows evidence that Stresemann remained a monarchist at heart but was unwilling to endanger the unity of the country in the pursuit of his ideals. One might perhaps call him a Churchillian democrat. *Nachlass,* 7014/H143923 (July 1922), and 7168/H155490 (April 1924).

[9] *Nationalversammlung, Verhandlungen,* Bd. 327 (July 4, 1919), 1291–92.

[10] *Ibid.,* Bd. 328 (July 30, 1919), 2106–7. The German People's Party voted finally against the entire constitution. See Stresemann's account and justification: Deutsche Volkspartei, *Bericht über den Zweiten Parteitag, am 18., 19., und 20. Oktober 1919 im Kristallpalast in Leipzig* (Berlin: Staatspolitischer Verlag, G.m.b.H., 1920), p. 15.

[11] *Reichstag, Verhandlungen,* Bd. 344 (June 30, 1920), 55.

[12] *Ibid.* (July 3, 1920), p. 184.

[13] *Ibid.,* Bd. 348 (March 8, 1921), 2723.

[14] *Ibid.,* Bd. 349 (April 28, 1921), 3463.

[15] *Ibid.* (May 3, 1921), p. 3558.

[16] *Frankfurter Zeitung,* January 7, 1923.

[17] See Freiherr v. Freytag von Loringhoven, *Die Weimarer Verfassung in Lehre und Wirklichkeit* (München, J. F. Lehmann, 1924), p. 70.

[18] May 12, 1921, *D'Abernon,* I, 177.

[19] Viscount D'Abernon, "Stresemann," *Foreign Affairs* (January 1930), VIII, 208–11. Another contemporary observer of the political scene noted that Stresemann was in firm control of the left wing of the People's Party, with Dr. Ernst Scholz controlling the center, and Dr. Reinhold Quaatz, Dr. Alfred Gildemeister, and Dr. Oskar Maretzky in control of the right wing. Since the center faction was personally attached to Stresemann, it was his continuous task to secure the support of that group in order to control the party. Johannes Fischart, "Neue Politikerköpfe," *Die Weltbühne* (October 9, 1924), XX, No. 41, 549. For a representative example of the foreign policy views prevailing in the People's Party at that time, see Freiherr v. Lersner, "Die Revision des Friedens von Versailles," *Deutsche Volkspartei, 3. Parteitag in Nürnberg, 3./4. Dezember, 1920* (Sonderbericht aus der "Nationalliberalen Korrespondenz").

[20] Edgar Stern-Rubarth, *Stresemann der Europäer* (Berlin: Verlag von Reimar Hobbing, 1930), pp. 42–43.

[21] *Frankfurter Zeitung,* November 15, 1924, p. 2.

[22] See Fritz K. Bieligk, *Stresemann, the German Liberal's Policy* (London: Hutchinson and Co., 1943), pp. 29–30. A bitter indictment of Stresemann, but in many respects, and unwittingly, a confirmation of theories presented in this study.

[23] January 18, 1916, Gustav Stresemann, *Michel Horch, der Seewind Pfeift,* pp. 58–59.

[24] *Reichstag, Verhandlungen,* Bd. 344 (July 28, 1926), I, 311.

[25] Stresemann, *Michel Horch*, p. 59.

[26] "Oh, wenn doch die Seele des Deutschen Volkes ein Saitenspiel in der Hand des Auswärtigen Amtes wäre, auf dem es zu spielen verstände." *Ibid.*, p. 64.

[27] *Ibid.*, p. 156; see also *Nachlass* 7147/H150850.

[28] Stresemann, *Deutsche Stimmen*, 29. Jhrg. (January 10, 1917), p. 213.

[29] Gustav Stresemann, *Warum Müssen Wir Durchhalten*, pp. 22–23.

[30] October 18, 1917, Stresemann, "Unsere Lage und das Deutsche Wirtschaftsleben," *Macht und Freiheit*, p. 105.

[31] Deutsche Volkspartei, *op. cit.*, p. 3.

[32] *Reichstag, Verhandlungen*, Bd. 344 (July 28, 1920), 310.

[33] *Ibid.*, Bd. 354 (March 29, 1922), 6645.

[34] *Ibid.*, Bd. 359 (April 17, 1923), 10575.

[35] See *Vermächtnis*, I–III. Press representatives with whom Stresemann maintained close relations were, among others, Wolf von Dewall (*Frankfurter Zeitung*), Dr. Fritz Klein (*Deutsche Allgemeine Zeitung*), Dr. Ruppel (*Berliner Tageblatt*), Victor Schiff (*Vorwärts*), Jimmy James (*New York Times*), Edgar A. Mowrer (*Chicago Daily News*), Robert Dell (*Manchester Guardian*), Wickham Steed (*The Times*, London), the French Correspondents, Marcel Ray, Jules Sauerwein, Henri de Jouvenal, Tabouis, and the Swiss, Dr. Oeri, Dr. Klötzli, and William Martin. Antonina Vallentin who contributed to the *Manchester Guardian* and Dr. Edgar Stern-Rubarth, Stresemann's personal friend and semiofficial mouthpiece, were prominent among his associates.

[36] See Edgar Stern-Rubarth, *Three Men Tried . . . Austen Chamberlain, Stresemann and Briand and Their Fight for a New Europe*, p. 180; see also *Nachlass*, 7122/H146676 and 7145/H150578.

[37] July 6, 1926, *Reden und Schriften*, II, 296.

[38] *Nationalversammlung, Verhandlungen*, Bd. 330 (October 23, 1919), 3352.

[39] April 10, 1925, *Vermächtnis*, II, 89.

[40] November 24, 1926, *Reichstag, Anlagen*, Bd. 411, No. 2700.

[41] *Reichstag, Verhandlungen*, Bd. 391 (December 17, 1926), 8640. See also Richard Lewinsohn (Morus), *Das Geld in der Politik* (Berlin: S. Fischer Verlag, 1931), p. 222; and *Nachlass*, 7147/H150816.

[42] See Appendixes A, B, and C.

[43] *Frankfurter Zeitung*, February 2, 1929; see also Appendixes A, B, and C.

[44] Stresemann to Held, September 9, 1925, *Nachlass*, 7415/H175610; Stresemann-Müller correspondence, July 16, and 23, 1927, *Nachlass*, 7414/H175331–32; and *Reichstag, Verhandlungen*, Bd. 425 (June 24, 1928), 816. Some interesting speculations are found in: Lewinsohn, *op. cit.*, 230.

[45] September 14, 1925, *Vermächtnis*, II, 172.

[46] December 25, 1924, *ibid.*, I, 606.

[47] February 17, 1924, *ibid.*, p. 299; see also *Nachlass*, 7414/H175358.

[48] November 29, 1924, *ibid.*, pp. 600–601.

[49] Gustav Stresemann, *Politische Gedanken zum Bismarck Gedenktag* (Berlin: Flugschriften der Deutschen Volkspartei, 1925), p. 9.

[50] *Reichstag, Verhandlungen*, Bd. 344 (July 28, 1920), 315; *ibid.*, Bd. 354 (March 29, 1922), 6643.

[51] Deutsche Volkspartei, *op. cit.*, p. 3.

[52] *Reichstag, Verhandlungen,* Bd. 357 (November 25, 1922), 9158.

[53] March 28, 1920, Stresemann, "Der Aufstand Kapps," *Reden und Schriften,* I, 327.

[54] *Reichstag, Verhandlungen,* Bd. 344 (June 30, 1920), 58.

[55] Deutsche Volkspartei, *op. cit.,* p. 3. In December 1919, he had hinted that his party was prepared to support a move to join the newly established Soviet Union in an action against Anglo-Saxon capitalism if the European powers persisted in their policy of isolating Germany. *Deutsche Stimmen,* 31. Jhrg. (December 7, 1919), p. 837.

[56] *Nationalversammlung, Verhandlungen,* Bd. 330 (October 8, 1919), 2917.

[57] March 15, 1910, *Reden und Schriften,* I, 74.

[58] Gustav Stresemann, *Das Deutsche Wirtschaftsleben im Kriege,* p. 57.

[59] April 9, 1916, Stresemann, *Michel Horch,* p. 108.

[60] Gustav Stresemann, *Industrie und Krieg,* p. 13. See also Lutz, *op. cit.,* I, 784. June 1, 1918, *Deutsche Stimmen,* 30. Jhrg. (June 16, 1918), p. 407.

[61] *Nationalversammlung, Verhandlungen,* Bd. 330 (October 8, 1919), 2911, 2917–18.

[62] *Reichstag, Verhandlungen,* Bd. 344 (July 28, 1920), 316.

[63] *Ibid.,* Bd. 349 (April 28, 1921), 3470.

[64] Gustav Stresemann, *Deutsche Gegenwart und Zukunft,* p. 11.

[65] *Reichstag, Verhandlungen,* Bd. 349 (April 28, 1921), 3468.

[66] *Ibid.,* Bd. 359 (April 17, 1923), 10576.

[67] June 29, 1927, Stresemann, *The Way of the New Germany* (Berlin: Carl Heymann's Verlag, 1927), p. 12.

[68] September 9, 1929, League of Nations, *Official Journal Special Supplement,* No. 75.

[69] Edgar Stern-Rubarth, "Der Stresemann Weg," *Preussische Jahrbücher,* Bd. CCII (December 1925), 454–60.

[70] Dr. Walther Schotte, "Die Stresemann Linie," *ibid.* (October 1925), pp. 96–97.

CHAPTER V

[1] The so-called question of war guilt, the *Kriegsschuldfrage,* arose primarily over the interpretation of the words "responsibility" and "cause" as laid down in Article 231 of the Treaty of Versailles: "The Allied and Associated Governments affirm and Germany accepts the responsibility of Germany and her Allies for causing all the loss and damage to which the Allied and Associated Powers and their nationals have been subjected as a consequence of the war imposed upon them by the aggression of Germany and her allies." *Versailles and After,* pp. 413 ff. The question is discussed in outline, *ibid.,* pp. 413–19. See also Ralph H. Lutz, *The Fall of the German Empire, 1914–1918,* Vol. I, chap. II; Alfred von Wegerer, *A Refutation of the Versailles War Guilt Thesis* (New York: Alfred A. Knopf, 1930); George P. Gooch, *Recent Revelations of European Diplomacy* (New York: Longmans, 1940), chap. I; Sidney B. Fay, *The Origins of the World War* (New York: Macmillan Co., rev. ed., 1947), pp. 3–32; Pierre Renouvin, *The Immediate Origins of the War* (New Haven: Yale University Press, 1928); Alfred von Wegerer, *Der*

Ausbruch des Weltkrieges, 1914 (Hamburg: Hanseatische Verlagsanstalt, 1939); and Charles Seymour, *The Intimate Papers of Colonel House* (Boston: Houghton Mifflin Company, 1928), IV, 409.

[2] See "Reply of the Allied and Associated Powers to the Observations of the German Delegation on the Conditions of Peace, and Ultimatum," June 16, 1919, *Versailles and After*, pp. 44–49.

[3] Address at the First Party Congress, April 13, 1919, *Deutsche Stimmen*, 31. Jhrg. (May 4, 1919), p. 317.

[4] Stresemann, "Politische Umschau," *Deutsche Stimmen*, 31. Jhrg. (September 28, 1919), p. 658.

[5] *Reichstag, Verhandlungen*, Bd. 348 (March 5, 1921), 2672–73.

[6] *Ibid.*, Bd. 349 (April 28, 1921), 3468. For purposes of advancing the argument against the war guilt accusation, the foreign ministry had established a Division on War Guilt. A monthly periodical was also published for purposes of propaganda and was entitled *Die Kriegsschuldfrage*; see Mildred S. Werthheimer, "Revision of the Versailles Treaty," *Foreign Policy Association*, V (June 26, 1929), 139–55. See also Friedrich Thimme, *Die Aktenpublikationen des Auswärtigen Amtes* (Berlin: Deutsche Verlagsgesellschaft für Politik und Geschichte, G.m.b.H., 1924). Karl Kautsky (ed.), *Outbreak of the World War, German Documents Collected by Karl Kautsky* (New York: Carnegie Endowment for International Peace, 1924). *Die Grosse Politik der Europäischen Kabinette, 1871–1914* (Berlin: Deutsche Verlagsgesellschaft, G.m.b.H., 1922–27).

[7] *Frankfurter Zeitung*, August 25, 1923, No. 626.

[8] *Ibid.*, September 3, 1923, No. 650.

[9] October 25, 1923, *Reden und Schriften*, II, 109 and 114.

[10] *Reichstag, Verhandlungen*, Bd. 381 (June 5, 1924), 108.

[11] *Ibid.* (June 6, 1924), p. 166.

[12] June 15, 1924, *Vermächtnis*, I, 432.

[13] See Stresemann to Chancellor Marx, September 6, 1924, *Vermächtnis*, I, 562.

[14] *D'Abernon*, III, 93–94.

[15] September 17, 1924, *Vermächtnis*, I, 314.

[16] *League of Nations, Monthly Summary*, December 1924, III–IV, 291.

[17] Note of the French government to the German government, June 16, 1925. See Great Britain, *Papers Respecting the Proposals for a Pact of Security Made by the German Government on February 9, 1925*, Cmd. 2435, Misc. No. 7, *Parliamentary Papers* (London: H.M. Stationery Office), Vol. XXX (1925).

[18] "German Oral Declaration to the Note of September 26, 1925," *ibid.*

[19] See Sir Charles A. Petrie, *The Life and Letters of the Right Hon. Sir Austen Chamberlain, K.G., P.C., M.P.* (London: Cassell and Co., Ltd., 1940), II, 285–86.

[20] October 6, 1925, *Vermächtnis*, II, 214.

[21] *Frankfurter Zeitung*, September 17, 1926, No. 694. According to Werthheimer, Stresemann interpreted Germany's unanimous election to the League Council as an indication that world public opinion no longer held the Reich responsible for the war. Mildred S. Werthheimer, *op. cit.*, p. 147; also, *Versailles and After*, p. 418.

[22] *Vermächtnis*, III, 198. For the text of the president's declaration, see

Die Kriegschuldfrage (October 1927), p. 931; also, Stresemann's interview with Jules Sauerwein, *Le Matin*, September 24, 1927.

[23] *Reichstag, Verhandlungen*, Bd. 425 (June 24, 1929), 2814–15.

[24] *Ibid.* (June 28, 1929), p. 2850.

[25] *Europäische Gespräche* (1929), No. 10, pp. 524–25.

CHAPTER VI

[1] "The measures which the Allied and Associated Powers shall have the right to take, in case of *voluntary* default by Germany, and which Germany agrees not to regard as acts of war, may include economic and financial prohibitions and reprisals and in general *such other measures* as the *respective Governments* may determine to be necessary in the circumstances." (Italics, author's), Paragraph 18, Part VIII: Annex II of the Treaty of Versailles, *Versailles and After*, p. 487. For a brief survey of the history of this paragraph, see W. M. Jordan, *Great Britain, France, and the German Problem* (London: Oxford University Press, 1943), pp. 69–70; also, Charles Seymour, *The Intimate Papers of Colonel House*, IV, 394.

[2] This German action was in violation of Articles 42 and 43 of the Treaty of Versailles. For the text of these articles, see *Versailles and After*, p. 159.

[3] For a discussion of the incident, see *United States Foreign Relations, 1920*, II, 297–327.

[4] For a brief survey dealing with the background of the Ruhr occupation, see *Versailles and After*, pp. 781–82. A valuable interpretation of the conflict is given in Arnold Wolfers, *Britain and France between Two Wars* (New York: Harcourt, Brace and Company, 1940), pp. 57–58.

[5] *Reichstag, Verhandlungen*, Bd. 348 (March 5, 1921), 2676.

[6] *United States, Foreign Relations, 1921*, II, 56–57.

[7] *Ibid.*

[8] *D'Abernon*, I, 172–73.

[9] This part of the ultimatum was subsequently incorporated into the Treaty of Versailles as Paragraph 19A; *Versailles and After*, p. 489.

[10] *D'Abernon*, I, 172.

[11] The second point of Stresemann's inquiry concerned the British Recovery Act of 1921. He inquired whether the Act, fixing the burden to be imposed upon German industry as not exceeding 26 percent, would be repealed once the ultimatum was accepted. *Ibid.*

[12] *Ibid.*, p. 173. The plebiscite in question was based upon Article 88 of the Treaty of Versailles. It was held on March 20, 1921. At the time of the above negotiations, the delimitation of the boundary had not yet been decided upon. See *Versailles and After*, pp. 210–15. Lord D'Abernon, in his report to the British foreign office, noted, "I am convinced that if [Stresemann] could be reassured on above points, he is persuaded that he can secure acceptance of our terms. It is of the utmost importance that I should receive an answer at the earliest possible moment, as the question of forming a government can scarcely be delayed beyond tomorrow."

[13] May 12, 1921, *ibid.*, pp. 176–77.

[14] Walther Rathenau, German foreign minister, committed to a policy of fulfillment, was shot and killed by assassins on June 24, 1922. Very much like Stresemann, he had been aware of "the conflict which any reasonable foreign policy must cause with regard to popular opinion in Germany." Harry Graf Kessler, *Walther Rathenau, Sein Leben und Sein Werk* (Berlin: Verlagsanstalt Hermann Klemm, A.G., 1928, p. 324.

[15] *D'Abernon*, I, 174–75.

[16] *Reichstag, Verhandlungen*, Bd. 349 (May 10, 1921), 3631–32.

[17] The vote was 220 for acceptance and 172 against, with one abstention; *ibid.* Stresemann notes in his diary that his candidacy for the chancellorship had been unsuccessful because of the split within the party. May 13, 1921, *Vermächtnis*, I, 20–21. Concerning the party situation at that critical moment, Lord D'Abernon observed that there was a bitter animosity between the Socialists and the People's Party. Both parties were needed to support a policy of fulfillment. While Stresemann was prepared to govern with the Socialists, a considerable segment within the party was opposed to such a coalition because of its effect on the relative strength of the People's Party as against the extremely rightist German National People's Party. It was feared that a coalition with the Socialists would start an exodus of voters and party members from the People's Party to the Nationalists. June 2, 1921, *D'Abernon*, I, 187.

[18] *Reichstag, Verhandlungen*, Bd. 349 (June 3, 1921), 3760–62.

[19] *Vermächtnis*, I, 29.

[20] See *United States, Foreign Relations*, 1923, II, 192–93; also, Great Britain, House of Commons, *Debates*, Vol. 161 (March 6, 1923), cols. 369–70.

[21] The parties concerned were the Center Party, German National People's Party, German People's Party, German Democratic Party, Bavarian People's Party, Bavarian Peasants Association, and the German-Hanoverian Party. *Reichstag, Verhandlungen*, Bd. 357 (January 13, 1923), 9422–23.

[22] *Vermächtnis*, I, 37.

[23] *Reichstag, Verhandlungen*, Bd. 358 (March 7, 1923), 9976–77.

[24] Stresemann, "Politik und Wirtschaft," *Die Zeit*, May 15, 1923, as reprinted in *Vermächtnis*, I, 63.

[25] *Reichstag, Verhandlungen*, Bd. 358 (March 7, 1923), 9975–82.

[26] *Ibid.*, Bd. 352 (February 11, 1922), 5792 and 5822; Richard Lewinsohn (Morus), *Das Geld in der Politik*, p. 93.

[27] Stern-Rubarth to the present writer, November 27, 1949.

[28] *Reichstag, Verhandlungen*, Bd. 359 (April 17, 1923), 10572–77.

[29] *Ibid.*, pp. 10577–79.

[30] April 22, 1923, *Vermächtnis*, I, 55.

[31] *Frankfurter Zeitung*, April 22, 1923, No. 297; also, *D'Abernon*, II, 218.

[32] Harold G. Nicolson, *Curzon: The Last Phase, 1919–1925* (New York: Houghton Mifflin Company, 1934), p. 367; see also Lord Curzon's address, House of Lords, *Debates*, Vol. 53 (April 20, 1923), col. 798.

[33] *Vermächtnis*, I, 43 and 63.

[34] *Reichstag, Verhandlungen*, Bd. 361 (August 9, 1923), 11772–75. Concerning Stresemann's extraordinary sense for propaganda, it is interesting to note that the same speech contained a warning addressed to German shipping circles to be more discreet in the launching of merchant ships. The suggestion was made to avoid the impression of a too rapid recovery by Germany at a time when he wanted to plead financial and economic distress. *Ibid.*, p. 11777.

[35] Great Britain, *Correspondence with the Allied Governments Respecting Reparation Payments by Germany*, Cmd. 1943, Misc. No. 5, *Parliamentary Papers*, Vol. XV (1923).

[36] August 12, 1923, *Vermächtnis*, I, 88; see also *Vossische Zeitung*, August 13, 1923, No. 380.

[37] *Reichstag, Verhandlungen*, Bd. 361 (August 14, 1923), 11840.

[38] Gustav Stresemann, *Der Wille zur Verständigung* (Berlin: Zentral Verlag, 1923), pp. 11–12.

[39] *D'Abernon*, II, 253.

[40] Stresemann, *op. cit.*, pp. 14–15.

[41] The German position demanded a moratorium on reparation payments for a given period at the end of which certain German industries and state properties would be offered as guaranty for future payments. The French counterproposal, while accepting the idea of industrial guaranty in principle, insisted, however, that the industries in question be limited to the Ruhr and Rhine areas. *Ibid.*, pp. 12–13.

[42] *Frankfurter Zeitung*, August 25, 1923, No. 626. (Address before the Deutscher Industrie- und Handelstag.)

[43] *Vermächtnis*, I, 114.

[44] Report to the cabinet on a conversation with Lord D'Abernon, September 18, 1913; *ibid.*, pp. 127–28.

[45] *Ibid.*, p. 134.

[46] *Reichstag, Verhandlungen*, Bd. 361 (October 8, 1923), 11985.

[47] September 2, 1923, *Vermächtnis*, I, 100.

[48] Sir Austen Chamberlain, *Down the Years* (London: Cassell and Co., Ltd., 1935), p. 158.

[49] Henry Bernhard, *Das Kabinett Stresemann* (Berlin: Staatspolitischer Verlag, G.m.b.H., 1924), p. 30.

[50] September 4, 1923, *Vermächtnis*, I, 106.

[51] *D'Abernon*, II, 264.

[52] Communication to the Belgian Ambassador, September 18, 1923, *Vermächtnis*, I, 125.

[53] Stresemann's notes on a cabinet meeting, September 15, 1923, *ibid.*, pp. 114–16, 123.

[54] October 29, 1923, *ibid.*, pp. 176–77.

[55] Bernhard, *op. cit.*, p. 31.

[56] Harold Nicolson considers this also Curzon's defeat at the hands of Poincaré. Nicolson, *op. cit.*, pp. 372–73.

[57] *Reichstag, Verhandlungen*, Bd. 361 (October 6, 1923), 11935.

[58] Address on cessation of passive resistance, Hagen, October 25, 1923, *Reden und Schriften*, II, 108. Article 241 provided that Germany was to undertake legislation necessary to give complete effect to the reparation provisions of the treaty. *Versailles and After*, p. 450. An official request by the German government for inter-Allied investigation of its financial resources had been dispatched on June 7, 1923. *United States, Foreign Relations*, 1923, II, 57–62.

[59] *Reichstag, Verhandlungen*, Bd. 361 (November 22, 1923), 12184.

[60] September 3, 1923, *Vermächtnis*, I, 102.

[61] September 6, 1923, *ibid.*, pp. 107–8.

[62] See Alfred Hugenberg, *Streiflichter aus der Vergangenheit* (Berlin: August Scherl, G.m.b.H., 1927).

[63] *Reichstag, Verhandlungen,* Bd. 361 (October 8, 1923), 11981–86.

[64] A prorepublican presentation of the internal struggle is given by Gustav Noske, *Erlebtes aus Aufstieg und Niedergang einer Demokratie* (Offenbach: Bollwerk Verlag, 1947).

[65] See Wolf von Dewall, *Der Kampf um den Frieden* (Frankfurt a/M: Frankfurter Sozietätsdruckerei, G.m.b.H., 1929), p. 390.

[66] See Stresemann to Marx, November 28, 1923, *Vermächtnis,* I, 248.

[67] *Reichstag, Verhandlungen,* Bd. 361 (November 22, 1923), 12180.

[68] Stresemann at a conference with foreign correspondents, November 23, 1923, *Vermächtnis,* I, 245.

CHAPTER VII

[1] September 7, 1925, *Vermächtnis,* II, 555. This letter has often been interpreted as giving evidence of Stresemann's allegedly monarchistic, even Machiavellian tendencies. The writer does not see any sinister motives or character traits in this letter but considers it instead a very astute appraisal of Germany's international position and of the political *dicta* arising from it. It represents undoubtedly the clearest expression of what a German foreign minister, planning his course without possible resort to armed might, had to do in order to restore Germany to her world position. For the opposing point of view, see G. Boas, "Stresemann," *Public Opinion Quarterly,* VIII, No. 2 (1944), 232–43. For a defense of Stresemann on that account, see the reply: Felix E. Hirsch, "Stresemann," *ibid.,* IX, No. 2 (1945), 258–60. Stresemann's biographer, Rudolf Olden, believes that the word *finassieren* conveys little else but certain recognized diplomatic procedures. Rudolf Olden, "Was Stresemann Sincere?" *The Contemporary Review,* Vol. 147 (May 1935), pp. 557–65.

[2] *United States, Foreign Relations,* 1923, II, 57–62; see also Great Britain, *Correspondence with the Allied Governments Respecting Reparation Payments by Germany,* Cmd. 1943, Misc. No. 5, *Parliamentary Papers,* XXV (1923), 391.

[3] Stresemann's reply to Karl Helfferich, *Frankfurter Zeitung,* March 9, 1924, No. 185.

[4] W. M. Jordan, *Great Britain, France, and the German Problem,* p. 129. Concerning the British attitude, Arnold Wolfers observes: "It was to the interest of businessmen and private creditors to scale down reparations . . . and to prevent the execution of the treaty from retarding the return of good will and economic initiative. Every shift to the economic side of the argument was therefore a victory for German, American, and British businessmen over French military strategists." Arnold Wolfers, *Britain and France between Two Wars,* p. 207; see also Earl of Ronaldshay, *The Life of Lord Curzon* (London: Ernest Benn, Ltd., 1928), III, 359; and Harold Nicolson, *Curzon: The Last Phase,* chap. VIII.

[5] Stresemann to Count von Brockdorff-Rantzau, German Ambassador at Moscow, December 1, 1923, *Vermächtnis,* I, 259.

[6] December 24, 1923, *D'Abernon,* II, 301–2.

[7] See Great Britain, *Reports of the Experts Committees Appointed by the*

Reparation Commission, Cmd. 2105, *Parliamentary Papers*, Vol. XXVII (1924).

⁸ January 19, 1924, *Vermächtnis*, I, 285.

⁹ Henry Bernhard, *Das Kabinett Stresemann*, p. 33.

¹⁰ *Reichstag, Verhandlungen*, Bd. 361 (February 28, 1924), 12527–29.

¹¹ See *Vermächtnis*, I, 233; also, Seeckt's letter to his wife, January 13, 1924, Friedrich von Rabenau, *Seeckt, Aus seinem Leben* (Leipzig: v. Hase und Köhler, 1941), p. 392; Bernhard, *op. cit.*, p. 36.

¹² Stresemann to Georg Wache, March 17, 1924, *Vermächtnis*, I, 355; also, *Frankfurter Zeitung*, March 13, 1924, No. 197.

¹³ Bernhard, *op. cit.*, p. 34.

¹⁴ *Reichstag, Verhandlungen*, Bd. 361 (February 28, 1924), 12528–29.

¹⁵ *Ibid.* (March 6, 1924), pp. 12634–37.

¹⁶ Address before the Sixth Land-Party Conference at Braunschweig, *Frankfurter Zeitung*, March 10, 1924, No. 185.

¹⁷ March 4, 1924, *D'Abernon*, III, 56. In a conversation with the British Ambassador, Stresemann predicted a swing to the Right in the then imminent election.

¹⁸ March 24, 1924, *Vermächtnis*, I, 271.

¹⁹ Address, "Through Work and Sacrifice to Freedom," given at the annual party conference at Hanover, March 3, 1924, *Reden und Schriften*, II, 175–77.

²⁰ *Frankfurter Zeitung*, March 30, 1924, No. 244, p. 2.

²¹ *Reden und Schriften*, II, 167.

²² Dr. Eduard Stadtler, *Bahn Frei für Hugenberg* (Berlin: Das Grossdeutsche Reich Verlags G.m.b.H., 1930), pp. 170–71.

²³ See *Frankfurter Zeitung*, April 1, 1924, No. 274, p. 2.

²⁴ *Ibid.*, April 28, 1924, No. 315.

²⁵ See *Ibid.*, April 29, 1924, No. 317; and *Vermächtnis*, I, 397.

²⁶ Stresemann's notes, September 17, 1926, *ibid.*, III, 19.

²⁷ Election Appeal, May 4, 1924, *D.V.P. Reichstag Wahlhandbuch*, II. Wahlperiode 1924, 315.

²⁸ May 30, 1924, *D'Abernon*, III, 68.

²⁹ Cmd. 2105, *op. cit.* The Dawes Plan, in order to create the conditions necessary for a resumption of reparation payments by Germany, recommended, among other things, a balanced budget and stabilization of currency. It further recommended a two-year moratorium and the granting of a loan of eight hundred million marks. It established an annual rate of payment which was to be based partly on the income from certain taxes and partly on the service of the German railway bonds. Great Britain, *Agreements Concluded between* . . . *(2) The Allied Governments and the German Government to Carry Out the Experts' Plan of April 9, 1924*, Cmd. 2259, *Parliamentary Papers*, XXVII (1924), 16 ff.

³⁰ Stresemann's notes on a conversation with Ambassador Houghton and Colonel Logan, June 4, 1924, *Vermächtnis*, I, 416.

³¹ Election campaign speech at Magdeburg, April 29, 1924, *ibid.*, p. 397; also, July 13, 1924, *ibid.*, p. 458.

³² The international situation at that time, as seen from a socialist point of view, is well represented in Friedrich Stampfer, *Die Vierzehn Jahre der ersten deutschen Republik* (Karlsbad: Verlagsanstalt Graphia, 1936), p. 363.

³³ Cf. Arnold Wolfers, *op. cit.*, pp. 86–89. The Labour Party's election

manifesto of November 17, 1923, declared that the party stood for "the immediate calling by the British Government of an International Conference to deal with the revision of the Treaty of Versailles," *The Times* (London), November 19, 1923, p. 21.

[34] *Reichstag, Verhandlungen*, Bd. 381 (June 6, 1924), 176–77.

[35] *Ibid.*, 223.

[36] June 16, 1924, *Vermächtnis*, I, 436.

[37] Stresemann's notes on a conversation with the British Ambassador, July 11, 1924, *ibid.*, p. 455; also, Stresemann to the German Ambassador at Paris, July 13, 1924, *ibid.*, p. 457.

[38] *Reichstag, Verhandlungen*, Bd. 381 (July 26, 1924), 766. For the text of the motion, see *Reichstag, Anlagen*, Bd. 383, No. 401.

[39] *Reichstag, Verhandlungen*, Bd. 381 (July 26, 1924), 738.

[40] July 11, 1924, *D'Abernon*, III, 79.

[41] August 8, 1924, *Vermächtnis*, I, 480.

[42] Dr. Paul Schmidt, *Statist auf der Diplomatischen Bühne*, pp. 56–61.

[43] Dr. Breitscheid, Social-Democratic member of the German delegation, reporting on his own conversation with Herriot, stated that the Premier had voiced a desire for a Franco-German security pact on August 7, 1924. *Vermächtnis*, I, 477. Sumner Welles, however, claims that Herriot told him of a proposal by Stresemann concerning a secret Franco-German alliance from which Great Britain was to be excluded. Sumner Welles, *The Time for Decision* (New York: Harper & Brothers, 1944), pp. 126–27. There is no mention of such a proposal in the unedited *Nachlass*; see 7175/H156791.

[44] August 11, 1924, *Vermächtnis*, I, 476–77; August 13, 1924, *ibid.*, pp. 491–97; also *Nachlass*, 7126/H147314.

[45] *Reichstag, Verhandlungen*, Bd. 361 (November 22, 1923), 12182.

[46] For the text of the letter of August 19, 1924, see *Reichstag, Anlagen*, Bd. 383, No. 446, 55. Chancellor Marx had addressed a letter to Herriot and Theunis, the prime minister of Belgium, wherein he had once more declared the Ruhr occupation to be illegal. This had been done primarily to appease the German opposition at home. For the text of that letter, see *ibid.*, p. 51, doc. 2.

[47] See *Vermächtnis*, I, 501.

[48] *Reichstag, Anlagen*, Bd. 382, No. 5, 47.

[49] *Reichstag, Verhandlungen*, Bd. 381 (August 23, 1924), 780 ff.

[50] *Ibid.* (August 25, 1924), p. 797.

[51] *Ibid.* (August 28, 1924), p. 1015.

[52] *Der Charakter der Deutschnationalen, dargestellt an Hand von 200 Deutschnationalen Versprechungen* (Berlin: Verlag der N.S.D.A.P., 1924), p. 16; also, *Kreuzzeitung*, August 30, 1924.

[53] Seeckt's letter to his wife, August 26, 1924, Rabenau, *op. cit.*, p. 404.

[54] Seeckt's letter to his wife, August 29, 1924, *ibid.*, p. 405.

[55] September 12, 1924, *Vermächtnis*, I, 565.

[56] *Reichstag, Verhandlungen*, Bd., 381 (August 29, 1924), 1125–34.

[57] *Ibid.*, Bd. 384 (February 7, 1925), 430. The following countries had agreed to waive their rights under Paragraph 18: Great Britain, Belgium, Italy, Yugoslavia, Czechoslovakia, Portugal, Japan, Peru, Canada; see *Versailles and After*, p. 488. For examples of trade treaties carrying the waiver, see Article 6, Treaty of Commerce and Navigation between Germany and the

Kingdom of Serbs, Croats, and Slovenes, December 13, 1927, *Reichsgesetz-blatt*, 1927, II, 1128; Article 10, Treaty of Commerce and Navigation between Germany and the United Kingdom of Great Britain and Ireland, *ibid.*, 1925, II, 777. For an interpretation of the latter treaty, see Minutes of the Meeting between British and German Representatives, held at 4 P.M. on the 2d of December, 1924, at the Foreign Office, London, for the purpose of Signing a Treaty of Commerce and Navigation, *ibid.*, p. 793.

CHAPTER VIII

¹ *Versailles and After*, pp. 304–5. For the text of the note, see *Reichstag, Anlagen*, "Materialien zur Entwaffnungsnote," Bd. 401, No. 971. The note charged Germany with violation of Articles 160, 162, 164–69, 174, and 211 of the Treaty of Versailles; see also chap. XIII, *infra*.

² December 29, 1924, *Vermächtnis*, I, 619.

³ December 30, 1924, *ibid.*, pp. 619–20; see also H. W. in *Göteborgs Handels och Sjöfarts Tidning* as reprinted in *The Living Age*, Vol. 324, p. 660; and, *Frankfurter Zeitung*, December 31, 1924, No. 975. A comparison of the first and the last source indicates that Stresemann did not associate himself personally with the "regret," as the second source would show.

⁴ January 3, 1925, *Vermächtnis*, II, 13. For a review of Anglo-French problems of that period, see J. Paul Selsam, *The Attempt to Form an Anglo-French Alliance, 1919–1924* (Philadelphia: University of Pennsylvania Press, 1936); see also Henry H. Cumming, *Franco-British Rivalry in the Post-War Near East* (London: Oxford University Press, 1938). The Cologne zone was not evacuated until one year later.

⁵ League of Nations, *Monthly Summary*, III–IV (December 1924), 291.

⁶ Address at a party rally, October 19, 1924, *Vermächtnis*, I, 597.

⁷ Letter to Hofrat Bickes, November 12, 1924, *ibid.*, p. 581.

⁸ See Friedrich Stampfer, *Die vierzehn Jahre der ersten deutschen Republik*, p. 402; also, Stresemann in *Hamburger Fremdenblatt*, December 25, 1924, as reprinted in *Vermächtnis*, I, 606–7.

⁹ *Frankfurter Zeitung*, December 27, 1924, No. 965. The new cabinet under Luther was formed on January 1.

¹⁰ December 28, 1924, *D'Abernon*, III, 119.

¹¹ March 5, 1925, *ibid.*, p. 146.

¹² Great Britain, *Papers Respecting the Proposals for a Security Pact Made by the German Government on February 9, 1925*, Cmd. 2435, Misc. No. 7, *Parliamentary Papers*, Vol. XXX (1925), Nos. 1 and 3.

¹³ *Vermächtnis*, II, 70; January 14, 1925, *D'Abernon*, III, 121; for a summary of the preliminary talks see *Nachlass*, 7135/H148917.

¹⁴ January 31, 1925; *ibid.*, p. 134.

¹⁵ Sir Austen Chamberlain to Lord Crewe, February 16, 1925, Sir Charles A. Petrie, *The Life and Letters of the Right Hon. Sir Austen Chamberlain, K.G., P.C., M.P.*, II, 258–59.

¹⁶ The documents relevant to the negotiations are given in Cmd. 2435, *op. cit.*; see also *Vermächtnis*, Vol. II, Part I; and *D'Abernon*, II, 121 ff.

A doctoral dissertation on the origins of the Locarno agreements, under which name the subsequent agreements became known, has been written by William McHenry Franklin, *The Origins of the Locarno Conference* (Fletcher School of Law and Diplomacy, 1941). See also Arnold Wolfers, *Britain and France between Two Wars,* chap. XVI.

[17] League of Nations, *Official Journal,* Records of the Fifth Assembly, 1924, Special Supplement, No. 26, Minutes of the Third Committee, Annex 9, p. 184. The minutes contain all of the debates, resolutions, and reports relating to the so-called Geneva Protocol. See also Great Britain, *Correspondence between His Majesty's Government and the League of Nations Respecting the Proposed Treaty of Mutual Assistance,* Cmd. 2200, Misc. No. 13, *Parliamentary Papers,* XXVII (1924), 265. Concerning Stresemann's own views on that matter, see press conference, March 7, 1925, *Vermächtnis,* II, 72; and *Kölnische Zeitung,* March 12, 1925, No. 190.

[18] W. M. Jordan, *Great Britain, France, and the German Problem,* p. 96; and concerning the United States attitude and its role in the negotiations leading up to the Geneva Protocol and the Locarno agreements, see *United States, Foreign Relations,* I (1925), 17–26.

[19] March 11, 1925, *Vermächtnis,* II, 81.

[20] Proposed French reply to the German memorandum, Cmd. 2435, *op. cit.,* No. 3, Sec. II, p. 9. See also Stresemann at the Bismarck celebration at Chemnitz, *Frankfurter Zeitung,* April 1, 1925, No. 244, p. 3. The proposed pact sought to "guarantee the present state of ownership in the Rhineland," and the powers were to oblige one another, "to respect, irrevocably, the inviolability of the present state of ownership." For the text of the German note, see Cmd. 2435, *op. cit.,* No. 1.

[21] *Ibid.,* No. 9, p. 46.

[22] See *ibid.,* p. 50; also, George Glasgow, *From Dawes to Locarno* (New York: Harper & Brothers, 1926), pp. 156–59; Stresemann's diary, July 1, 1925, *Vermächtnis,* II, 115.

[23] Stresemann's notes on a conversation with the Nationalist cabinet ministers, April 2, 1925, *ibid.,* p. 88.

[24] *Reichstag, Verhandlungen,* Bd. 385 (May 18, 1925), 188.

[25] Lord D'Abernon's notes on a conversation with Stresemann, June 10, 1925, *D'Abernon,* III, 168–69.

[26] *Vermächtnis,* II, 110, 135–36, 177, and 180.

[27] Stresemann's notes on a meeting of the party council, June 30, 1925, *ibid.,* p. 132.

[28] Seeckt to his wife, July 2, 1925, Friedrich von Rabenau, *Seeckt, Aus seinem Leben, 1918–1936,* p. 418.

[29] Great Britain, *Reply of the German Government to the Note Handed to Herr Stresemann by the French Ambassador at Berlin on June 16, 1925 Respecting the Proposals for a Pact of Security,* Cmd. 2468, *Parliamentary Papers,* XXX (1925), 3–4.

[30] *D'Abernon,* July 11, 1925, III, 175.

[31] Austen Chamberlain, *Down the Years,* p. 176; see also Stresemann's Locarno Diary, *Nachlass,* 7129/H147779 ff.

[32] Stresemann's notes on the Locarno Conference, October 15, 1925, *Vermächtnis,* II, 201.

[33] Stresemann's own notes on Locarno, October 12, 1925, *ibid.,* p. 194.

³⁴ For the text of the Locarno agreements, see League of Nations, *Treaty Series*, LIV (1926–27), 289–364; see also *Reichstag, Anlagen*, Bd. 405, No. 1515.

³⁵ Gustav Stresemann, *Das Werk von Locarno*, pp. 14–15; see also *Nachlass*, 7320/160614.

³⁶ Address before the Dresden press, October 31, 1925, *Vermächtnis*, II, 212.

³⁷ *Reichstag, Verhandlungen*, Bd. 388 (November 24, 1925), 4533.

³⁸ Radio address, November 3, 1925, *Reden und Schriften*, II, 215–16.

³⁹ *Reichstag, Verhandlungen*, Bd. 388 (November 24, 1925), 4533.

⁴⁰ Stresemann to Lord D'Abernon, November 8, 1925, *Vermächtnis*, II, 224–25.

⁴¹ Alfred Hugenberg, *Lokal Anzeiger*, November 15, 1925.

⁴² The *Nachlass* contains numerous documents which describe the high-pressure diplomacy of the Soviet government in their endeavor to obtain an Eastern security pact in compensation for Locarno. *Nachlass*, 7129/H147779 ff. See also chaps. XI and XIII, this study.

⁴³ *Frankfurter Zeitung*, November 3, 1925, No. 823.

⁴⁴ *Vermächtnis*, II, 526. Stresemann's Russian policy is generally summarized in *ibid.*, Part III, chap. III.

⁴⁵ See *Versailles and After*, pp. 723–24; *Reichstag, Verhandlungen*, Bd. 388 (January 28, 1926), 5228.

CHAPTER IX

¹ Alfred Hugenberg in *Der Tag*, January 9, 1926, as reprinted in *Streiflichter aus der Vergangenheit und Gegenwart*, p. 82.

² Julius Curtius, *Sechs Jahre Minister der deutschen Republik* (Heidelberg: Carl Winter Universitäts Verlag, 1948), p. 26.

³ See Friedrich Stampfer, *Die vierzehn Jahre der ersten deutschen Republik* (Karlsbad: Verlagsanstalt Graphia, 1936), pp. 391 and 395.

⁴ Concerning the details of this event, see George Scelle, *Une Crise de la Société des Nations* (Paris: Les Presses Universitaires de France, 1927), pp. 1–48. For a critical review of Stresemann's role at Geneva during the admission crisis, see Carl von Ossietzky in *Die Weltbühne*, XXII (April 20, 1926), No. 16, 604.

⁵ *Vermächtnis*, II, 433–37.

⁶ Stresemann before the Overseas Club at Hamburg, April 16, 1926, *Frankfurter Zeitung*, April 17, 1926, No. 283, p. 2.

⁷ Before a party rally at Stuttgart, *ibid.*, April 18, 1926, No. 287; see Robert M. W. Kempner, "Die Reichswehr und die Reichsregierung," *Der Monat*, I (March 1944), No. 6, 103–5.

⁸ July 23, 1926, *Hannoverscher Kurier*, as reprinted in *Vermächtnis*, II, 460; also, Stresemann to Professor Hesnard, Briand's confidant, August 5, 1926, *ibid.*, pp. 463–66.

⁹ See Andrew McFadeyan, *Reparation Reviewed* (London: E. Benn, Ltd., 1930), pp. 113–15; also, Stresemann's notes on Thoiry, September 17, 1926,

Vermächtnis, III, 21; see also Franco-American Funding Agreement, *United States, Statutes at Large* (1929–31), XLVI, Part I, 48.

[10] *Vermächtnis*, III, 16–17; see also *Nachlass*, 7331/H162450.

[11] Stresemann's interview with Jules Sauerwein, *Le Matin*, as reprinted in *Frankfurter Zeitung*, September 28, 1926, No. 721, p. 2; Deutsche Volkspartei, *Siebenter Reichs-Parteitag am 2. u. 3. Oktober in Köln* (Sonderausgabe der National-Liberalen Korrespondenz, 1926), p. 4; McFadeyan, *op. cit.*, pp. 113–15; Deutsche Volkspartei, *op. cit.*, p. 2.

[12] Stresemann's notes on Thoiry, September 17, 1926, *Vermächtnis*, III, 21; *Nachlass*, 7331/H162454.

[13] *Ibid.*, pp. 84 ff.; see also Seeckt's own account of the incident, Friedrich v. Rabenau, Seeckt, *Aus seinem Leben, 1918–1936*, pp. 558 f.

[14] *Reichstag, Verhandlungen*, Bd. 391 (December 16, 1926), 8577 ff.

[15] January 31, 1927, *Vermächtnis*, III, 104, and January 14, 1927, *ibid.*, pp. 95–97.

[16] *Reichstag, Verhandlungen*, Bd. 394 (February 1, 1928), 12559.

[17] *Ibid.*, Bd.. 392 (March 22, 1927), 4815.

[18] Stresemann's notes on a conference with the British foreign secretary, June 18, 1927, *Vermächtnis*, III, 160; see also Great Britain, House of Commons, *Debates*, Vol. 208 (July 6, 1927), col. 1243; and *Reichstag, Verhandlungen*, Bd. 393 (June 23, 1927), 11009.

[19] *Ibid.*, 11006.

[20] Campaign talk by Stresemann in Bavaria, April 24, 1928, *Frankfurter Zeitung*, April 26, 1928, No. 310, p. 2.

[21] Deutsche Volkspartei, *Wahlhandbuch, 1928* (Berlin: Staatspolitischer Verlag, G.m.b.H.), pp. 74–76.

[22] For the text of the preliminary diplomatic exchanges and of the pact itself, see Germany, Foreign Ministry, "Materialien zum Kriegsächtungspakt" (Weissbuch des Ministeriums des Äusseren, Berlin: Reichsdruckerei, 1929), *Reichstag, Anlagen*, Bd. 434, I, supplement to No. 785; see also Hunter Miller, *The Peace Pact of Paris* (New York: G. P. Putnam's Sons, 1928).

[23] *Ibid.*, document No. 12, p. 194. This passage was cited at the Nuremberg trials after World War II as evidence of Germany's peaceful intentions. Professor Dr. Jahrreis, counsel for the defense of General Jodl, International Military Tribunal, *Trials of the Major War Criminals before the International Military Tribunal; Nuremberg, 14 November 1945–1 October 1946* (Nuremberg, Germany, 1947), XVII, 470.

[24] *Frankfurter Zeitung*, August 26, 1928, No. 639, p. 2.

[25] *Vermächtnis*, III, 364–66.

[26] *Ibid.*, pp. 376–82.

[27] Interview for the *Baltimore Sun* of December 27, 1928, as reprinted in *Frankfurter Zeitung*, December 27, 1928, No. 965. For an interpretation of Article 431 by a British statesman, see Sir Austen Chamberlain, Great Britain, House of Commons, *Debates*, Vol. 223 (December 5, 1928), col. 1191; also, Great Britain, House of Lords, *Debates*, Vol. 72 (December 10, 1928), col. 461.

[28] *Reichstag, Verhandlungen*, Bd. 423 (February 2, 1929), 992–93.

[29] *Versailles and After*, pp. 388–89. The six governments joined in inviting Owen D. Young and J. P. Morgan to be the American members with the approval of the United States government. The committee of experts met for the first time on February 4, 1929, and dated its report, named after the chair-

man, Mr. Young, June 7, 1929. For the text of the report, see Great Britain, *Report of the Committee of Experts on Reparations*, Cmd. 3343, *Parliamentary Papers* (London: H.M. Stationery Office, 1930), XVII, 507.

[30] *Vermächtnis*, III, 436–38.

[31] *Reichstag, Verhandlungen*, Bd. 425 (June 24, 1929), 2814.

[32] *Vermächtnis*, III, 555–57.

[33] League of Nations, *Treaty Series*, Vol. 104, p. 473; *Versailles and After*, p. 722.

[34] *Ibid.*, p. 487; see also *Reichstag, Verhandlungen*, Bd. 425 (June 24, 1929), 2814.

[35] *Ibid.*, Bd. 426 (November 30, 1929), 3374.

[36] *Reichstag, Anlagen*, Bd. 438, No. 1429.

CHAPTER X

[1] Cf. chap. III, *supra.* "First Party Conference of the People's Party, Jena, April 13, 1919," *Deutsche Stimmen,* 31. Jhrg. (May 4, 1919), No. 18, p. 320.

[2] *Reichstag, Verhandlungen*, Bd. 361 (February 28, 1924), 12530.

[3] Address before the German League at Geneva (the so-called "Gambrinus Speech"), September 21, 1926, *Vermächtnis*, III, 29. For an adverse comment on the all-too-patriotic speech, see Carl von Ossietzky, *Die Weltbühne,* XXII (September 28, 1926), No. 39, 480.

[4] *Reichstag, Verhandlungen*, Bd. 391 (November 23, 1926), 8145.

[5] League of Nations, *Official Journal, Council,* VIII (March 12, 1927), No. 4, 406–7.

[6] *Reichstag, Verhandlungen*, Bd. 392 (March 22, 1927), 9815.

[7] *Ibid.* (March 23, 1927), p. 9877.

[8] *Frankfurter Zeitung,* July 9, 1929, No. 503, p. 2.

[9] *Vermächtnis*, III, 562; see also Franz von Papen's testimony on behalf of his own defense, International Military Tribunal, *Trials of the Major War Criminals before the International Military Tribunal; Nuremberg, 14 November 1945–1 October 1946*, XVI, 240–41.

[10] League of Nations, *Official Journal, Assembly,* X, *Special Supplement,* No. 75 (September 9, 1929), 68.

[11] Treaty of Versailles, Article 34, *Versailles and After,* pp. 140–41.

[12] June 10, 1925, Stresemann to Lord D'Abernon, *Vermächtnis,* II, 102.

[13] D'Abernon quoting Stresemann, February 3, 1926, *D'Abernon,* III, 222; see also Stresemann's statement to the correspondent for the *Gazetta del Popolo* as reported in *Frankfurter Zeitung,* September 3, 1926, No. 657, p. 4.

[14] Stresemann's notes on a conference with Briand's confidant, Professor Hesnard, August 5, 1926, *Vermächtnis,* II, 464.

[15] Stresemann's notes on a conversation with the French Chargé d'Affaires, Laboulaye, August 22, 1926, *ibid.*, pp. 467–68.

[16] *Ibid.*, p. 468.

[17] *Ibid.*, III, 368, 376, 392, and 406.

[18] *Versailles and After,* p. 142.

[19] The Saar plebiscite was held as scheduled, on January 13, 1935. Of the 528,705 votes cast, 477,119 were in favor of union with Germany, 46,613 for retention of the League of Nations regime, and 2,124 for union with France. *Ibid.,* p. 179. The Saar was transferred to Germany on March 1, 1935. Germany, *Reichsgesetzblatt,* 1935, II, 135. Eupen-Malmédy's status remained unchanged until 1940, when German troops occupied Belgium.

CHAPTER XI

[1] Treaty of Versailles, Articles 87–108, *Versailles and After,* pp. 208–62.

[2] *Reichstag, Verhandlungen,* Bd. 344 (July 28, 1920), Part I, 317. The researcher cannot afford to ignore the very portentous document 7117/H145801 in the *Nachlass.* It represents a memorandum sent to Brockdorff-Rantzau by Stresemann's secretary, Bernhard, on July 28, 1923. The document was not used in this study because it is not clear as to whether its contents represent Stresemann's or someone else's views on Germany's Eastern policy.

[3] See *D'Abernon,* I, 145 and 172–73.

[4] *Ibid.,* III, 101.

[5] April 15, 1925, *Vermächtnis,* II, 513.

[6] See General von Seeckt, "Deutschlands Stellung zum russischen Problem; Antwort auf ein Promemoria des Grafen Br[ockdorff]-R[antzau] an den Reichskanzler, 11, 9, 1922," *Der Monat,* I (November 1948), No. 2, 46.

[7] Stresemann's letter to the ex-Crown Prince, September 7, 1925, *Vermächtnis,* II, 553.

[8] Stresemann's notes on a conversation with Chicherin, *Nachlass,* 7129/H147984–95.

[9] *Kölnische Zeitung,* March 13, 1925, No. 190.

[10] April 10, 1925, *Vermächtnis,* Vol. II, 91–93.

[11] Stresemann's Locarno Diary, *Nachlass,* 7129/H147984–95. It is of course quite possible that Brockdorff-Rantzau had actually made such an offer or had implied that Stresemann could be won over to accept it and that Chicherin had been the victim of a diplomatic miscue.

[12] *Nachlass,* 7129/H147859.

[13] *Reichstag, Verhandlungen,* Bd. 388 (July 20, 1925), 4534.

[14] See the German note of July 20, 1925, in reply to the French answer of June 16 to the original security pact offer of February 9, *Papers Respecting the Proposals for a Security Pact Made by the German Government on February 9, 1925,* Cmd. 2435, *Parliamentary Papers* (London: H.M. Stationery Office, 1925), Vol. XXX (1925); and *Reply of the German Government to the Note Handed to Herr Stresemann by the French Ambassador at Berlin, on June 16, 1925,* July 20, 1925, Cmd. 2468, *Parliamentary Papers,* Vol. XXX (1925).

[15] *Vermächtnis,* II, 106–7 and 117.

[16] *League of Nations, Treaty Series,* LIV (1926–27), No. 129, 329–31, Article 1; and No. 1296, pp. 343 and 345 (Treaty of Arbitration between Germany and Poland). The treaties provided for the establishment of a permanent

conciliation commission. Of greatest significance, from a political point of view, was Article 17, which provided that disputes not amenable to settlement by conciliation should, at the request of either party to the dispute, be brought before the Council of the League of Nations. The latter organization was to deal with the disputes so submitted in accordance with Article 15 of the Covenant. *Ibid.*, No. 129, p. 331, Article 2; *ibid.*, p. 337, Part II, Article 18. Article 15 of the Covenant set up the machinery for the settlement of disputes. See *The Covenant of the League of Nations with a Commentary Thereon,* Cmd. 151, Misc. No. 3, *Parliamentary Papers,* LIII (1919), 14–16.

[17] July 1, 1925, *Vermächtnis,* II, 115.

[18] Cmd. 2435, *op. cit.,* p. 50.

[19] *League of Nations, Treaty Series,* LIV (1926–27), No. 1295, Article 18, 337; and *ibid.*, No. 1296, p. 351.

[20] *Ibid.,* Nos. 1297 and 1289, pp. 354–63.

[21] December 14, 1925, *Vermächtnis,* II, 235–36.

[22] League of Nations, *op. cit.,* p. 355.

[23] *Vermächtnis,* II, 235–36.

[24] *Nachlass,* 7129/H147859.

[25] Stresemann to the press, April 26, 1926, *Vermächtnis,* II, 504–11; *D'Abernon,* III, 253; *Reden und Schriften,* II, 256.

[26] Krestinsky to Litvinov, October 14, 1926, *Nachlass,* 7334/H162770. For the text of the Treaty of Berlin, signed April 26, 1926, see Germany *Reichsgesetzblatt,* II (1926), 360.

[27] *Vermächtnis,* III, 217.

[28] League of Nations, *Official Journal, Council,* VII (September 20, 1927), No. 10, 1413; *ibid.* (September 27, 1927), pp. 1433–34.

[29] Stresemann's notes on a press conference at Geneva, September 7, 1927, *Vermächtnis,* III, 179.

[30] For the text of the resolution, see League of Nations, *Official Journal, Assembly,* Vol. IX (September 1927), *Special Supplement,* No. 54 (September 9, 1927), p. 84; and *ibid.* (September 24, 1927), p. 156.

[31] Stresemann to Chancellor Marx, September 21, 1927, *Vermächtnis,* III, 195; and League of Nations, *op. cit.,* p. 80.

[32] *Vermächtnis,* III, 179.

[33] December 15, 1927, *ibid.,* p. 246; also, Julius Curtius, *Sechs Jahre Minister der deutschen Republik,* p. 244.

[34] Stresemann to Sthamer, German Ambassador at London, April 19, 1926, *Nachlass,* 7414/H175393.

[35] Stresemann to Marx, November 24, 1927, *Vermächtnis,* III, 237.

[36] Address at Königsberg in East Prussia, December 16, 1927, *ibid.,* p. 247; also, Bernhard, *op. cit.,* p. 279. For a public reaction to his approach, see *Frankfurter Zeitung,* December 17, 1927, No. 938, p. 2.

[37] *Ibid.,* December 20, 1927, No. 945, p. 3.

[38] See Table II, chap. IX, *supra.*

[39] For Stresemann's attitude toward a cabinet of the "Great Coalition," see Stresemann to Chancellor Hermann Müller, June 23, 1928, *Vermächtnis,* III, 298.

[40] See Wilhelm Dittmann, *Das politische Deutschland vor Hitler* (New York: Europa Zurich Verlag, 1945) [Plate V]. The German National People's Party polled 39.2 percent of the total vote in East Prussia in the election of

1924. In 1928, they polled 31.4 percent. To this should be added the 6.2 percent cast for the National-Socialists in 1924. Thus, from 1924 to the election of 1928, the Right commanded 45.4 percent of the total vote in East Prussia as against 23.5 percent in all of Germany. The picture was even more favorable for the Right in the Province of Pomerania. There, the combined total of the German National People's Party and the National-Socialists, in the election of 1924, was 53.3 percent of the votes cast. Pomerania's boundary with Poland made up more than one-third of the total of that frontier. The electoral district of Frankfurt on the Oder, also bordering on Poland, showed a total strength of the Right of 41.5 percent. Only the electoral districts of Silesia showed a predominantly Socialist and Center vote. This latter fact might partly explain why Stresemann, always sensitive to votes, did not assign a priority to boundary changes in that area. All of the above election data have been taken from Dittmann, *op. cit.* (tables on election districts: 1, 5, 6, 7, 8, and 9).

CHAPTER XII

[1] See Part II of the Treaty of Versailles, *Versailles and After*, pp. 122–34. Countries which received German minorities as a result of the peace settlement were (percentages indicated after the country's name refer to the ratio of the ceded area to the total prewar area of Germany) : Poland (8.53), France (2.69), Denmark (0.74), Lithuania (0.49), Danzig (0.35), Belgium (0.19), and Czechoslovakia (0.06). To be added to that is the Saar territory (0.36). Thus a total of 13.41 percent of the prewar area of Germany was ceded to neighboring countries. United States, Department of State, *International Transfers of Territory in Europe* (Washington: Government Printing Office, 1937), Table VII, p. 75.

The ceded populations were distributed as follows:

Poland	3,854,971
France	1,874,014
Denmark	166,348
Lithuania (Memel)	141,238
Danzig	330,630
Belgium	60,003
Czechoslovakia	48,446
Saar (until 1935)	569,376
Total	7,045,026

German speaking: 3,558,023 (former German nationals who claimed German as their mother tongue at the census of 1910).

Source: Germany, Statistisches Reichsamt, Sonderhefte zu Wirtschaft und Statistik, 5. Jhrg., Sonderheft No. 2, *Vorläufige Ergebnisse der Volkszählung im Deutschen Reich vom 16. Juni 1925 mit einem Anhang: Die Abgetretenen Gebiete und das Abstimmungsgebiet in der Saar nach den Ergebnissen der Volkszählung vom I, XII, 1910.* (Bearbeitet im Statistischen Reichsamt) (Berlin: Verlag von Reimar Hobbing, 1925), p. 66.

[2] United States, Foreign Relations, *The Paris Peace Conference, 1919* (Washington: Government Printing Office, 1946), VI, 941.

[3] "Reply of the Allied and Associated Powers to the Observations of the German Delegation on the Conditions of Peace and Ultimatum," June 16, 1919, *Versailles and After*, pp. 44–54.

[4] See Paragraph 1, Article 12 of the Treaty of June 28, 1919, between the principal Allied and Associated Powers and Poland, *ibid.*, p. 801. The League of Nations published the following compilations of minority obligations and rights: *Protection of Linguistic, Racial, and Religious Minorities by the League of Nations* (Publications of the League of Nations, I.B. Minorities, Geneva, 1927), I.B. 2; and *Extracts from the Minutes of the Council, Resolutions, and Reports Adopted by the Assembly Relating to the Procedure to be Followed in Questions Concerning the Protection of Minorities, ibid.,* 1931, I.B. 1; see also *Versailles and After*, pp. 117–19.

[5] Stresemann to Hofrat Bickes, November 12, 1924, *Vermächtnis*, I, 581–82; see also *Nachlass*, 7415/H175709–27.

[6] Stresemann to ex-Crown Prince, September 7, 1925, *ibid.*, II, 553. It might be stated at this point that Stresemann never seriously attempted to effect the so-called *Anschluss* of Austria with Germany. The gist of his policy in this regard is contained in an anonymous article contributed to the *Hamburger Fremdenblatt*, wherein he wrote: "Germany must do pioneer work in the sphere of the right of self-determination of people, a right which has been rendered illusory by the Allies in the question of *Anschluss* in a most cynical manner." September 14, 1925, *Vermächtnis*, II, 172. Stresemann was very much aware of the fact that a strong independence movement had developed in Austria and that the question of *Anschluss* had to be postponed until a more opportune time. Stresemann to Löbe, February 18, 1928, *ibid.*, III, 331. By 1928, he had given up all hope, provided that he ever seriously contemplated the move, that Austria would join Germany. *Ibid.* Also, Stresemann to Poincaré, August 17, 1928, *ibid.*, pp. 359–60. It appears from the scant evidence available that he contented himself with keeping the flame burning by vigorous insistence on self-determination. Ideals which the earlier Stresemann harbored appear to have given way to stern realities. Concerning Stresemann's earlier views on the role Austria was to play in the Central European area, see Gustav Stresemann, "Zollunion," *Nord und Süd*, Vol. 155 (October 1915), p. 493; *Deutsche Stimmen*, 30. Jhrg. (June 16, 1918), No. 24, pp. 408–9; Gustav Stresemann, "Altes und Neues Deutschland," *Reden und Schriften*, I, 237; *Deutsche Stimmen*, 31. Jhrg. (February 22, 1919), No. 9, p. 138; *ibid.* (May 4, 1919), No. 18, p. 320; *Nationalversammlung, Verhandlungen*, Bd. 330 (October 8, 1919), 2917; Stresemann, *Deutsche Volkspartei und Regierungspolitik*, pp. 28–29; *Reichstag, Verhandlungen*, Bd. 384 (February 20, 1925), 809.

[7] Stresemann to the ex-Crown Prince, September 7, 1925, *Vermächtnis*, II, 554.

[8] Stresemann in an anonymous article in the *Hamburger Fremdenblatt*, September 14, 1925; *Vermächtnis*, II, 172.

[9] *Ibid.*, pp. 774–75.

[10] Gustav Stresemann, *Das Werk von Locarno*, p. 11.

[11] December 14, 1925, *Vermächtnis*, II, 243; *Reichstag, Verhandlungen*, Bd. 388 (November 21, 1925), 4468.

[12] February 3, 1926, *Vermächtnis*, II, 556; *Nachlass*, 7415/H175602.

[13] *Reichstag, Verhandlungen*, Bd. 388 (February 9, 1926), 5362–65.

[14] February 22, 1926, *D'Abernon*, III, 226–27.

[15] Stresemann to D'Abernon, August 11, 1926, *Vermächtnis*, II, 585–86.

[16] *Frankfurter Zeitung*, March 17, 1926, No. 206, p.. 2. With reference to the Brazilian refusal to support Germany's candidacy for a Council seat, Stresemann observed bitterly (when the Brazilian president could apparently not be reached for comment): "The President cannot be reached because he has gone into the jungle to swing from tree to tree." Edgar Stern-Rubarth, *Three Men Tried . . . Austen Chamberlain, Stresemann, Briand, and Their Fight for a New Europe*, p. 107.

[17] March 22, 1926, *D'Abernon*, III, 240; *Reichstag, Verhandlungen*, Bd. 389 (March 22, 1926), 6449.

[18] Stresemann's notes on a cabinet meeting, August 26, 1926, *Vermächtnis*, II, 589.

[19] Berthold Jacob, leading German pacifist, claimed that Stresemann, on August 25, 1926, made a secret agreement with several nationalist leaders, whereby the latter would abstain from obstructing his League policy. A member of the army command, and Franz Seldte, leader of a paramilitary organization, *Der Stahlhelm*, were allegedly present at the meeting. In return for nationalist co-operation, Stresemann allegedly promised to abstain from interfering with secret arrangements whereby paramilitary organizations were being trained by the regular army. "Stahlhelm und Stresemann," *Die Weltbühne*, Vol. XXII (September 28, 1926), No. 39.

[20] Stresemann to the press, September 22, 1926, *Vermächtnis*, III, 32; *Frankfurter Zeitung*, September 22, 1926, No. 708.

[21] *Reichstag, Verhandlungen*, Bd. 392 (March 22, 1927), 9815.

[22] Elizabeth Wiskemann, *Czechs and Germans* (London: Oxford University Press, 1938), p. 129.

[23] League of Nations, *Official Journal, Council*, Vol. 129 (June 9, 1926), p. 897; and *ibid.* (October 1926), pp. 1271–78.

[24] *Berliner Tageblatt*, January 12, 1927, No. 18, pp. 2–3.

[25] League of Nations, *Official Journal, Assembly, Special Supplement* (September 9, 1927), No. 54, p. 81; also, Stresemann to Marx, September 21, 1927, *Vermächtnis*, III, 196.

[26] League of Nations, *Official Journal, Council*, X (January 1929), 68–70.

[27] Stresemann to Kahl, March 13, 1929, *Vermächtnis*, III, 438.

[28] League of Nations, *Official Journal, Council*, X (April 1929), 520–22.

[29] *Ibid.*, p. 526.

[30] *Ibid.*, p. 521.

[31] *Ibid., Special Supplement*, No. 74 (June 11, 1929), p. 29.

[32] "Documents Relating to the Protection of Minorities by the League of Nations," *ibid.*, Annex I, pp. 21–30; see also Rauscher to Stresemann, June 20, 1929, *Nachlass*, 7415/H175618.

[33] *Reichstag, Verhandlungen*, Bd. 425 (June 24, 1929), 2881.

[34] League of Nations, *Official Journal, Assembly*, X, *Special Supplement*, No. 75 (September 9, 1929), 69–70.

CHAPTER XIII

[1] Part V of the Treaty of Versailles, "Military, Naval, and Air Clauses," Articles 159–213, *Versailles and After*, pp. 301–65. For a summary of the negotiations leading to these provisions, see W. M. Jordan, *Great Britain, France, and the German Problem*, chap. XI; Harold W. Temperley (ed.), *A History of the Peace Conference of Paris* (London: H. Frowde, and Hodder and Stoughton, 1920–24), II, 131–36.

[2] *Versailles and After*, p. 309; see also Charles Seymour, *The Intimate Papers of Colonel House*, IV, 156 and 194.

[3] J. Hartman Morgan, *Assize of Arms* (London: Methuen & Co., 1945), I, 302–3.

[4] "Politische Umschau," *Deutsche Stimmen*, 31. Jhrg. (June 19, 1919), No. 26, p. 444.

[5] *Reichstag, Verhandlungen*, Bd. 344 (June 30, 1920), 58.

[6] *Ibid.* (July 28, 1920), p. 311.

[7] *D'Abernon*, III, 76–77.

[8] Memorandum by the German government addressed to the ten nations represented in the League of Nations Council, League of Nations, *Official Journal, Monthly Summary*, III–IV (December 1924), 291.

[9] For the text of the note, see *Reichstag, Anlagen*, "Materialien zur Entwaffnungsnote," Bd. 401, No. 971. The note charged Germany with violation of Articles 160, 162, 164–69, 174, and 211 of the Treaty of Versailles.

[10] Stresemann to Konrad Adenauer, Lord Mayor of Cologne, January 7, 1925, *Vermächtnis*, II, 25.

[11] March 7, 1925, *D'Abernon*, III, 146–47; *Kölnische Zeitung*, March 13, 1925, No. 190.

[12] *Reichstag, Verhandlungen*, Bd. 385 (May 18, 1925), 1879.

[13] October 8, 1925, *Vermächtnis*, II, 191–92.

[14] Stresemann's maiden speech before the League Assembly, League of Nations, *Official Journal, Assembly* (1926), *Special Supplement*, No. 44 (September 10, 1926), p. 52.

[15] *Reichstag, Verhandlungen*, Bd. 391 (November 23, 1926), 8142–43.

[16] Stresemann's notes on a conversation with Sir Ronald Lindsay, British Ambassador at Berlin, November 24, 1926, *Vermächtnis*, III, 65.

[17] *Reichstag, Verhandlungen*, Bd. 391 (November 23, 1926), 8142.

[18] October 23, 1925; Great Britain, *Correspondence between the Ambassadors Conference and the German Ambassador at Paris Respecting German Disarmament, Evacuation of Cologne, and Modification in the Rhineland Regime*, Cmd. 2527, Misc. No. 12, *Parliamentary Papers* (London: H.M. Stationery Office, 1925), Vol. XXX (1925).

[19] Conference with *Reichswehrminister* Gessler and with leaders of the Social-Democratic Party, January 1927 (?), *Nachlass*, 7337/H163462; and February 6, 1926, *ibid.*, 7138/H149467. For an account of the secret operations of the *Reichswehr* in the Soviet Union and for a discussion and reports on the trade in ammunition and equipment, see Julius Epstein, "Der Seeckt Plan: aus unveröffentlichten Dokumenten," *Der Monat*, I (November 1948), No. 2, 48–50; Stresemann to Gessler, June 18, 1924, *Nachlass*, 7414/H175333; *ibid.*, 7128/H147736; *ibid.*, 7137/H149293.

[20] *Nachlass*, 7414/H175350 and 175352; 7138/H149451.

[21] Minutes of a conference at the foreign ministry, December 1, 1926, Robert M. W. Kempner, "Die Reichswehr und die Reichsregierung," *Der Monat*, I (March 1949), No. 6, 103–5; see also *Nachlass* (August 11, 1926), 7137/H149293; and *ibid.* (January 5, 1927), 7337/H163495, H163462.

[22] Protocol of December 12, 1926, League of Nations, *Official Journal, Council*, VIII, No. 2 (February 1927), 162.

[23] Stresemann to the press, December 14, 1926, *Vermächtnis*, III, 74.

[24] *Frankfurter Zeitung*, December 21, 1926, No. 948.

[25] Seeckt to his wife, May 22, 1927, Friedrich von Rabenau, *Seeckt, aus seinem Leben*, p. 627. (Italics, author's.)

[26] League of Nations, *Official Journal, Assembly*, VIII, *Special Supplement*, No. 54 (September 9, 1927), 81 and 164.

[27] *Reichstag, Verhandlungen*, Bd. 394 (January 30, 1928), 12491; see also "Observations of the German Government on the Programme of the Work of the Committee on Arbitration and Security," League of Nations, *Official Journal, Asembly*, Vol. VIII (1928) (Document C.A.S. 10, p. 651; and, Stresemann at the banquet of the foreign press at Berlin, *Frankfurter Zeitung*, March 29, 1928, No. 240.

[28] A foreign ministry memorandum, submitted to Stresemann on December 30, 1927, warned against a too rigid presentation of that thesis. It pointed out that the French thesis (first security, then disarmament) met with the approval of public opinion the world over and that it would be necessary for Germany to take the lead in the discussions on collective security before action could be taken in the field of disarmament. The memorandum continued to point out that it would not be in the interest of Germany to permit the conclusion of a regional security pact because such a pact would inevitably lead to commitments on the eastern frontiers and would tend to prejudice the *Anschluss. Nachlass*, 7415/H175657. Concerning the level of disarmament to which the powers could possibly agree, Stresemann had known, ever since Locarno, that neither Britain nor France was prepared to disarm to Germany's level. Great Britain, *Parliamentary Debates, House of Commons*, Vol. 281 (November 7, 1933), col. 91; and *Nachlass*, 7319/H160169.

[29] Dr. Walter Siemers, counsel for the defense of Admiral Raeder, International Military Tribunal, *Trial of the Major War Criminals before the International Military Tribunal, 14 November 1945–1 October 1946*, XVIII, 377.

[30] Admiral Raeder in his own defense, *ibid.*, XIII, 621–22.

[31] *Ibid.*, XIV, 255.

[32] *Reichstag, Verhandlungen*, Bd. 423 (November 19, 1928), 415.

[33] Stresemann to the press, August 10, 1929, *Vermächtnis*, III, 548–49.

[34] *Frankfurter Zeitung*, July 14, 1929, No. 518.

[35] *Vermächtnis*, III, 574–75.

BIBLIOGRAPHY

PRIMARY SOURCES

Books and Pamphlets

BERNHARD, HENRY. *Das Kabinett Stresemann*. Berlin: Staatspolitischer Verlag, G.m.b.H., 1924.

———— (ed.). *Gustav Stresemann; Vermächtnis: Der Nachlass in drei Bänden*. 3 vols. Berlin: Verlag Ullstein, 1932.

LUTHER, DR. PAUL. *Stresemann Buch: Aussprüche und Aufsätze*. Berlin: Staatspolitischer Verlag, G.m.b.H., 1923.

STRESEMANN, GUSTAV. *Addresses at the Ceremony of Conferring Honorary Degrees upon the Foreign Minister, Dr. Stresemann, and the Ambassador of the United States, Dr. Schurman, in the Convocation Hall of Heidelberg University, May 5, 1928*. Heidelberg: C. Winter, 1928.

————. *Deutsche Gegenwart und Zukunft: Vortrag gehalten in Stuttgart am 18. November 1917*. Stuttgart: Julius Hoffmann, 1917.

————. *Deutsches Ringen und Deutsches Hoffen*. Berlin: Reichsverlag Herrmann Kalkoff, 1914.

————. *Deutsche Volkspartei und Regierungspolitik: Rede Dr. Stresemanns gehalten auf dem 3. Parteitag der DVP in Nürnberg, Dezember 3, 1920*. Berlin: Staatspolitischer Verlag, G.m.b.H., 1921.

————. *Das Deutsche Wirtschaftsleben im Kriege*. Leipzig: S. Hirzel, 1915.

————. *Drei Völkerbundsreden*. Bielefeld: Velhagen und Klasing, 1929.

————. *Englands Wirtschaftskrieg gegen Deutschland*. Stuttgart: Deutsche Verlagsanstalt, 1916.

————. *Essays and Speeches*. Preface by the Rt. Hon. Sir Austen Chamberlain, K.C., M.P.; Introductory Life by Baron Rochus von Rheinbaben. London: Thornton Butterworth, Ltd., 1930.

————. *Goethe und Napoleon: Ein Vortrag mit Anhang: "Weimarer Tagebuch."* Berlin: Staatspolitischer Verlag, G.m.b.H., 1921.

————. *Industrie und Krieg: Rede gehalten auf der 18ten Hauptversammlung des Bundes der Industriellen am 24. Okt. 1916 in Berlin*. Berlin: Selbstverlag des Bundes der Industriellen, 1916.

————. *Macht und Freiheit*. Halle: Carl Marhold, 1918.

————. *Die Märzereignisse und die Deutsche Volkspartei*. Berlin: Staatspolitischer Verlag, G.m.b.H., 1920.

————. *Michel Horch, Der Seewind Pfeift: Kriegsbetrachtungen*. Berlin: Hermann Kalkoff, 1916.

————. *Nationale Realpolitik: Rede des Dr. Stresemann gehalten auf dem 6ten Parteitag der Deutschen Volkspartei in Dortmund am 14. November 1924*. Berlin: Staatspolitischer Verlag, G.m.b.H., 1924.

————. *Die Politik der Deutschen Volkspartei.* Berlin: Staatspolitischer Verlag, G.m.b.H., 1919.

————. *Politische Gedanken zum Bismarck Gedenktage.* Berlin: Staatspolitischer Verlag, G.m.b.H., 1925.

————. *Reden und Schriften: Politik, Geschichte, Literatur 1897–1926.* 2 vols. Dresden: Carl Reissner Verlag, 1926.

————. *Schutz der Verfassung.* Berlin: Staatspolitischer Verlag, G.m..b.H., 1922.

————. *Der Völkerbund vor dem Reichstag.* Berlin: Staatspolitischer Verlag, G.m.b.H., 1926.

————. *Von der Revolution bis zum Frieden von Versailles: Reden und Aufsätze.* Berlin: Staatspolitischer Verlag, G.m.b.H., 1919.

————. *Warum Müssen Wir Durchhalten?* Berlin: Kriegspresse Amt, 1917.

————. *The Way of the New Germany: An Address Delivered on June 29, 1927 in the Hall of the Oslo University on the Invitation of the Storthing Nobel-Committee.* Berlin: Carl Heymanns Verlag, 1927.

————. *Der Wille zur Verständigung: Rede des Deutschen Reichskanzlers Dr. Stresemann vor dem "Deutschen Industrie- und Handelstag" am 24. August 1923.* Berlin: Zentral Verlag, 1923.

————. *Weimar und die Politik.* Berlin: Staatspolitischer Verlag, G.m.b.H., 1919.

————. *Das Werk von Locarno.* Berlin: Staatspolitischer Verlag, 1925.

SUTTON, ERIC. *Gustav Stresemann: His Diaries, Letters, and Papers.* 3 vols. New York: The Macmillan Co., 1935–40.

Articles

STRESEMANN, GUSTAV. "The Economic Restoration of the World," *Foreign Affairs* (New York), II (June 15, 1924), No. 4, 552–57.

————. "Trade of Germany and Canada," *Industrial Canada*, XIII (November 1912), No. 4, 621–22.

————. "Zollunion," *Nord und Süd*, CLV (October 1915), 493.

Microfilm

Germany, Auswärtiges Amt, Politisches Archiv. *Nachlass des Reichsministers Dr. Gustav Stresemann.* National Archives, Washington, D.C.

SECONDARY SOURCES

Books and Pamphlets

BAUER, HEINRICH. *Stresemann: Ein deutscher Staatsmann.* Berlin: Verlag von Georg Stilke, 1930.

BIELIGH, FRITZ K. *Stresemann: The German Liberal's Foreign Policy.* London: Hutchinson and Co., 1943.

CURTIUS, DR. JULIUS. *Memorial to Gustav Stresemann.* Worcester, Mass.: Carnegie Endowment for International Peace, Division of Intercourse and Education, 1930.

GÖRLITZ, WALTER. *Stresemann.* Heidelberg: Ähren Verlag, 1947.

HIRTH, FRIEDRICH. *Stresemann.* Paris: Les Editions des Portiques, 1930.

LÖWENSTEIN, HUBERTUS PRINZ ZU. *Stresemann. Das deutsche Schicksal im Spiegel seines Lebens.* Frankfurt a/M: Verlag Heinrich Scheffler, 1952.

MIETHKE, FRANZ. *Dr. Gustav Stresemann, Der Wirtschaftspolitiker.* Dresden: Verlagsanstalt Sachsen, 1919.

OLDEN, RUDOLF. *Stresemann.* New York: E. P. Dutton & Co., Inc., 1930.

REBER, JAMES Q. *Stresemann's Foreign Policy.* Master's Thesis, University of Chicago, August 1935.

REVENTLOW, GRAF ERNST CHRISTIAN EINAR LUDWIG DETLOW ZU. *Minister Stresemann als Staatsmann und Anwalt des Weltgewissens.* München: J. F. Lehmann, 1926.

RHEINBABEN, BARON ROCHUS VON. *Stresemann: The Man and the Statesman.* New York: D. Appleton and Co., 1929.

STERN-RUBARTH, EDGAR. *Drei Männer suchen Europa.* München: Willi Weismann Verlag, 1947.

————. *Stresemann der Europäer.* Berlin: Verlag von Reimar Hobbing, 1930.

————. *Three Men Tried . . . Austen Chamberlain, Stresemann, Briand, and Their Fight for a New Europe.* London: Duckworth, 1939.

VALLENTIN, ANTONIA. *Stresemann.* London: Constable and Co., Ltd., 1931.

WOLF-DESSAU, HANS. *Stresemann's Weg: Untergang oder Befreiung.* Berlin: R. Bredow, 1925.

Articles

BOAS, G. "Stresemann," *Public Opinion Quarterly,* VIII (1944), No. 2, 232–43.

D'ABERNON, VISCOUNT EDGAR V. "Stresemann," *Foreign Affairs,* VIII (January 1930), 2, pp. 208–11.

DEWALL, WOLF VON. "Stresemann der Staatsmann," *Zeitschrift für Völkerrecht,* XV (1930), 387–409.

HIRSCH, FELIX E. "Stresemann," *Public Opinion Quarterly,* Vol. IX (1945), No. 2, 258–60.

OLDEN, RUDOLF. "Was Stresemann Sincere?" *The Contemporary Review,* CXLVII (May 1935), 557–65.

SAUERWEIN, JULES. "Stresemann and France," *The Living Age* (November 15, 1926), Vol. 331, pp. 291–95.

SCHOTTE, DR. WALTHER. "Die Stresemann Linie," *Preussische Jahrbücher,* CCII (October 1925), 91–101.

STERN-RUBARTH, EDGAR. "Der Stresemann Weg," *Preussische Jahrbücher,* CCII (December 1925), 454–60.

INDEX

Advertising, 29
Air force, German, 138; airports, 93
Alemania Illustrada Gaceta de Munich, 37
Allied and Associated Powers, 11, 18, 20, 23, 41, 42, 46, 79, 83, 84, 126; armed forces of, 73; Conference of Ambassadors, 103, 143; disunity, 22–23, 39, 60, 73, 90, 107; Supreme Council of, 55; treaty with Poland, 127–28; war aims of, 20
Allied conferences of Spa, Boulogne-sur-Mer, and San Remo, 140
Allied Reparation Commission, *see* Reparation Commission
Alsace-Lorraine, 20, 38, 43, 94, 103
Anglo-French relations, 60–61, 73–74, 86, 87, 90
Anglo-German relations, 12, 56, 61, 64, 65, 73, 91
Anschluss, see Austro-German relations
Antwerp, 17
Arbitration, 61, 119; treaties of, 89, 93, 94–95, 119–20; *see also* Locarno
Arbitration Tribunal, 84, 119
Armaments, 47; *see also* Demilitarization, Disarmament, Russo-German relations
Armistice, 1918, 6, 18–23, 58, 139; negotiations, 21–23, 60
Army, French, 103
Army, German, 102, 117, 140, 142; chief of the army command, 83, 143; collaboration with USSR, 11, 100, 102, 144; and disarmament, 144, 146, 147; high command, 19, 143; military intelligence, 144; minister of armed forces, 102, 146; ministry of armed forces, 144; press office, 33; supreme command, 93; training of troops, 93; *see also* Russo-German relations, Disarmament
"Army-in-being" concept, 146
Asia, 39
Association of German Chocolate Manufacturers, 4, 5

Austria, 47, 128
Austria-Hungary, 41
Austro-German relations: *Anschluss* with Germany, 21, 22, 38, 127; treaty with Germany, 95

Baden, Prince Max von, *see* Max, Prince von Baden
Balkans, 39
Ballin, Albert, 5
Bassermann, Ernst, 4, 5, 6
Bavarian People's Party (BVP), 123
Belgium, 34, 38, 81, 93, 106, 113; German occupation of, 114; neutrality of, 17, 33, 120
Berchtold, Count Leopold von, 47
Berlin, Treaty of, 121
Bernhard, Georg, 5
Bernhard, Henry, 4, 35
Bethmann-Hollweg, Chancellor Theobald von, 6, 33, 120
Bismarck, Prince Otto von, 27, 39
Boundaries, east German, 38, 90, 94, 99, 103, 117, 118, 120, 121, 122, 124, 127, 141; west German, 89, 93, 94, 105, 113
Brest-Litovsk, Treaty of, 17, 18
Briand, Aristide, 13–14, 51, 89, 100–102, 103, 105, 107, 111, 112, 113–14, 134, 146–47; *see also* Franco-German relations, League of Nations, Thoiry
Briey, 16–17
British Empire, 86
Brockdorff-Rantzau, Count Ulrich von, 5, 11
Bülow, Prince Bernhard von, 10
Bulgaria, 41
Bundesrat, 27

Center Party (Z), 7, 68, 72, 82
Central Europe, 41
Central Union of German Industrialists, *see* Pan-German League
Chamberlain, Sir Austen, 13, 50, 90, 103, 117, 133
Chicherin, Grigori V., 118